Admiral Sir Francis Bridgeman

The Life and Times of an Officer and a Gentleman

Stewart Ross

The right of Stewart Ross to be identified as author of this
work has been asserted by him in accordance with the
Copyright, Designs and Patents Act 1988

ISBN 0 9523628 8 0

Published by Baily's 1998
© Pearson Publishing Limited 1998
Text © Stewart Ross 1998

Baily's, Chesterton Mill, French's Road, Cambridge CB4 3NP
Tel 01223 350555 Fax 01223 356484
Baily's is an imprint of Pearson Publishing Ltd

For Dar

1904 – 1991

At last

Contents

Admiral Sir Francis Charles Bridgeman GCB GC VO

Foreword by Jan Morris

The Royal Navy of the late Victorian and Edwardian eras – the Navy that reached a late anti-climax in the battle of Jutland – is chiefly remembered in the public mind for its excesses. It was excessively big. It was excessively splendid. Overwhelmingly self-confident, it is now seen to have been somewhat self-delusory too, and its affairs were studded with scandal and dispute. Its roster of senior officers was astonishingly rich in flamboyance, eccentricity and humour, and immortalized in funny nicknames – "The Swell of the Ocean Wave", "'Old 'Ard 'Art". There was certainly nothing dull about the Navy then, as it moved with decidedly mixed feelings out of Nelson's age of sail towards the twentieth century of steel and steam.

By no means all its officers, though, were buffoons, show-offs or old reactionaries. Although the Royal Navy generally preferred to let other navies set the pace in technological change, its officer corps included many men genuinely devoted to their profession. Its seamanship was superb, its courage seldom doubted, and a sense of integrity and honour generally underlay even the worst of its hyperbole. In many ways characteristic of the thousands of diligent, modest, thoroughly professional and now mostly forgotten officers who pursued a naval career around the turn of the nineteenth century was Francis Charles Bridgeman, who became, for one brief and disconcerting year in his sixties, the professional head of the Navy, and who is now honourably commemorated in this book.

Its subtitle is just right. Bridgeman was quintessentially an officer and a gentleman, not at all one of your naval "characters" of the Victorian *fin-de-siècle*, with their peculiar habits and often hilarious reputations – he did not even *have* a nick-name! For most of his life his progress was steady and unspectacular. He sailed in many seas but, in the heyday of the *Pax Britannica*, saw almost no action. Happily married rather late in life, to an older and conveniently wealthy wife, his personal conduct was exemplary. He was a good-looking man, a Freemason with friends in high places, and intellectually he was just what you might expect of an upper-class Englishman of his time, thrown into a naval career in boyhood – no Philistine fool but certainly no man of culture.

Mr Ross presents this likeable personality to us without apology. He recognizes that Bridgeman did not possess star quality, and tells us the story of his long naval career with sympathetic frankness. What makes the tale so different from any other biography of a British naval officer is that one startling year near the end of it: for then this unassuming professional, a model sea officer with no enemies, found himself thrown into the metropolitan cauldron of politics, rivalry and subterfuge that lay behind the Navy's glittering presence. He could be unknown to the public no longer: having risen so steadily to the top ranks of the Royal Navy, with such well-mannered restraint, in 1911 he was summoned from the Home Fleet to the ultimate appointment of them all, First Sea Lord to Winston Churchill's First Lord of the Admiralty.

Now the officer and gentleman found himself in a very different ambiance, a pit prowled around by formidable powers and predators: Churchill himself, young, brilliant and terrifically ambitious, "Jackie" Fisher a kind of conspiratorial genius, the irrepressible Lord Charles Beresford, who was both an outrageously argumentative admiral and a member of Parliament, and a host of political activists, journalists, self-seekers and gossips. What resulted, described here in vivid detail, was the one great controversy of Bridgeman's life – the one great event, one might say. For a few weeks Francis Bridgeman was famous, and then he was forgotten.

This extraordinary climax to an unexceptional life gives the book true dramatic impact, and Mr Ross has paced it perfectly. Was Bridgeman himself tainted by his late experience of life at the heart of things? Perhaps a little, but it was as the archetypal country squire, all the same, that he went to his grave: a hunting, shooting Justice of the Peace, good to his employees, generous to his parish, as far removed as one can imagine from all the back-biting and half-truths of life at the Admiralty in the last fateful years before the Great War. The grand old Royal Navy would soon be gone for ever: and perhaps between the lines Bridgeman's story records too, as in allegory, the life and death of the Officer and Gentleman.

Introduction and Acknowledgements

Sir Francis Bridgeman (1848-1929) needs some introduction. If his near contemporary Bonar Law is the forgotten Prime Minister, then Bridgeman is the forgotten First Sea Lord. He had the misfortune to work with mighty stars – Jackie Fisher and Winston Churchill to name but two – beside whose radiance his own modest glow was barely visible. Nor did he wish it otherwise. He was a modest man who throughout his life stuck to the principles of honesty and decency on which he had been raised. His life was spent doing his Christian and patriotic duty to the best of his ability, not seeking glory or status. Indeed, when offered the post of First Sea Lord, the most powerful position in the Royal Navy, he begged that the honour be given to another. He was not a startlingly able or original man either. Although a fine sailor and a very good fleet commander, he lacked the panache of a Beatty or the computer-like mind of a Jellicoe. But that did not make him any less valuable to the Service to which he devoted 51 years of his life. In rough seas the best hand on the wheel is a steady one.

When Bridgeman joined the Navy, in 1861 the Service was beginning the longest and most dramatic period of change in its entire history. He was taught to shoot cannon balls, splice ropes, furl sails and watch the wind as if his life depended on it. Which sometimes it did. He saw men flogged till their backs were raw and spin headlong to their deaths from the rigging. Despite the appearance of the first belching, wheezing steam engines and an ironclad, there had been little fundamental change from the time of Nelson. The ghost of the country's naval genius haunted every quarter-deck in the fleet; his signal about duty was imprinted on every sailor's mind. When Bridgeman retired on the eve of the First World War the spirit of Nelson might not have gone, but that was all of the age of tar that remained. The modern Navy was turbine, steel and electricity. The warship had become a technological marvel, whether as a submarine prowling beneath the waves or a dreadnought ploughing above at speeds previously reached only by cavalry. The enemy was unseen, his ships no more than a periscope or a silhouette. All this Bridgeman witnessed and adapted to better than most. For that alone his life is worth exploring.

Bridgeman hit the headlines only once, at the time of his resignation in December 1912. Had he really been asked to leave because of failing health or had he been pushed out of the nest because, like a cuckoo, First Lord Churchill wished to be surrounded only by his own kind? The question was debated in the Commons just before Christmas and for a few hours the career of one of the most brilliant, domineering politicians of his day looked as if it might topple. But Churchill survived, probably as Bridgeman hoped he would, and the unfortunate Admiral retired to his Yorkshire estate in dignified silence. But many questions remained unanswered.

The Bridgeman-Churchill confrontation was a clash of personality, of style, of generations, even of morality. Old-fashioned naval decency was out-manoeuvred by political guile; steadfastness overcome by genius. And it was probably better for the country that it turned out that way. Bridgeman, like his heroes Captain Scott and Admiral Cradock, was a gallant loser. Churchill was a born winner, at any price. With war imminent, that was the type the country needed.

Because most of his private papers and correspondence have disappeared, Bridgeman's life is extremely difficult to piece together. Official records and occasional newspaper articles provide a bare outline, but the man behind remains elusive. I have done my best to paint an accurate picture in the limited time at my disposal but am only too aware of the unsightly areas of bare canvas remaining. These would have been wider still without the generous assistance of the following: Mrs Alastair Graham; Mrs Barbara Wray; Frank and Margaret Stacey; Mrs Jean Jones; Andrew Buchannan; Mrs Joan Huddart; Leonard Axelby; Lady Blacker; Lady and Sir James Graham, Bt; Anthony Boynton Wood; Mrs Priscilla Napier; Claire Cumming of Weston Park; Sarah Costley and the staff of the West

Yorkshire Archive Service, Wakefield; Ann Heath and the staff of the Sheffield City Archives; Miss Pamela Clark of the Royal Archives, Windsor Castle; W J Connor of the West Yorkshire Archive Service; Lord Patrick Beresford; Sir Philip Duncombe, Bt; Lord Feversham; Peregrine Chadwyck-Healey; Matthew Sheldon of the Admiralty Library, Portsmouth; the staff of the Public Record Office, Kew; the staff of the Bodleian Library, Oxford; Mrs G M A Randall of the Staffordshire Archive Service; Adrian Honstock of the Nottinghamshire Archives; Rob Hyre of the Warwickshire County Record Office; M Y Ashcroft of the North Yorkshire County Archives; John Keeley of the House of Commons Information Office; Richard Childs of the West Sussex County Archives; and Mr Guy Reed for allowing me to snoop around Copgrove Hall.

I should also like to extend my gratitude to HMSO for permission to quote from the letters to Admiral Sir Francis Bridgeman from Winston Churchill. Also to the Imperial War Museum, National Maritime Museum, National Portrait Gallery, Popperfoto and York Minster Library and Archives for supplying photographic material.

I am particularly indebted to Mary and Rob Hastings-Trew for bed and board in the best Yorkshire tradition; Commander Michael Saunders Watson for kindly digging through his personal archive and providing me with some fascinating snippets of information; Sir Josslyn Gore-Booth, Bt, for allowing me access to his family papers and showing me much kindness during my visit; Mark Tewfik for hours of valuable research; Mrs Walter Hingston for invaluable stories, photographs and other fascinating Bridgeman miscellany.

Thanks to the efforts of Admiral of the Fleet Sir Henry Leach, GCB, DL, Mr R Suddaby of the Imperial War Museum and, most particularly, Alan J Giddings of the National Maritime Museum, all of whom most kindly gave of their time to read the manuscript, hence many inaccuracies and inelegancies were removed from early drafts. Those that remain are, of course, entirely my responsibility. I would also like to thank Rod Suddaby and Alan Giddings for their friendliness, help and guidance with my researches.

A special mention must be made of Bridgeman's original (unpublished) biographer, Captain Sam Lombard-Hobson RN, who generously gave me full access to the fruits of his extensive research. Several chapters of this book rest upon the foundations he so painstakingly laid.

Finally, I would like to record my sincere thanks to my family, particularly my wife Lucy, for tolerating my eccentric hours and absences and reading the manuscript with penetrating insight; and above all to Lady Loch (Bina) great-great niece of Sir Francis Bridgeman, without whose drive, enthusiasm and support this book would never have been conceived, let alone written.

PROTRACTED AND CONTRACTED SURNAMES

The marriage of Sir Henry Bridgeman, Baron Bradford (b. 1725) with Elizabeth Simpson (b. 1735) produced three sons. The second, Orlando, kept the name Bridgeman, while his two brothers, Henry and John, both MPs, assumed their mother's surname of Simpson. The children of John's second marriage appear to have called themselves Bridgeman-Simpson, even adding an extra 'Bridgeman' to ensure that the original family name did not fall into disuse. The future Admiral, Francis Charles, a grandson of John Bridgeman-Simpson, is recorded in the early *Navy Lists* as Francis Charles Bridgeman-Bridgeman-Simpson – the longest name in the register. In the 1870s, however, he appeared in Australian newspapers as plain 'Sub-Lieutenant Simpson', suggesting either that colonial reporters had no time for pompous Old-World hyphenation or that Francis himself preferred a simpler surname. In 1896 he changed his surname by deed poll to Bridgeman but added an extra 'Bridgeman' to his forenames, i.e. Francis Charles Bridgeman Bridgeman. For the sake of clarity in the pages that follow he is generally called 'Bridgeman'; '(Sir) Francis' or 'Francey' appear only where appropriate or where to do otherwise would only add to the confusion.

A FAMILY NOTE

In 1985 my mother, Dar Wright, discovered a bundle of some 30 letters inherited from her mother, Sybil Powerscourt, who had died very suddenly in 1946. On reading them and realising their importance, she looked around for help. It was to Sam Lombard-Hobson, a very great friend, that she turned, and who subsequently offered to compile a book around them (*Never Go to Sea*). I cannot stress strongly enough my mother's debt of gratitude to him, and mine also, for nigh on 10 years work.

But then a new phase – my inheritance of the letters and introduction to Pearson Publishing. I am deeply grateful to George and Mark Pearson for their interest, and when they introduced me to Stewart Ross, I was lost. His charm, enthusiasm, diligence and professionalism have gone far beyond the call of duty. Thank you Stewart. I hope Uncle Francey would be proud of all our efforts.

Bina Loch (Admiral Sir Francis Bridgeman's great-great niece)

Victorian values – Rev William Bridgeman-Simpson (right) and members of his family on the lawns of Babworth Rectory c.1870

1 Britannia

Francis Charles Bridgeman-Simpson was born on 7 December 1848 and baptised at All Saints, Babworth on 4 February the following year. The two-month delay is a mystery. It was not caused by practical considerations, for the child's father, Rev William Bridgeman-Simpson, was rector of Babworth and his sprawling Victorian rectory stood only a 3-minute walk from the church.[1] Perhaps the onset of Christmas, when the Bridgeman-Simpsons invariably played host to friends and relatives, led Rev William to put off the ceremony.

Another, more intriguing possibility is that the child was sick. If this were so, then it established a precedent of more than parochial significance. On several subsequent occasions Francis would be let down by real or imagined ill-health that eventually brought his distinguished career to its spectacular, premature demise.

A more likely reason for the delay was the time it took to assemble the chosen godparents. Written invitations were sent as soon as the gender of Lady Frances Laura Bridgeman-Simpson's fourth child was known. There was no problem arranging for his 52-year-old unmarried aunt Charlotte to be present, but because of their professional duties the two male sponsors were less easily accommodated at short notice. One was his great-uncle, the Hon Charles Orlando Bridgeman, who celebrated his 58th birthday the day after the christening. The second was Charles Ramsden, RN. As Uncle Charles, from whom Francis probably took his second name, was an even more distinguished naval officer, a Vice-Admiral no less, it was clear from the moment he was born that Francis Bridgeman-Simpson was destined for the sea.

The Bridgemans, like most English families, could boast their fair share of naval service. They had their origins in the sea-faring county of Devon and first appear as a family of consequence during the reign of Elizabeth I, when an Edward Bridgeman was appointed sheriff of Exeter. Edward's son

Jasper, Registrar of the Admiralty of Devon, was the first Bridgeman with a recorded link with the Royal Navy. The family's upward mobility was maintained by the sheriff's grandchildren. John Bridgeman, a chaplain to James I, became Bishop of Chester and in the 1620s his brother Edward sat in the Commons as MP for Wigan and Liverpool. Following the restoration of the monarchy in 1660, the bishop's royalist descendants flourished. Sir Orlando Bridgeman became Lord Keeper of the Great Seal for Charles II and Bishop Henry presided, at least nominally, over the uninspiring see of Sodor and Man. William re-established the family's links with the sea by serving as Secretary to the Admiralty during the reigns of James II and William III.

The Bridgemans, by now based in Shropshire, marked time for much of the eighteenth century. They worked as barristers and clergymen and were frequently returned to the Commons as MPs for Wigan. Their maritime experiences were limited to the unfortunate drowning of Sir Orlando Bridgeman in the Thames in 1738 as he was leaving to take up his post as Governor of Barbados, and the death on board ship of his son, Sir Francis Bridgeman, also bound for Barbados. In the latter half of the century the marriage of Sir Henry Bridgeman, Baron Bradford, to the wealthy heiress Elizabeth Simpson revived family fortunes. Elizabeth was the great-granddaughter of the celebrated Admiral Benbow and the marriage seems to have awakened dormant family interest in ships and the sea. Henceforward, for more than a century, there was always at least one Bridgeman in the Senior Service. While not one of them displayed the dash of a Benbow, who in late seventeenth century had battled almost single-handed with a French squadron in the West Indies, neither did they share the dubious reputation for cowardice earned by Admiral Byng, whose ancestor Hon Lucy Byng married Sir Orlando Bridgeman, second Baron Bradford.

The baron's younger brother, John Bridgeman-Simpson (1763-1850), inherited not only the Simpson property in Nottinghamshire, including Babworth Hall and the living of All Souls, but also estates in Warwickshire left to him by Charlotte Addison, daughter of the celebrated essayist and a distant ancestor of the seventeenth-century Lord Keeper.

John, grandfather of Francis, the future First Sea Lord, married twice and had a large family. Born on 9 September 1813, Rev William Bridgeman-Simpson, Rector of Babworth, was probably his thirteenth and last child. His brother Arthur, born the previous year, joined the Royal Navy in his early teens and died of fever in the Cape Verde Islands while serving as a midshipman in the *Tweed*. What bearing this tragedy had on William's decision to send one of his own sons to sea, we shall never know; but Francis' entry into Navy may have been a form of tribute to the lost brother.

On 23 June 1837, at St George's, Hanover Square, Rev William Bridgeman-Simpson married Lady Frances Laura Fitzwilliam, second daughter of Charles, 5th Earl Fitzwilliam. Bride and groom were both 24. The marriage strengthened the Bridgeman-Simpsons' ties with the landed aristocracy, bringing them close to the Douglas Earls of Morton as well as the Fitzwilliams. In an age when advancement, particularly in the armed forces, depended as much on family connection as talent, Francis Bridgeman-Simpson would have a smoother upward path than many of his contemporaries.

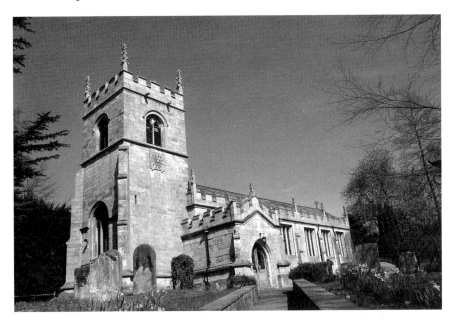

All Saints, Babworth

Rev William Bridgeman-Simpson and Lady Frances in 1863, a year after Francis left Britannia

Lack of evidence makes it impossible to speak about Francis' home background with any certainty. Although his parents were comfortably off and lived in a house that today is little short of a stately home, apparently they found it difficult to maintain the lifestyle to which they had been accustomed before their marriage. If family hearsay is to be believed, for much of his naval career Francis was always short of funds.[2] Rev William received a £3000 marriage settlement and a further substantial sum on his father's death. His brothers and sisters were originally bequeathed £6000 each, twice as much as William, suggesting that Lady Frances had money of her own.[3] In 1845 the bequest to William's eldest brother Henry, master of nearby Babworth Hall, was reduced to nothing but 'wines' and 'comestibles' and his share made over to William. In the third codicil of his father's will Henry was replaced as an executor by the Earl of Yarborough, to whom the Honourable John Bridgeman-Simpson was related through a daughter by his first marriage.

Whether this alteration in their father's will was a symptom or cause

Wentworth Woodhouse, Rotherham - Francis' mother's spectacular family home

we cannot tell, but by the 1850s a bitter feud raged between the lord of the manor and his rector brother. Money probably played a part in their mutual antipathy, for Henry's marriage to Frances Baring was childless and William appears to have resented his brother's unwillingness to help support his many nephews and nieces. There are also suggestions in the diaries of Georgiana, the brothers' youngest sister, that Henry's lifestyle shocked the sober and respectable sensibilities of the rector and his family.[4] In 1853, Georgiana, wife of the distinguished soldier Major-General Sir William Eyre, spent Christmas at Babworth Hall with her son Arthur, her brother, his future heir Henry Denison and her brother-in-law Charles Eyre. A highly-strung, emotional woman, Georgiana was not in the best of spirits following her husband's call-up in anticipation of the outbreak of hostilities with Russia. Her mood did not lighten when, moving down to the rectory in February, she found that her brother and sister-in-law ('Willie' and 'Fanny' as they were always known in family circles), were away in London 'on business'. Nor did things improve on their return. On 2 April the two brothers confronted each other in the church. Georgiana recalled Henry 'actually sitting over the vault that contains the remains of both our beloved parents'. She obviously thought her eldest brother almost beyond redemption. 'Oh my god turn his heart,' she wailed with scant regard for punctuation, 'for I believe truly that nothing now but Divine Grace can rescue him from the evil passions that have got domination over his soul'. The nature of those 'evil passions' remains a mystery. They were sufficiently wicked for William, whom Georgiana believed was 'very much to be pitied', to be 'quite at a loss' to know how to effect a reconciliation.[5] Henry's hatred extended to the rector's children, whom he drove from his lands when they strayed there with their ponies.[6] One wonders, given his childlessness and the strength of the rector's reaction to his nameless sins, whether Henry Bridgeman-Simpson may have been homosexual.

Cadet Bridgeman-Simpson, complete with telescope and sword, 1864

Family tradition speaks of Rev William as the archetypal Victorian father – stern, remote and insistent that his children should be seen and not heard. Apparently, even when his sons were grown men, William refused to let them invite young ladies into the family home. The tyrannical embargo is said to explain why, apart from the irrepressible Orlando, none of them married until after their father's death.[7] There may well be some truth in this picture of William, for in a remarkably frank and illuminating conversation with his young nephew Arthur Eyre, the rector wondered sadly why his children were not more open with him. 'But is he not to blame?' Arthur reflected that evening. 'Has he not always treated them as children? Has he ever opened out to them as he ought?'[8] If this is an accurate assessment, then it is not hard to see where the introverted, undemonstrative side of Francis' personality came from.

As befitted the rector of a parish once presided over by Richard Clyfton, one of the future Pilgrim Fathers, William Bridgeman-Simpson was an effective preacher. In the pulpit his reticence left him and he was able to give vent to his inner thoughts and feelings. Arthur Eyre, who was quite prepared to speak his mind in the privacy of his diary, was particularly impressed by his uncle's 'beautiful' sermon on the subject of 'true religion and cant', delivered on 3 December 1871. 'I don't know when I listened more attentively to a sermon than I did to that one', the young infantry officer concluded. William's moral homilies must have lodged in Francis' young heart, too. We don't have much evidence of his love for true religion (a luxury, together with fresh food and water, that most sailors learned to live without), but cant, dishonesty and double-dealing he abhorred.

William may have found it difficult outwardly to express emotion and have had strange views on his sons' need for celibacy, but there is no evidence to suggest that he was unduly harsh in other matters. Indeed the few facts we possess indicate that Babworth Rectory was a warm and friendly home. The informal poses and touching inscriptions in faded but lovingly prepared family photograph albums, in which Francis' brothers and sisters are given their pet names (Orlando, for example, was 'Oey', Caroline 'Carly' and Beatrice 'Bea'), hint at an atmosphere far removed

Imly (William), 1867

Bea (Beatrice), 1867

Carly (Caroline), 1867

Georgey (George), 1866

from the dour rectitude popularly associated with Victorian clergy families. A comment in Georgiana's diary for April 1860, in which she noted that 'the dear children [were] all much improved in every way – much more engaging,' implies, reassuringly, that on previous visits she had found them tiresomely ill-disciplined.[9]

Given William's introversion, it is likely that Fanny was responsible for the parental warmth that filled the family home. She seems to have been an attractive, good-natured woman with a kind heart and ready smile.[10] Although she may not have possessed great intellectual qualities, she imbued in her children a strong sense of fun, which was most pronounced in Orlando.[11] If it was less obvious in Francis, whose principal joy in later life lay in riding to hounds, then he was certainly indebted to her for his handsome looks and instinctive charm.

None of William or Lady Frances' correspondence survives, but there are hints that they took a normal and healthy interest in their children's welfare. When Orlando left for his round-the-world trip in 1870, the 57-year-old William accompanied him to London to see him off, and Francis' return from Australia in 1871 seems to have been a source of universal excitement at the rectory.[12] It is a credit to both parents that the children grew up remarkably lacking in prejudice and armed with an instinctive sense of right and wrong.

Besides the gallivanting Orlando, Francis had three brothers and three sisters.[13] Lancelot (born 1854) died young. William, five years' Francis' senior, left the family home at an early age and spent most of his subsequent life as a bachelor in Toronto, Canada. George (born 1846) is a somewhat shadowy, anonymous figure. Appointed Registrar of the District Probate Registry at Wakefield, like Francis he did not marry until after his father's death and left no issue. When his travelling days were over, Orlando enjoyed a period of service as a Major in the West Yorkshire Yeomanry and worked as an agent for his uncle Lord Fitzwilliam at Coolattin, County Wicklow. He married Catherine Cotes in 1873 and had three daughters.

Babworth, 1868, by when Rev William had the females of the family almost entirely to himself

All we know of the Bridgeman-Simpson boys' education is that Orlando spent time at Harrow and Francis must have had some sort of schooling in order to gain entry into the Navy. All but one of Rev William's sons spent long periods of time as far from Babworth as possible.

Mary, the fairest and favourite child of the rectory, married Walter Pleydell-Bouverie in 1876. She died four years later, aged 29, giving birth to her third child. Her syphilitic husband, by all accounts something of a bounder, remarried before succumbing to his illness at the age of 42. Mary and Francis may well have been very close in childhood, for Walter's five daughters and their families were some of his dearest companions in his later years. Caroline Bridgeman-Simpson, born a year after Mary in 1852, died unmarried in the same year as her father. Beatrice, the youngest child, married Adolphus Duncombe, son of the Dean of York, shortly before Christmas, 1881. The couple were childless.

As well as the children, the rectory was usually refuge to at least one maiden aunt. Apart from the detested Henry and faceless John, an unmarried officer in the Horse Guards, all William's brothers died young. Not so his sisters. Two got married, Louisa and the highly-strung Georgiana. That left Francis' godmother Charlotte and her sisters Caroline, Isabella and Emily to fill their leisurely lives as best they could in an age when women of their social standing rarely undertook gainful employment. Caroline died before Francis was born, but the dark silk shadows of her unmarried sisters, two of whom survived into their nineties, were still gliding about the rectory long after Francis had gone to sea.

Aunt Georgiana was anything but a shadow. Passionately devoted to her soldier husband, who followed distinguished but debilitating service in the Crimea with a period as Commander-in-Chief, Canada, she was thrown into paroxysms of grief when he died at Bilton Hall in September 1859. Once her sorrow had abated somewhat, she devoted her considerable energies to furthering the career of her son Arthur and to restoring her

Orlando Bridgeman-Simpson in characteristic confident pose, 1866

depleted fortunes. First, she tried to get the Crown to increase her widow's pension. When this failed, she turned her attention to her mother-in-law's will. The outcome of these exertions is not recorded, but they certainly drew the disapproval of her brother William, who objected 'very strongly' to her pleadings.[14]

William may have had reasons other than propriety for objecting to his sister's conduct. Georgiana's father-in-law, Sir George Eyre, KCB, had been a highly respected Vice-Admiral in the Royal Navy. Francis having recently entered the Service, his father obviously wished to keep in with the Eyres and anyone else with influence in naval circles.

Francis joined the Royal Navy's officer training ship *Britannia* in September 1861, aged nearly 13.[15] Regulations promulgated in 1773 stipulated that only the sons of noblemen and gentlemen were eligible for service as naval officers and to ensure this class bias was maintained, all would-be cadets required the nomination of an officer of the rank of captain or above. We do not know who put forward Francis' name but, as we have seen, the family was not short of naval contacts. As well as his godparents and the Eyres, there was also the possibility (albeit somewhat remote, given William's fraught relationship with his eldest brother) of using the Baring connection – Henry's wife Frances was closely related to the leading Whig politician Sir Francis Thornhill Baring (1796-1866), the future Baron Northbrook, who had served as First Lord of the Admiralty from 1849 to 1852. Although Francis may not have sought the help of his aunt's family at this stage in his career (two years' previously things had come to such as pass between the two brothers that William had contemplated leaving the rectory and taking a house in Boulogne!), they almost certainly assisted him 20 years later.[16]

As well as needing nomination, to enter *Britannia* cadets had to be between the ages of 12 and 14, in good health and able to pass a written examination at the Royal Naval College, Portsmouth.[17] This required writing clear and legible English from dictation, dictionary-assisted translation from Latin or a modern foreign language and basic geography, mathematics and geometry, including knowledge of the famous First Book of Euclid. Where Francis acquired this knowledge, we don't know. But he passed the exam and so stepped, full of teenage trepidation, onto the first rung of the long and tradition-crusted ladder of a naval career. As he climbed aboard *Britannia*, men who had served with Lord Nelson were still drawing their pay.

Britannia was a sort of floating minor public school. The ship itself was an ancient wooden three-decker, cleared out, painted in black and yellow to look like the *Victory* and converted by the addition of a massive greenhouse-like structure over a good part of the upper deck. For years the vessel had been moored in Portsmouth harbour, which one cadet believed was 'a very unhealthy spot because of the mud and drains of Gosport'.[18] This criticism was borne out by the epidemics that periodically swept through the crowded ship, culminating in several deaths from typhus in the autumn of 1861. Because the lives of well-connected young gentlemen were at stake, rather than those of ordinary seamen (some 15% of whom had died during a shipboard cholera outbreak when *Britannia* was flagship to the British Black Sea Fleet during the Crimean War), upon the advice of a team of inspectors the hulk was moved, first to Portland and then to the River Dart. Cadet Bridgeman, it

The stern quarters of HMS Britannia, *the Navy's antiquated and insanitary officers' training ship, c.1864*

National Maritime Museum, London

seems, was on board during the temporary sojourn of the ship at Portland. Not until 1898 was the 'damp and evil-smelling' vessel finally abandoned and the cadets moved to healthier and more spacious accommodation ashore.[19]

Cadets entered in batches of about 50 every three months – 'Cheeky New Fellows', 'Three Monthers', 'Six Monthers' and 'Nine Monthers' or 'Passing Out Numbers' – and stayed for four terms.[20] The ship's academic routine was well organised and high standards attainable, though not necessarily demanded. An able student like James Sisson, who attended voluntary extra lessons, found himself fully stretched and reacted favourably to the encouragement and enthusiasm of the 'very able' staff, one of whom lent James his room for private study.[21] Sisson, however, was an exception and the majority of the cadets, including Francis Bridgeman, muddled along towards their final exams only because they were the passport to a more exciting life beyond.

The cadets were divided into two watches, port and starboard, each of which comprised seven classes of 12 cadets. A senior cadet, known as a 'Captain', was attached to each class and given the powers of a prefect in a normal school of the time, which included using a bit of cord, or 'togie', on recalcitrant juniors.[22] Cadets rose at about 6 am and did drill or practical work before breakfast at 8 am. Lessons ran from 9 am to midday and from 2.00 pm to 4.30 pm, theoretical and practical work alternating. Wednesdays and Saturdays were half-holidays. Tea was served at 6 pm, after which cadets could retire to their hammocks when they wished. Francis' rectory upbringing was challenged as soon as he went aboard – on *Britannia* evening prayers were optional.

The academic syllabus was free from the obsession with the Classics that distorted British education until the second half of the twentieth century. In *Britannia* the emphasis was heavily on the practical. Many hours were devoted to seamanship (working with sails, spars, rigging and rope, with knots taught by the Captain!) and such algebra, trigonometry and astronomy as were necessary to make the cadets skilled navigators.[23] Each cadet had to provide himself with his own sextant, which he took with him when he left. Geography was, of course, compulsory, as were the less obviously practical subjects of history, scripture and French. In an understandable hang-over from the pre-photographic era, which annoyed the future Admiral Reginald Bacon, an inordinate amount of time was devoted to drawing.[24] Far more lamentable, as far as the long-term development of the Navy was concerned, was the absence of any training in engineering and the practicalities of steam power. The cadets of Bridgeman's generation, many of whom would one day command turreted steel battleships capable of sinking an entire fleet of triple-deckers while it was scarcely more than a speck on the horizon, left *Britannia* ready to furl the heaviest sail on the highest yard in the roughest weather, but almost totally ignorant of trajectory, horsepower, armour plate and coal consumption.

Ambitious cadets worked hard, attending voluntary evening classes that could earn them an extra 5% to be added to their final marks. There was some incentive for the less well-off to apply themselves diligently too, for those who obtained 75% in all subjects were awarded a first-class certificate and immediate automatic promotion to the rank of midshipman. As such, they were paid more and allowed to display a white patch instead of the white cord of a naval cadet. The conscientious James Sisson and Reginald Custance, who one day would replace Francis Bridgeman as Commander-in-Chief of the Home Fleet, made flying starts to their naval careers by getting firsts.[25] Bridgeman took a second-class certificate.[26] If he was to rise to a high rank, at some stage he was clearly going to have to learn to work.

Looking back, officers who had started their naval careers in *Britannia* were as divided as any group when questioned about their schooldays. H L Fleet remembered the single-sex dancing and Saturday evening sing-songs and concluded that 'the *Britannia* days offered a good deal of pleasure and happiness'.[27] Seymour Fortescue, on the other hand, reckoned there was no period in his life he looked back upon with such distaste as the time he spent in the *Britannia*.[28] Compared with the rigors of the late-Victorian public school, the cadets seem to have been treated with unusual civility. They had servants, a weekly allowance and plentiful food. Even James Sisson, whose Swiss upbringing had made him something of a gourmet, was pleased with the plentiful pies, hams, puddings and tarts, all washed down with beer and cocoa. There were confirmation classes to succour the souls of the spiritually inclined and plenty of opportunity for swimming and messing about in small boats. The Christmas and summer holidays were each more than a month long, and although regulations were tightened up after cadets were reported swaggering about town smoking pipes, passes were readily granted for long week-ends ashore.[29] Both Sisson and Fleet reported little bullying and no 'immorality'.[30]

Nevertheless, life in the training ship certainly had its unpleasant side as cadets were introduced to naval harshness and snobbery. Sisson encountered the latter shortly after his arrival, writing home to his father that he stood no chance of being invited to one of Captain Harris' special parties as he was not one of the favoured 'lords and honourables'. Others were occasionally invited but only if they were 'sons of influential persons or sons of his friends'. Lord Beresford, who would later make a name for himself as a celebrated naval maverick and sworn opponent of First Sea Lord Jackie Fisher, was 'always invited'.[31] Whatever his intellectual capacities, armed with a title, vigour and charm, Beresford was already destined to go far.

Equally galling and a sign of its espousal of ultimately irrelevant criteria was the Navy's growing obsession with appearance. From 1861 onwards cadets were obliged to wear (and keep spotless) impractical white trousers, specially steam laundered in London. To the distorted naval mind, clean pants rapidly became an indication of a cadet's aptitude to high command.

While snobbery and attention to appearance might have been depressing, at least they were not dangerous. Not so disease which, as we have already seen, constantly lurked in the cramped, insanitary living quarters. Furthermore, the ceaseless round of climbing and hauling in all weathers led to frequent injuries, some serious. The boys devised their own rigors, too. To prove their skill and bravery, by the end of their second term all new entrants were supposed to reach the topmast by scaling the futtock shrouds round the outside of the observation platform, rather than taking the easier and much safer route through the 'lubbers' hole' in the platform itself.[32] Furthermore, whatever Sisson and Fleet might have declared, senior cadets, some tattooed and many with an incipient drink problem, enjoyed throwing their weight about.

The physical and psychological demands of *Britannia* were excused as preparation for what was to come – a cadet who could not stand the pace in *Britannia* stood little chance of surviving long in a man o' war. The ultimate test, as in most schools of the time, was the ability to take punishment. Percy Scott, who became one of the most forward-thinking officers of his generation, heartily approved of the practice of frequently birching cadets 'publicly with great ceremony'.[33] To witness a beating, all cadets were paraded four deep on the main deck, where a stout table covered with a mattress was placed between two gunports. Proceedings were supervised by the commander, attended by the ship's surgeon and a sick-bay orderly, who brought along water and 'other paraphernalia' needed to treat the offender. When all was ready, the Master-at-Arms and a corporal brought the culprit forward.

> 'The Commander then made a short address in which he emphasised the heinousness of the offence. The wrists and ankles of the offender were securely fastened to the legs of the table, a sufficient portion of his anatomy exposed, and the corporal did the rest by laying on 15 of the best with a formidable birch.'[34]

It was, in our eyes, a barbaric practice. But it was nothing to the punishment the cadets would see meted out to erring able seamen.

Before they left *Britannia*, cadets were asked where they wished to serve. The choice was not as simple as it may sound. The most favoured posting was the Mediterranean, where it was rumoured there was nothing to do but 'go to parties – etc'. But the Mediterranean was also the 'extravagant station', open only to those who were well-connected and had sufficient private income to enable them to live far more grandly than they could ever do on their meagre naval pay.[35]

Francis Bridgeman, naval cadet second class, left *Britannia* on 26 November 1862.[36] A year and a half later he was posted to the Mediterranean.

NOTES

1   Like many large Victorian houses, in the twentieth century Babworth Rectory proved too expensive for ordinary domestic use. It was requisitioned by the Army during World War II, served as a pump maintenance training school for a while and now, whitewashed outside and arrayed with bars and sporting prints inside, it operates as the Haygarth House Conference Centre.

2   I am deeply indebted to Mrs Walter Hingston for a great deal of oral evidence about the Bridgeman-Simpsons. Where it has been possible to check her stories with authentic sources, they usually turn out to have a sound basis in fact.

3   Will of the Hon John Bridgeman-Simpson, Nottinghamshire County Archives.

4   Georgiana's diaries, uncatalogued, are in the Sheffield Archives, 1992/61.

5   *Ibid.*

6   Story related by Mrs Walter Hingston.

7   Mrs Walter Hingston.

8   31/8/1869, *Diary of A H Eyre*, Sheffield Archives, 1992/61.

9   Sheffield Archives, 1992/61.

10   'A Riddle by Lady Frances Fitzwilliam', recorded in the journal of her friend Mary Thompson, 12/10/1835, is the only example of Fanny's writing to have survived. It reads,

> *Three fourths of a cross and a circle complete*
> *Two semi-circles and a perpendicular meet*
> *A triangle standing on two feet*
> *Two semi-circles and a circle complete*
> = *TOBACCO*

11   See below, p. 59 et seq.

12   *Diary of A H Eyre*, Sheffield Archives, 1992/61.

13   21/12/1861, *Diary of Georgiana Eyre*, Sheffield Archives, 1992/61.

14   *Ibid.*

15   The Admiralty records are not clear. They state Bridgeman was in *Britannia* from 9/09/1862 to 26/11/1862, with '6 months sea time in Britannia Queens Regns'. As cadets served for four terms (i.e. about 15 months) in *Britannia*, it is likely that Bridgeman joined in the autumn of 1861. This would tie in with his Service Record which says that he entered service' on 9/12/1862, presumably on leaving *Britannia*. See PRO ADM 196/17 & 196/39 (II).

16   1860, *Diary of Georgiana Eyre*, Sheffield Archives, 1992/61.

17   *Navy List*, 1862.

18   10/11/1861, James Sisson to his father, the English pastor in Lausanne, NMM SIS/7.

19   Scott, *Fifty Years in the Navy*, p. 4.

20   Fleet, *My Life and a Few Yarns*, p. 23.

21 *Ibid.*, p. 25; 28/9/1860, NMM SIS/7.
22 Scott, *Fifty Years in the Navy*, p. 23.
23 Kerr, *The Navy in My Time*, p. 10.
24 Bacon, *A Naval Scrapbook*, p. 9. Although the need to draw unfamiliar coastlines and headlands was rapidly diminishing, training in the basic principles of art at least gave officers something to do during long, tedious voyages. The standard of illustration in many surviving logbooks and journals is surprisingly high and adds considerably to the pleasure of reading them.
25 12/12/61, NMM SIS/7.
26 PRO ADM 196/17.
27 *My Life and a Few Yarns*, p. 27.
28 *Looking Back,* p. 19.
29 24/1/1861, NMM SIS/7.
30 *Ibid.*, 28/9/1860; Fleet, *My Life and a Few Yarns*, p. 23.
31 24/1/1861, NMM, SIS/7. For Beresford's career, see Chapter 7.
32 Bacon, *A Naval Scrapbook*, p. 9.
33 Scott, *Fifty Years in the Navy*, p. 4.
34 Fleet, *My Life and a Few Yarns*, p. 24.
35 20/10/1861, NMM, SIS/7.
36 PRO ADM 196/17.

2 'The Queen's Navee'[1]

During his time in *Britannia* Bridgeman showed no great ambition and only average ability. When he left there was nothing to suggest he had the makings of anything other than a run-of-the-mill officer. Nor is there evidence that he took steps to make up for this in the years immediately following. Indeed, for some time he was marked out from the dozens of other cadets of his generation only by having the longest name in the service – Francis Charles Bridgeman-Bridgeman-Simpson.[2]

After a two-month break, on 29 January 1863 the 15-year-old cadet reported to the *Victory*, the doughty yet ancient and anchored flagship of the equally doughty but rather less ancient Commander-in-Chief at Portsmouth, Vice-Admiral Sir Michael Seymour.[3] In many ways Seymour's career epitomised what the mid-Victorian Navy was all about. At the age of 11 he had joined his father, captain of the *Hannibal*, for the last two years of the Napoleonic Wars. Having returned to school after the war, he rejoined the Navy in 1816 and, after various adventures, which included

HMS Victory *in Portsmouth Harbour c.1870*

losing a ship on the coast of Chile and an eye in the Baltic, in 1856 travelled overland to Hong Kong to take command of the China Station. Here he distinguished himself by capturing Canton and a string of forts near Tientsin, before returning home, laden with honours, to sit as MP for Devonport until 1863.

When he took up his command at Portsmouth, Sir Michael re-joined the large band of ageing senior officers whose naval expertise had been set fast in the time of Nelson. They performed well their limited tasks, which consisted primarily of flying the flag, helping maintain and expand the empire and acting, as one admiral rather grandly put it, as a 'World Police Force' – patrolling the seas and acting against slavers, pirates and others who threatened to disrupt the *Pax Britannica*. However, unlike their mentor, Lord Nelson, the naval grandees were instinctively conservative regarding most aspects of their profession. Particularly marked was their deep suspicion of new technology – Sir Michael had lost his eye when peering at a strange-looking object his crew had fished aboard off Kronsdadt. It turned out to be a mine.

Writers of the post-imperial era have had great and easy sport criticising the men, material and methods of Sir Michael's generation.[4] Indeed, as the immediate popularity of W S Gilbert's *HMS Pinafore* (1878) illustrated, it was a pastime also enjoyed by the Victorians themselves. In some respects, as we shall see, the criticism was wholly justified, particularly as the Navy often fell far short of the standards it set itself.

The prestige of the Royal Navy was universally recognised as 'beyond plausible challenge'.[5] Its position as undisputed Mistress of the Seas rested partly on its sheer size and partly on its reputation. It was also earned by default. When Bridgeman joined the *Victory* neither Germany nor Italy were united and none of the separate states of which they were comprised came even remotely near to being a first-class naval power. The Ottoman and Austro-Hungarian Empires were not interested in building up their naval strengths to a point where they might have threatened Britain's. The United States was torn by civil war, China was locked in a spiral of decline and Japan's remarkable modernisation had scarcely begun. Until the last quarter of the century, only France, with a smaller though technically more advanced navy, had the potential to challenge the Royal Navy. Even so, French interest in naval affairs was inconsistent and the cross-Channel threat was rarely an exacting yardstick by which the British Navy needed to measure its effectiveness.

Lack of serious competition and the over-confidence that it bred underlay the Navy's unwillingness to change during the leisurely 40-year decline after 1815. One effect was the 'Trafalgar syndrome': a conviction that what had been good enough for Nelson was good enough for subsequent generations. A second repercussion of the great events of 21 October 1805 was an unwillingness to weed out admirals who had served under Nelson and were now well past their sell-by date. Although First Lord Childers began getting rid of a few in 1868, others remained on the active list well into the 1870s. Another problem was promotion above the rank of captain by seniority. Although perhaps acceptable in wartime, when the death-rate was high, in peacetime it put the service in the hands of elderly and often backward-looking men, like the captain who objected to the introduction of steam power not on technical grounds but because it made officers indistinguishable from chimney sweeps.[6] Attitudes of this sort were far from uncommon. Under-educated and drawn from a narrow social clique, many officers had little regard for either the technology that might modernise their Service or for those with the skills to effect such a modernisation. Finally, until the 1880s the country showed little interest in naval affairs. Forts and soldiers were considered sufficient defence against invasion and as long as the Navy went on servicing the empire and recording the occasional morale-boosting victory over outgunned junks, the press and the government were content to leave it to its own eccentric devices.

Bridgeman was fortunate to have joined the Navy when he did. Thanks to outside pressure and to the efforts of the Duke of Somerset, who began a seven-year term as First Lord of the Admiralty in 1859, by the early 1860s some of the Service's worst abuses were at last being reformed. The days of the press gang were over and since 1851 able seamen had enjoyed continuous service, rather than being signed on and off with each ship they sailed in. Even so, the Navy was still an archaic, insensitive organisation.

Although sailors no longer felt they were being held against their will 'like convicts' (as a petition to the Lords of the Admiralty had claimed earlier in the century), leave was still a privilege and when a ship was in harbour the crew were frequently kept on board to avoid desertion.[7] 20 years' service, without a break, was required before a seaman earned a pension. Promotion to officer from the ranks was almost unheard of.

Conditions below decks were as sordid and insanitary as anyone who has visited Portsmouth harbour and ventured into the dark recesses of the *Victory* can imagine. Men slept in hammocks packed so close that the incumbents could not avoid touching each other. In bad weather, when the ports were closed, the air was so foul and the stench so powerful that officers frequently resented having to visit the crew's quarters. During Bridgeman's last year in *Britannia*, a report noted, not surprisingly, that 'consumption is the most uniform and persistent cause of the destruction of life' in the Royal Navy. Accident was not far behind.[8] Captain O W Andrews, who joined the Navy as a surgeon ten years later, estimated that in the 1870s about one man a week was lost in falls from the rigging.[9] Less serious accidents were commonplace. As only officers were permitted to wear shoes on board ship, after a few years of splinters, broken toes and crushed bones a sailor's feet resembled gnarled and misshapen gargoyles.

Before the establishment of a Cookery School in 1873, naval food was notoriously foul. In 1870 a cask of salt beef dated 1805 was still in store waiting to provision some unsuspecting vessel.[10] One ship's cadets were expected to present 24 dead cockroaches when they fell in for the morning parade, or face a beating.[11] During a long voyage drinking water stored in wooden barrels rapidly deteriorated to the point where consumption would have brought certain sickness. Temporary alleviation might be obtained from the daily ration of half a pint of rum, but this brought its own problems. Reginald Bacon remembered a lieutenant on board *Britannia* being so drunk he could hardly read the lesson at evening prayers, a misdemeanour which, as far as we know, was so unremarkable as not to merit punishment.[12] A combination of continual heavy drinking, the thunder of the guns at close quarters and constant slabbing of the head against low beams drove many sailors out of their minds. The more fortunate ones ended their days in the Navy's private lunatic asylum at Hoxton in London.

No survey of the turbulent, vicious life into which the young Bridgeman was thrown would be complete without at least a passing reference to that most infamous aspect of the Victorian Navy – punishment. As one historian has observed, 'Philosophically the naval establishment conformed to the classic conservative view about the worth of an individual: man was basically evil'.[13] One might add the rider that 'man' meant an ordinary seaman, not an officer. Given the type of recruit generally drawn into the Navy before 1860 (in 1831, for example, Admiral Codrington had been obliged to take into his ships all the unwanted criminals from London's jails), the officer class' contempt for their men is understandable, if not excusable. Barbaric and violent men, they argued, could be kept in check only by barbaric and violent means.

Until just before Bridgeman joined the Navy, corporal punishment was the 'principal method' of maintaining discipline.[14] Equally unnerving, the punishment system was totally lacking in regulation and basic justice. Each captain did as he thought fit. Some considered drunkenness the most serious crime (yet still gave the men their intoxicating daily rum ration) and punished accordingly. Sentences were both over-severe and over-lenient. On occasion a man was even tried for one offence and punished for another.[15]

Minor misdemeanours were dealt with by short-term detainment or cancellation of privileges. For more serious offences, ranging from rudeness to an officer to attempted desertion, the standard punishment was a flogging. In some ships men were flogged simply for being the last off the rigging. There was no appeal. The sentence was carried out with the 'cat', a wooden-handled whip with nine cord 'tails', each 28" long and knotted twice at the end. The whole ship's company was mustered to watch. The task of the surgeon was not to minister to the victim but to keep him conscious (and even alive) as long as possible. A dozen lashes was the minimum sentence, 36 was normal, 60 frequent and sentences of 100, 300 or even 1,000 were recorded, the latter being merely a particularly cruel form of death sentence.

Cruelty harms more than its victims and floggings barbarised the entire Service. The future First Sea Lord Jackie Fisher, a decent, humane man, fainted with horror the first time he saw the cat in action, then himself sentenced a man to 36 lashes five years later.[16] Percy Scott, in most respects a forward-thinking reformer, recalled a man receiving four dozen lashes on Monday and a further four dozen the following Saturday and commented favourably on the fact that he 'took them without a murmur' in 'the spirit which made this great country'.[17] As a young man Bridgeman witnessed several floggings.[18] Although the custom had been abolished by the time he was senior enough to have ordered it, the influence of the vicious regime of his early years may help explain why as a senior officer he was regarded as a strict disciplinarian and once reprimanded for unnecessarily clapping a man in irons.[19]

Some of the more glaring injustices of the Navy's disciplinary system were being reformed as Bridgeman joined. The Naval Discipline Act of 1860 had prepared the way for improved leave and pay, as well as setting up a formal Ship's Police. Corporal punishment was limited and the Table of Summary Punishments (1862) formalised sentences. All punishments were to be recorded in a Defaulters' Book and reported in a ship's Quarterly Returns. Gagging was outlawed in 1867 and 12 years later, following parliamentary debate and prominent coverage during an election campaign, use of the cat was finally suspended in peacetime. However, as in all institutions, there remained a gap between theory and practice. Officers in the more traditional or less tightly-run vessels continued to administer unofficial and off-hand punishment. Scott, for example, recorded one bullying commander exiling cadets and midshipmen to the masthead for minor misdemeanours. It was not such a gruelling experience in fine weather, when the boys could sit aloft with a book, but in stormy conditions it was both unpleasant and extremely dangerous.[20]

Along with the regulation of punishment went a parallel regulation of attire. Until the 1850s a ship's crew were dressed as the captain wished. Most seamen still appeared in 'Number Ones' similar to those worn in Nelson's day and in wet weather officers sported hopelessly impractical glazed straw hats. This notwithstanding, 'eccentricity to the point of madness was not uncommon'.[21] At his own expense, the captain of the *Harlequin* dressed his crew in multi-coloured uniforms suggested by their ship's name. When the men of *HMS Blazer* appeared in eccentrically striped jackets in 1843, the design was so popular that soon all fashion-conscious young men ashore were sporting 'blazers' of their own! Even after the dress regulations were tightened, a degree of variety inconceivable today was tolerated. It extended from a refusal to do up the requisite number of jacket buttons to the captain who made a 'tall white Ascot hat' an invariable part of his couture.[22]

In response to the damning reports of medical officers, from the 1860s onwards the Navy made a serious attempt to improve standards of on-board hygiene. As well as moving *Britannia* from the insalubrious mudflats of Gosport to more bracing anchorages at Portland and then Dartmouth, steps were taken to ensure that cadets were trained in high standards of personal hygiene. With a typical service dislike of half-measures, washing and cleanliness were elevated almost to fetish status. When Bridgeman was serving in the *Bellerophon* as a midshipman, at their daily muster on the aft deck the ship's boys were inspected by a senior lieutenant who ordered 'one or more boys to strip each day, to see they [were] cleanly in their persons'. Washing was done in twice-weekly shifts, 'using the appropriate side of the Head to that in use by the ship's company', and supervised by the seaman schoolmaster or the strips corporal. Part of his brief – unimaginable today – was to make sure that the boys stripped and washed one another.[23]

As with the men, so with the ships themselves: appearance and cleanliness became an obsession. By the 1880s it was customary for a commander to spend half his pay buying paint for his vessel as 'the only road to promotion'.[24] Nuts and bolts were gilded, magazine keys electroplated and on the smartest vessels gun carriages were French polished and cannon balls painted blue with a gold band round the middle. The Admiralty banned the practice only when it discovered that it increased the circumference of the projectiles to the point where they were too large to fit into the gun barrels![25]

We have only the thinnest outline of Bridgeman's time as a cadet. We know the ships he was attached to, but not what he did or where he went. In March 1864 he transferred from the *Victory* for a short and probably unpleasant spell in the iron troopship *Himalaya*, then under the command of Edward Lacy. Life perked up considerably in June when he moved to Captain William Rolland's steam corvette *Cossack*, possibly for the trip out to the Mediterranean where on 26 July he joined the *Liffey*.[26]

A cadet's life was not easy. The crew, particularly hardened seamen, had little respect for privileged teenagers with a minimal knowledge of sea. To midshipmen and junior lieutenants the new arrivals from *Britannia* were obvious targets for bullying – a common trick, apparently, was to mark their noses with two broad arrows.[27] Cadets continued their naval education, after a fashion, under the supervision of a seaman schoolmaster and were subject to continual scrutiny by all the officers on board, who were obliged to report immediately,

> 'any want of promptness in obeying an order or the slightest attempt at a reply on receiving one, swearing, dirty habits and anything improper.'

Officers were also asked to note 'those Boys who by their intelligence, alacrity, and smartness are deserving of advancement'.[28] We have no report of anyone suggesting at this stage that Cadet Bridgeman was 'deserving of advancement'! Indeed, it is likely that in his early years, like most teenage boys, he was more interested in having a good time than in furthering his career.[29]

And good times there were, too. Percy Scott, not a sentimental man and one who fought hard to bring the service he loved up to date, retained a close affection for the days of wood and sail. He delighted at the memory of sailing in a man-of-war in fine weather. With the sea drumming against the hull, the wind thrumming the rigging and the great white sails billowing like clouds in the breeze, it was like being in a 'gigantic yacht'.[30] Equally memorable were the evening ship-board sing-songs when, in a massive exercise in male bonding, the whole crew – as many as 800-strong – came together on deck to bellow out a traditional medley of verses sentimental, humorous and, to use the Victorian expression, 'strong'.[31] It was at such heady occasions, when the air was thick with addictive emotion, that the hardships, dangers and deprivations of a naval career were set aside and replaced in the sailors' hearts by a deep affection for the sea that frequently endured for the rest of their lives.

Nothing better illustrates the enormous adaptability required of Bridgeman and the naval officers of his generation than the fact that he began his career afloat in two 4,000-ton wooden hulks, the *Britannia* and *Victory*, and ended it almost half a century later in a 19,900-ton, all-steel battleship *Neptune*. The magnitude of the changes in ship design, construction and performance and the corresponding changes in thinking required of those who commanded them cannot not be underestimated. In *Britannia* and as a cadet Bridgeman was taught to think in terms of sail patterns, cannon fire, cutlass drill and knots (so vital a subject, it will be recalled, that it had been handled by no less a person than the captain himself). Even more significant, he had been taught to accept an order without question and to feel secure in the traditions (or, rather, the perceived traditions) that had triumphed at Trafalgar; in other words, not to think for himself, not to question, not to challenge. The wonder was not perhaps that the Navy found it hard to adapt to the age of iron and steam, but that it managed to adapt at all.

Warship design probably changed more between 1825 and 1900 than it had done in its entire previous history. The revolution was based on steam power, iron and steel construction, screw propulsion, high-velocity, shell-firing-breech-loading guns and electricity. At the suggestion of Marc Brunel, father of the more famous Isambard, the Navy first considered using steam power in 1814. The plan, which was for seaworthy steam tugs to tow battleships out to sea, was dropped as too fanciful. It was left to the

United States, which launched the first steam-powered warship the following year, to begin the power revolution. The Navy ordered its first paddle-steamer seven years later and by the end of the decade was beginning, slowly and with great uncertainty, to equip a limited number of ships with auxiliary steam engines. Some measure of the reluctance with which the step was taken can by gathered from the fact that although steam vessels first appeared in the *Navy List* in 1827, 35 years afterwards steam propulsion still hardly featured in cadets' education.

Opposition to steam came on many fronts. There were those, like Lord Melville, who objected simply because it was new and therefore untested. 'The introduction of steam,' grumbled the Tory First Lord of the Admiralty in 1828, 'is calculated to strike a fatal blow to the naval supremacy of the Empire'.[32] More considered reservation focused on the weight and space occupied by the engine and its concomitant means of propulsion, as (particularly with paddle wheels) armament had to be reduced to accommodate them. Others had doubts about steam's reliability, its vulnerability in battle and its limited range. A second controversy raged about whether paddle or screw was the best way of driving a steam-powered vessel. In 1845 the Navy arranged a tug-o-war between the two forms of propulsion and the screw won. That should have settled the matter, particularly as a screw propeller was almost invulnerable in action and left a ship's sides clear for cannon. But ever cautious (or just plain inefficient), the Service continued with a mixture of sail, screw and paddle for another 20 years. The *Liffey*, which Bridgeman joined in August 1864, was a 4,000-ton, eight-year-old paddle frigate that had been built at Devonport 11 years after the screw-paddle tug-o-war. The following year, now a midshipman, Bridgeman transferred to the *Topaze*, a fully-rigged frigate with an auxiliary engine and screw. Nine years later, with the appearance of the trend-setting 9,300-ton *Devastation*, fitted with two engines and two screws and only a single, stumpy iron mast, the sail versus steam battle was as good as over. There were, however, still ancient captains who, on entering port and ordering the sails to be lowered, wondered why their ships did not stop, and for a time vessels on long-range patrol continued to use wind power to conserve fuel.[33] But by and large, only 15 years after Bridgeman had left *Britannia*, much of the practical seamanship he had acquired there was totally redundant.

The second part of the nineteenth-century naval revolution was in design and construction. The British tradition in this field was not to pioneer, but to watch others and learn by their mistakes.[34] Although in many respects a wise policy, it positively discouraged innovative thinking at a time when technology was opening up all sorts of possibilities in the field of naval architecture. As a result, by the middle of the century even the Royal Navy's new ships were alarmingly old-fashioned. Three years before Bridgeman's birth, for example, *HMS Sanspareil* was laid down to a French design prepared 50 years earlier![35]

By the mid-1850s 20% of all new ships were iron-hulled. Nevertheless, the world's navies still preferred wood, for the very obvious reason that wood floats and iron sinks. A single well-aimed shot, it was argued, could sink an iron vessel, while its wooden counterpart could be easily patched and kept afloat. Another argument in favour of wood was its longevity. As we have seen, the vessels of Nelson's navy might remain in service for 60 years or more. Most iron ships were rusty hulks in half that time.

The French solved some of the problems by cladding a wooden-hulled vessel with iron plates several inches thick. *La Gloire* (launched in 1859) and Britain's first ironclad *Warrior* (launched 1861) initiated a series of dramatic changes in ship design and performance that 'entirely altered, not only the nature of the fleet, but the character of the naval profession'.[36] Later ironclads, defended by armour up to one foot thick and capable of 14 knots, had sufficient fire-power to destroy an entire fleet of Nelsonian triple-deckers single handed. The Navy laid down no large wooden ship after 1866. Soon ironclads gave way to ships with iron then steel hulls, protected by compound armour and armed with massive guns in turrets or barbettes.[37] As the ironclads and their successors rendered Britain's entire fleet obsolete, in a few years her proud lead in capital ships was destroyed. In response, the naval estimates rose by 25% to £12 million between 1858 and 1861 and remained at a consistently high level for the rest of the decade. Expenditure meant taxation, which dragged the Royal Navy into the political arena. From now on, particularly when expenditure again rose sharply towards the end of the century, it was not enough for a senior admiral to be just a good seaman. He was also required to be a first-class administrator and a sharp political operator. These, too, were skills in which Bridgeman and his contemporaries had received virtually no formal training. A man like Admiral Fisher made up the deficiency with a natural instinct for politics. But it left Bridgeman, to whom politics was a shifty game played by untrustworthy cads, painfully ill-equipped for the tasks he was expected to perform.[38]

A revolution in gunnery ran parallel to those in ship design and propulsion. Four factors held back development. One was the huge prize money, as much as £200 for an ordinary seaman, paid for the capture of an enemy ship intact. By the end of the century, when modernisers were recognising that future naval battles would be fought between fleets thousands of yards apart, British warships still carried a full complement of cutlasses and were trained to repel borders as effectively as they dodged torpedoes.

Another problem was that until 1886 the Navy and the Army were both supplied with guns by the War Office, which gave priority to designs favoured by the latter. This meant, for example, that the Navy often had to make do with muzzle loaders when breech loaders, for obvious reasons, would have been better suited to conditions at sea, particularly when large guns were housed in turrets or barbettes.

Thirdly, for a time the naval authorities were uncertain whether an ironclad was better suited to attacking an enemy by gunfire or ramming. Lastly, the standard of gunnery training was so lamentable that, however powerful their weapons, those firing them were unlikely to hit the target at anything but point-blank range.[39] When sailing with his brother in the *Blanche*, Orlando Bridgeman noted scornfully that in a heavy swell balls from the ship's guns travelled only 15 yards before hitting the water and ricocheting off 'a long way'.[40] Eleven years later Jackie Fisher was infuriated to find practice at *Excellent*, the gunnery school that the Navy had established in 1830, being carried out with old-fashioned smooth bore guns.

During Bridgeman's first 20 years in the service technical developments produced heavier projectiles but little improvement in accuracy. The way forward might have been shown by the breech-loading, rifled Armstrong gun, introduced in 1858. Unfortunately, although potentially a considerable improvement over the Navy's traditional smooth-bore, muzzle-loading 32-pounders, its breech was so unreliable that the gun frequently fired backwards. Thereafter, the Navy shunned heavy breech-loaders until 1882. The drawbacks of muzzle loading are well illustrated by the four 80-ton Woolwich Infants, which had been winched into *Inflexible* the previous year. Because the barrels had to be short enough to be withdrawn into their turret for reloading, the guns' range and accuracy were woeful. Recalling gunnery practice of the time, Admiral Penrose Fitzgerald was scathing about the hotchpotch of gun calibres and weights and the poor engineering that often led to broken guns or projectiles that 'turned end over end and went in any direction but the right one'.[41] There had clearly been almost no improvement since 1872, when the authorities had arranged a duel between two heavy-gun monitors and found that the Navy's best gunner missed his target by 200 yards.

As if trying to make up for its inability to fire straight, the Navy pressed ahead with heavier and heavier projectiles. The nine-inch guns of the *Bellerophon*, which Bridgeman joined the year after she was launched in 1865, fired shells four times heavier than those in use five years earlier. The *Dreadnought*, launched ten years after that, sported $12^{1}/_{2}$" guns and ten years later still, the *Benbow* boasted gigantic $16^{1}/_{2}$" guns, each weighing $110^{1}/_{2}$ tons. Thereafter, with the development of improved explosives, barrel diameter came down again.[42]

Bridgeman was in the paddle frigate *Liffey* from July 1864 to October 1865. As far as we know, he saw no action. Apart from the obvious excitement the 16-year-old must have felt at visiting the Mediterranean for the first time, the only event of personal note occurred on 21 August 1864, when Captain George Parker raised him to the rank of midshipman. As all cadets who had passed through *Britannia* were promoted automatically (unless they had stepped seriously out of line), we cannot read any significance into the promotion.

Bridgeman's education did not stop now that he had moved up a rung. In 18 months' time he faced the midshipman's intermediate exams in which he was expected to show proficiency in navigation and charts, French, rigging, sails, masts gunnery and small arms. He also had to prove that he was a 'fair practical observer' and keep a daily log which, in theory, was examined daily by the captain. Finally, if he was in a ship fitted with an engine, he was expected to understand how it worked.[43] Examinations took place on board and successful candidates were allowed to go forward to the final exams for promotion to the rank of lieutenant two years' later.

Back in England, on 1 November 1865 Bridgeman travelled down to Devonport to join the nearly completed *Topaze*.[44] Captained by Michael de Courcy, the fully-rigged, 2,600-ton steam frigate was undergoing trials before leaving for the Pacific station. We have no idea what Bridgeman did during the two months he was attached to her. One would like to think he use the time to brush up on his increasingly purposeless knowledge of sails, rigging and masts in preparation for his lieutenant's exams, but it is unlikely. At this stage of his career the good-looking boy showed little ambition and he probably found more amusing ways of passing his time than swotting.[45]

In January Bridgeman was on the move again, this time to Plymouth to join the *Royal Adelaide*. The old (1828) 104-gun 1st rate ship-of-the-line was now the flagship of another of the distinguished Seymour clan, Admiral Frederick Beauchamp Paget Seymour. One of the great eccentrics of the Victorian Navy affectionately known as the 'Ocean Swell', Seymour had distinguished himself during the Crimean War by negotiating the passage of the floating battery *Meteor* out to the Black Sea and back without major incident. He had also commanded the Australia Station and may possibly have encouraged Bridgeman to do the same when an opportunity arose.

After two months at Plymouth, on 21 March Bridgeman was off to sea again, this time aboard one of the Navy's most prestigious vessels, *HMS Bellerophon*.[46] The 7,500-ton warship, one of the largest afloat, had been launched the previous year and was only now fully operational. She was a transition ship, a personification of the Navy of her day. Her all-iron construction, with a 14-knot steam-assisted top speed and 10 9" and five 7" guns all pointed to the future, while her full rigging harked back to the past.

In the absence of more personal evidence, we can only build up a picture of Bridgeman's life in the *Bellerophon* from the ship's Order Book, which happily survives from this period.[47] The ship was commanded by Edward Tatham of the Channel Fleet (replaced in September 1867 by Captain Reginald Macdonald) with Harry W Brent as the Executive Officer. Petty rules abounded, such as the order that no one was to bathe on Sundays as it was not a working day and another that allocated two bags of potatoes to each watch and stipulated exactly when they were to be opened. Punishment was harsh, the most severe example being the 48 lashes and one year's hard labour given to James Adams ('alias Cororan') for an unspecified crime on 10 September 1867. Not surprisingly, the ship had the highest number of leave breakers in the Channel Fleet.

HMS Bellerophon, *a compromise of sail and screw*

The day began at 5.30 am (4.30 on Tuesdays for some inexplicable reason) when the crew had to rise and stow their hammocks before breakfast at 6 am. On a normal day the entire morning was spent cleaning the ship – polishing brass, scrubbing the decks and so forth. Dinner was taken at noon, followed by grog and a suitable rest period for its effects to wear off. Small arms were cleaned at 3.50 pm and supper served at 4.30 pm. The day closed with 'hammocks down' at 7.30 pm, lights out at 9.00 pm and 'pipe down' (i.e. silence) half an hour later. The Order Book makes no provision for regular gunnery practice.

The two highlights of Bridgeman's time in the *Bellerophon* came in July and November 1867. On the first occasion the ship escorted the Sultan of Turkey across the Channel as part of an Anglo-French show of solidarity with their ex-Crimean War ally. On the second the ship sailed up the Tagus and docked at Lisbon after stormy steam trials with the rest of the fleet in the Bay of Biscay. Released ashore, the British sailors drew a formal complaint from the governor of the Portuguese capital for their 'riotous & disorderly behaviour & indecent behaviour & assaulting police'.

One word in the official Admiralty records from Bridgeman's time in the *Bellerophon* is intriguing. Injury and illness were common enough on board ship and 'Hospital' next to Bridgeman's name clearly referred to no more than a temporary incapacity.[48] But it set an ominous precedent.

NOTES

1   *When I was a lad I served a term*
    As an office boy to an Attorney's firm.
    I cleaned the windows and I swept the floor,
    And I polished up the handle of the big front door.
    I polished up the handle so carefullee
    That now I am the Ruler of the Queen's Navee!
    W S Gilbert, *HMS Pinafore*, 1878, Act I.

2   *Navy List.*

3   Seymour was born in 1802, by when his future flagship was already 65 years old.

4   Many of the more horrifying and amusing details are collected in Bonnett, *The Price of Admiralty.*

5   Gordon, *The Rules of the Game*, p. 163.

6   Woodward, *The Age of Reform*, p. 273.

7   Bonnett, *The Price of Admiralty*, p. 16.

8   *Ibid.*, p.82.

9   *Seamarks and Landmarks*, p. 8.

10 Bonnett, *The Price of Admiralty*, p. 85.

11 *Ibid.*

12 Bacon, *A Naval Scrapbook*, p. 40.

13 Rasor, *Reform in the Royal Navy*, p.16.

14 *Ibid.*, p.42.

15 Briggs, *Naval Administrations*, pp. 146-7.

16 Bonnett, *The Price of Admiralty*, Chapter 3, has all the grisly details of Navy floggings one could wish for.

17 *Fifty Years in the Navy*, p. 8.

18 See below, e.g. p. 57.

19 'Disapproval expressed at Capt Bridgeman Simpson's action in imprisoning Acting ERAP Henderson in irons while awaiting Courts Martial. My Lords consider there was no necessity for such an action.' PRO ADM 196/17.

20 *Fifty Years in the Navy*, p. 8.

21 Bacon, *A Naval Scrapbook*, p. 17.

22 Scott, *Fifty Years in the Navy*, p. 12.

23 Order Book of *Bellerophon*, NMM BNT/3.

24 Scott, *Fifty Years in the Navy*, p. 60,

25 *Ibid.*, pp. 10-11.

26 PRO ADM 196/17.

27 Order Book of *Bellerophon*, NMM BNT/3.

28 *Ibid.*

29 See below, p. 71.

30 *Fifty Years in the Navy*, p. 6.

31 *Ibid.*, p. 7.

32 Cited in Bonnett, *The Price of Admiralty*, p. 51.

33 Bacon, *A Naval Scrapbook*, p. 32.

34 Incidentally, one of the major criticisms of the Navy's decision to go ahead with the revolutionary all-big-gun battleship *Dreadnought* (launched 1906) was that it broke with this tradition by producing new designs for others to benefit from and improve on.

35 Woodward, *The Age of Reform*, p. 27.

36 Briggs, *Naval Administrations*, p. 141.

37 A barbette was a fixed protective cylinder behind which guns rotated.

38 See below, Chapters 8-12.

39 See below, p. 93. One of the more remarkable gunnery stories was told by Percy Scott. When the 50-gun frigate he was serving on captured an Arab slaving dhow, they took off the slaves and crew and used their ship for target practice. When they had fruitlessly expended a quarter of the frigate's ammunition in inaccurate blasting, they gave up and sank the dhow by ramming it! Scott, *Fifty Years in the Navy*, p. 9.

40 19/4/1871, *Diaries*, Sheffield archives, 1992/61.

41 Fitzgerald, *Memories of the Sea*, p. 298.

42 See Chapter 5.

43 *Navy List*, 1865.

44 PRO ADM 196/17.

45 For more on the *Topaze*, see below, p. 69.

46 PRO ADM 196/17.

47 NMM BNT/3. All the information in the paragraphs that follow is from the same source.

48 PRO ADM 196/17

3 Blanche *and the Pacific*

Admiralty records state that Bridgeman left the *Bellerophon* on 10 February 1868 and transferred immediately to the *Blanche*, a steam corvette nearing completion in Chatham dockyard. One wonders, if he managed to get home for a few days between ships, what impression he created. His parents must have been proud of their handsome son. He was now 20 and, with a six-year unblemished if undistinguished naval record, safely on his way to promotion to sub-lieutenant. He had stories to tell – not all of them suitable for the vicarage table – and an air of maturity that must have left his mother wondering what had become of the little Francey whom only yesterday it seemed she had watched playing in the woods behind the rectory.

Francey off duty in Sydney, 1871

But did Lady Frances notice another, perhaps less welcome change? Over several years her son had been subjected daily to coarseness and brutality that were inconceivable amid the the clean linen and affectionate smiles of the rectory. He had been taught to obey, not question, to sublimate feeling to duty, that most misunderstood catchword of the revered Lord Nelson.[1] The impressionable young midshipman had witnessed drunken debauchery in the streets of Lisbon, sailors killed in falls from the rigging and flogged until their backs were raw flesh. Bullying and harshness had been his bedfellows. How had he received them? He was not an artist or an academic, able to escape into a cerebral world. Nor was he, by all accounts, a confident extrovert who might turn his back on the immediate darkness to fix his gaze on a distant star. Sensitive, slightly introverted (like his father) and perhaps short on intellectual confidence, over the years Bridgeman probably learned to protect the more vulnerable aspects of his personality behind a shield of formal discipline and good manners. The former guided him when his instinct might have failed; the latter made him universally appreciated, something valued by all who are not quite sure of their own abilities. The shield was not infallible – no self-imposed personality limitations ever are – and the most obvious manifestation of its failing was, not uncommonly, physical illness.

The 1,755-ton *Blanche* had been designed specially for service in distant corners of the Empire. 185 feet long and 36 in the beam, she was both attractive looking and capable of withstanding the heaviest seas. A projecting prow that in the eyes of one newspaper reporter 'gave her the appearance of a ram', featured a retractable bowsprit, allowing a gun to be fired forwards when the spar was stowed.[2] She was built of wood over an iron frame, making her both stronger and roomier than all-wood ships. The hollow iron lower masts doubled as ventilators to the lower decks, a provision that was very welcome in the tropics.

A single four-blade screw, designed to offer minimum resistance when under sail, driven by a twin-boiler engine could push the vessel to about 13 knots in favourable conditions. However, as the 250 tons of coal

HMS Blanche, *whose projecting prow was sometimes mistaken for a ram*

she carried were soon consumed, the engines were used sparingly. However irrelevant sail power was becoming in European and American waters, where there were ample coaling stations, self-sufficiency was still essential for ships cruising elsewhere, particularly in the empty vastness of the Pacific, which was where the *Blanche* was headed.

The *Blanche's* tour of duty on the Australia Station is the only part of Bridgeman's career for which we have evidence of his daily activities. This alone makes it worth recording in some detail. Furthermore, the almost Gilbertian exploits of the ill-fated corvette and her crew offer such a wonderful insight into the workings of the Royal Navy during Bridgeman's formative years that it would be perverse not to record them in some detail.

On 11 February, the *Blanche* steamed down to Sheerness to take on powder and shell. After a few days' trials, at 2.45 pm on 23 February she proceeded to sea, swung round North Foreland into the Channel and set course for Farm Cove, Sydney in the colony of New South Wales.[3] Aboard were 188 men and 21 officers, including 'Midshipman F C B Simpson' (as Bridgeman was inexplicably known in the ship's records and the Australian press), the shadowy and incompetent Captain James

Montgomerie, First Lieutenant Albert Markham, a domineering martinet, and Sub-Lieutenant Lewis Beaumont, whom Bridgeman had met in the *Bellerophon*.[4]

By early March, travelling anything between 52 and 239 miles a day, they were at Madeira. Two weeks later they crossed the equator with the 'usual ceremonies', lurched past the Cape of Good Hope in heavy seas on 26 March and put into Simon's Town to take on coal and provisions and refit some of the rigging.[5] Markham was delighted with the performance of his new ship, declaring it to be a 'perfect success as a steamer, besides sailing very well'.[6] Later, when Orlando Bridgeman joined the ship, he was nowhere near so impressed. He complained that the *Blanche* rolled heavily and did not behave well when sailing close to the wind. Captain Montgomerie, he felt, was 'very nervous' and shortened sail unnecessarily whenever the wind got up. Moreover, his navigation was not what one would have expected of a naval officer. His ship frequently missed its intended destination by a wide margin and touched bottom on several occasions.[7]

Albert Markham as a rear-admiral, 1893. Although stalked by disaster, he enjoyed a surprisingly successful naval career

From South Africa, where Markham had disciplined engineer McDougall 'for absenting himself from the ship without leave', the *Blanche* set out on the long haul to Australia.[8] To relieve the tedium of the voyage, the first lieutenant organised endless rounds of cutlass, rifle and gunnery drills (but no firing), washing, making and mending clothes, painting, cleaning and maintaining the vessel. On 7 May they had their first fatal accident when Leading Seaman William Allen fell from topmast rigging, 'receiving serious injuries'. He died the following day and his body was committed to the deep.[9] His last words – 'Poor, poor Smith!' – caused some consternation, not least to the superstitious Seaman Albert Smith, who from that time onwards regarded himself as jinxed.[10]

The *Blanche* steamed into Princess Royal Harbour in King George's Sound (Albany) on 28 May. After riding at anchor for a few days, where the crew practised firing live ammunition for the first time (albeit while stationary), she moved on to Sydney, where she arrived on 23 June. Sadly, Bridgeman had not done anything worthy of inclusion in Markham's log, journal or scrapbook. All we know is that he was quartered in the shell room, was attached to a rifle company and the ship's five-ton pinnace for drills, watched the starboard cable when the ship was mooring and during normal sailing was responsible for activity on and around the mainmast. In case of fire, his station was 'at the fire' itself, suggesting that his bravery and practicality were highly regarded.[11]

The *Blanche* remained on the Australia Station for three years. Although not exactly ideal preparation for the latter stages of his career, they must have been among the most interesting and perhaps enjoyable in Bridgeman's entire life. June and July were spent exercising, patching up the ship after the ravages of the outward voyage (this included replacing a fair bit of 'bad iron' used in her construction) and participating in several flag-showing activities, such as receiving the Governor of New South Wales, and firing salutes and dressing ship to mark various royal occasions. Then, in the middle of August, orders were received for the ship to proceed to the Solomons to 'redress certain grievances that had taken place' there.[12]

At first sight the lightly-armed *Blanche* was hardly the ideal ship to send on a mission that might involve gunfire. She carried only six guns, two seven-inch cannon mounted on swivels and four 64-pounders that could fire either 158-pound shells or 115 pound solid shot. The maximum official range for these weapons was 5,000 yards, although the chance of hitting anything at that distance was negligible. She also had a 12-pounder for use on land, a 24-pounder for the boats, two rockets and numerous small arms. By European standards, the *Blanche* was only just a warship. But she had been designed not to fight naval engagements but to police the Empire, and her few heavy guns were quite sufficient to overawe recalcitrants armed with no more than hand-held weapons. Besides, she also displayed the most effective deterrent of all: the white ensign.

First stop was Port de France, New Caledonia, where they hoped to meet up with Bishop Pattison, but he was nowhere to be found. Before they left, Markham observed a partial eclipse of the sun and the *Blanche* tried to help the French frigate *Alceste*, which had run aground. The mission was thwarted by a combination of broken hawsers, a malfunctioning boiler and Chatham's 'bad iron', and the *Alceste* was eventually rescued by another British warship.[13]

Quite what happened next is a bit confusing. It seems as if at some time during the past year a group of Fijians had taken it into their own hands to tackle a band of slavers who had been shipping their illegal cargo around the Eastern Pacific in the schooner *Marion Remy*.[14] Captain Rae and most of his dubious crew were lured ashore on Rubeana Island with the assurance that 'there were plenty men to be had'. The landing party then disappeared and the schooner was attacked. The chief purpose of *Blanche*'s 'reparations cruise' was to punish those who had taken the law into their own hands.[15]

The story is complicated by a comment in Orlando's diary, written three years later, in which he stated that the *Blanche* had been sent to collect a $3,000 fine for murder imposed on the 'Old King's Party' of Savii. As far as Orlando was able to gather, French priests had persuaded the islanders not to pay the fine, upon which Captain Montgomerie had given them further time to pay. 'This was very bad policy,' ventured Orlando, who rarely lost an opportunity to criticise the Navy, 'for they have no intention of ever paying'.[16] Whether this fine was related to the *Marion Remy* incident is not clear. Interestingly, Orlando also noted that the islanders were very keen to be ruled by either the British or the Americans, for they found French and German administrators harsh and exploitative.

Be that as it may, by September the *Blanche* reached Guadalcanal Island in the Solomons, where 'natives came off in great numbers in canoes and traded, bartering cocoa nuts, yams and warlike weapons for pipes, tobacco, etc'. She then moved on to Banquetta Island. Here she anchored and fired a blank 'to frighten a body of natives assembled on the beach, which effectively did so'.[17] The next stop was Rubeana Island, where the *Marion Remy* incident had taken place. The islanders, Markham observed, 'seemed to know what we had come for'. What happened next was an example of imperial justice at its roughest.

On the evening of 10 September a shell was fired towards a light on the shore, which was instantly extinguished. At dawn the following day the pinnace (Bridgeman's boat – was he on board?) was sent ashore with a party of armed marines and sailors. At eight o'clock the *Blanche* opened fire with shot and shell at a village at the head of Rondora Bay. As they were firing at a stationary target at short range from a ship riding at anchor, some hits must have been scored, but to make sure the job was done properly further armed men, bringing the total to 60, were sent ashore to destroy the village. The Fiji press said 'three or four chiefs' were shot.[18] Markham's journal says only that the landing party returned at 11.35 am, bearing the body of Seaman George Eastough who had been killed by a pistol shot. Before burning the huts not destroyed in the bombardment, they had found 35 skulls, five of which were European. This unsavoury incident was the only active service Bridgeman saw in his entire 51-year naval career.

The *Blanche* spent the rest of the month pottering about the Solomons and New Hebrides. From time to time she fired her guns, partly to impress the islanders and partly to brush up on her gunnery. On 22 September she picked up a couple of intrepid missionaries and set out for Sydney six days later. The day before she arrived Montgomerie and Markham felt it necessary to give William Cole 30 lashes, 'for theft'.[19] By now, although still legal, use of the cat was almost obsolete and its use can have done little for the crew's morale.[20] It was probably no coincidence that as soon as they docked in Sydney the recalcitrant Engineer McDougall again went off without permission.[21]

After a month's flag-showing in Sydney, the *Blanche* went down to Wellington, New Zealand, where she arrived on 29 November, 1868. Whatever we may think of the ship's harsh discipline, its superficial manifestations certainly impressed her new hosts. 'Everything throughout the ship, not excepting the engine room, is scrupulously clean,' wondered the *Taranaki New Herald*, 'so much so that a stranger feels ashamed to touch the bright brass handrails, etc'. As well as the cleanliness, visitors were surprised to see a bookcase amidships 'filled with works from the best authors, available for all hands', and two baths, one for the men and a second for the engineers 'who enjoy the choice of hot and cold water in theirs'. The crew's ability to raise the top gallant masts and set the sails in two-and-a-half minutes and launch the pinnace in three minutes (well done Midshipman Bridgeman!) were also noted with approval. Civilian observers, like many in the naval hierarchy, clearly believed neat appearance and meticulous time-keeping were an essential concomitant of first-rate strategy, tactics and fighting skills.

The New Zealanders' warm reception of the *Blanche* was tinged with relief. For eight years the islands had been troubled by conflict between the European settlers and the native inhabitants. After a lull, skirmishing had broken out again, particularly in the region of Waikato where British and Maori possessions overlapped. As overland travel in the colony was still slow and difficult, an extra warship on the station was most welcome. Not only did it enable men and supplies to be moved easily to where they were most needed, but it was a powerful symbol of Britain's power and determination to stand by her colonists. In these circumstances perhaps Montgomerie and Markham's endless burnishing and drills were not altogether pointless – the very presence of a glittering, ensign-flying warship that could launch its cannon-firing pinnace in three minutes was enough to sow doubt in rebel minds and boost the spirits of those it had come to defend.

Accordingly, in December the *Blanche* made a stately, attention-attracting cruise up the eastern coast of North Island, calling in at Hawkes Bay, Poverty Bay, Hick's Bay, the Bay of Plenty and Maketu Sound. Supplies were dropped off and guns fired 'for the edification of friendly chiefs'.[22] After celebrating Christmas with athletic sports at Te Papa, the ship returned to Wellington early in 1869. The first two months of the new year were spent putting on an entertainment in the Odd Fellows Hall, ferrying military 'swells' up to Wanganui on the west coast and receiving the Governor of New Zealand, His Excellency Sir George Bowen.

Quite what Montgomerie and his men made of the distinguished scholar and lawyer who liked to draw parallels between the territory he governed and Classical Arcadia, we do not know, but he did not remain on board for long. Certainly he had more important business to attend to than pretending to be interested in naval brasswork, and when he went off to negotiate with the Maoris (whom he romantically compared with Jacobite Scottish Highlanders), the *Blanche* weighed anchor and headed south for the Auckland Isles to look for the crew of the missing merchant vessel *Matoaka*.

Although the bleak and inhospitable Auckland Isles had already been claimed for the British crown by the *Victorious*, Montgomerie was either not aware of this or he chose to ignore it, for on 16 March, as the *Blanche* lay at anchor in Sarah's Bosom, a haven in Ross Island, Markham recorded that they formally 'took possession of the Auckland Islands in the name of her Most Gracious Majesty Queen Victoria. [They then] fired a *feu de joie* and gave Three Cheers'.[23] The next few days were spent exploring and charting, making what were rather grandly described as 'roads', replenishing the islands' supply depots and looking vainly for signs of the crew of the *Matoaka*. On 20th they were driven onto rocks by heavy seas and were fortunate to get away without serious damage. The autumn storm lasted throughout the voyage back to Auckland, rolling the ship past the maximum extent of its roll pendulum (30°) and carrying away the forward staysail.

Bridgeman left for this little voyage of exploration a midshipman and returned a sub-lieutenant. His promotion took place on 24 March.[24] With the *Blanche* battling with the gales and massive waves of the South Pacific, there can have been little time for ceremony. At this stage he was only an acting sub-lieutenant, for to acquire the full rank he needed to spend time at the gunnery school *Excellent* and study navigation at the Royal Naval College, Portsmouth.[25] To receive promotion he was required to pass practical exams, supervised by three captains. For those, like Bridgeman, unable to obtain the services of three captains, provision was made for examination by a single captain and other suitably qualified officers. Presumably, therefore, Bridgeman was examined by Montgomerie and Markham. Since they managed to ground the *Blanche* several times during her stay on the Australian Station and were not always quite sure of their exact position, the standard they set was probably not too exacting.[26]

After a diver had examined the *Blanche*'s hull and found the Auckland Island rocks had done no serious damage, on 21 April 1869 she was ordered to Port Lyttleton, Christchurch. Here she picked up the Governor and his distinguished guest, the Duke of Edinburgh, for passage first to Port Chalmers (just north of Otago) then back up to Wellington, where they arrived on 2 May. The 25-year-old duke was no less a person than Prince Alfred, second son of Queen Victoria. In accordance with his own and his father's wish that he should experience normal life, Alfred had chosen a naval career. Needless to say, he was not treated normally and after passing through *Britannia* he was raised to the rank of captain in 1866, aged 22. His visit to New Zealand was part of an extended tour of Australasia and South America in the *Galatea*, which for some reason he had left in Wellington when he came south. We do not know whether Bridgeman and the duke exchanged many words together, but certainly contact with the Navy's most distinguished recruit, who went on ably to command the Channel and Mediterranean Fleets (1883-89), cannot have done the young sub-lieutenant any harm. Moreover, Prince Alfred was a friend and contemporary of Bridgeman's future mentor, Sir Michael Culme-Seymour. Perhaps, after an exchange of formal pleasantries on the gleaming decks of the *Blanche*, Francis Bridgeman had been noted as the sort of well-connected, reliable young gentleman whose career was worth advancing.

To the obvious delight and pride of the European settlers, there were now no less than six Royal Navy warships in New Zealand waters: the *Blanche*, *Galatea*, *Challenger*, *Virago*, *Clio* and *Rossario*. The *Galatea* left to resume her Pacific cruise on 1 June and a few weeks later the *Blanche* made one of her periodic flag-showing forays into the Pacific, this time to Samoa and Fiji. At Bau they received a visit from King Thakembau – a 'fine looking old fellow' – before sailing to Sydney for a full refit.[27]

It was now 18 months since the ship had left England and the strain was beginning to tell. Two sailors, one of them certainly the worse for drink, fell into Wellington Harbour. Acting First Lieutenant McKenzie was arrested for being too drunk to keep his morning watch and the irrepressible McDougall was finally dismissed the service, presumably for taking yet another of his unauthorised leaves. Of Bridgeman, however, no mention is made, either favourable or otherwise.[28]

The next four months were marked by a string of minor mishaps. In September the *Blanche*'s attempt to tow the New Zealand schooner *Edith* from Sydney to Wellington failed when the hawser parted. A small-arms shooting match against the No. 1 Company Wellington Rife Volunteers ended in humiliating defeat, 425 hits to 267. Two of the *Blanche*'s vaunted marksmen recorded no hits at all at 500 yards. 'We were licked' recorded Markham with dismal honesty.[29] Three weeks later Cadet Maynard was given 24 cuts with the birch for some unspecified misdemeanour, and the ship twice hit rocks on a flying pre-Christmas visit to Fiji. Worse was to come.

The first two months of 1870 were spent supporting anti-Maori operations around Te Papa. Then, after a spell in dry dock to patch up the various dents and scrapes along her hull, on 8 March the *Blanche*, with 25 native police on board, set sail for Cape York in north-east Australia. A request for help had been received from the local magistrate, Mr Chester, who had reported that 'some white people' might have been 'detained as prisoners by the natives of Prince of Wales Island'.[30] A glance at the map will show that the direct passage from Sydney to the Torres Straits takes a vessel straight through the Great Barrier Reef. Given the *Blanche*'s unenviable record for collision with natural obstacles, it would have been difficult to have devised a more ominous mission.

The voyage up to Somerset, a small port just below the Cape, passed off with only one mishap – the temporary loss of the ship's fire engine overboard 'through the carelessness of the officer of the watch'.[31] The native police then easily sorted out the little local difficulty and on 12 April the *Blanche* turned for home.

At 9.40 that evening, as the corvette was steaming south at a steady seven knots, she suddenly came to a juddering halt on Campbell Reef.[32] The captain went astern and tried in vain to back off. The starboard bilge keel remained stuck fast on a submerged rock which, Markham claimed, had not been shown on the chart. With a stiff easterly breeze threatening to blow the vessel towards a reef looming to starboard, it was essential to free her before the wind got up any more. When listing and rolling the ship by moving the guns about had no effect, they tried hauling her off with hawsers attached to anchors. This resulted only in broken hawsers and the loss of two anchors. The native police were taken off in the cutter to Mount Earnest Island and the exhausted crew turned in for the night.

At high water the following morning, Wednesday 13 April, a further attempt was made to haul the ship clear. As before, it got nowhere. Despite lightening the ship by dropping surplus chain over the side and making a raft of spare spars, as she settled onto the reef that afternoon the iron stanchions and bulkheads of the coal bunkers started to buckle alarmingly. At 10.15 that night a third unsuccessful attempt was made to haul her free.

By the morning of the 14th the *Blanche* was in serious danger. The decks had risen five inches and the main steam pipe was close to fracturing. If it did so, all power would be lost and the ship would certainly founder. In desperation, further spars were added to the raft and tons of coal and shot were jettisoned. The exhausted crew lowered the masts and moved them to the stern of the ship with the sails and all equipment light enough to be manhandled. At 5.30 pm the aptly-named ketch *Retrieve* came out from Somerset and anchored nearby, ready to lend assistance. Finally, at 10.38 that night, with the engines going full astern, hawsers straining and the crews of the pinnace and cutter rowing for all they were worth, the *Blanche* came off the reef and slipped out into deeper water. Just as everyone was congratulating themselves on their success, the raft that had been made out of the ship's spars drifted off into the darkness and disappeared.

The extraordinary pantomime continued for a further week. Although the wind was still threatening to blow his ship onto the reef at any moment, Captain Montgomerie insisted on fishing up from the sea bed as much of his abandoned equipment as he could find. In the process the cutter was holed and saved from sinking only by running it up onto the raft, which fortunately had not been carried too far off. Eventually, minus only one anchor and a few shot, lengths of hawser and chain, the *Blanche* picked her way gingerly down to Brisbane, where she arrived on 10 May. Before entering the harbour, Montgomerie fired a gun to signal that he required a pilot. Even in well-charted waters, he was not taking any further chances.

It took the Sydney shipyard the rest of May and all of June to restore the battered *Blanche* to her former glory. Her rigging was replaced, the hull and decks were caulked and, where possible, the twisted iron was straightened. Markham kept the men occupied with the usual, mind-numbingly tedious rounds of washing, exercising, drills and so forth, while the officers enjoyed the occasional croquet party or 'hop' with the élite of Sydney society.

In early July, much to the Captain's dismay, news came that a fire had been seen on one of the Auckland Islands, suggesting that there were indeed survivors from the *Matoaka* lurking there. The croquet mallets were packed away and once again the *Blanche* headed towards the stormy south. 40 miles east of Sydney she ran into a violent storm and was apparently saved only by Markham's foresight.[33] To cheer themselves up on arrival, the officers went 'pig hunting' before they began looking for castaways.[34]

The visit was as dismal as the last. No Crusoes were found and a great deal of time was wasted dragging for an anchor and chain lost during their previous visit. It was freezing cold, with heavy seas and a cruel wind driving snow flurries up from the Antarctic. Shortly before they left, Seaman Thomas Green was sentenced to 48 lashes. When they returned to Wellington in August, Sub-Lieutenant McKenzie was court-martialled and dismissed the service. Whatever the charges levelled against Green and McKenzie, it seems quite clear that the *Blanche* was not a happy ship. One would like to think that whatever else Bridgeman picked up from his extraordinary experience on the Australia Station, at least he saw how a ship should not be run.

Armed Maori opposition to European rule was almost over, although Chief Tito Kowaru caused a bit of a scare in September and October by rumbling fully-armed around the Taranaki region. The *Blanche* ferried constables up from Wellington and hung around off shore for a while as a glittering warning to Tito Kowaru of the 'might of Her Majesty', then slipped back to Wellington.[35]

An incident now occurred that 'cast a universal gloom over the whole ship'. One afternoon a sailor working at the fore topmast slipped and fell, cracking open his head on the boom before tumbling into the harbour and drowning. The accident itself was horrible, especially as bits of the man's skull were found embedded into the wood of the boom. But what really shook the crew was the victim's name: Albert Smith. The prophesy of the dying William Allen, made over two years previously, had been fulfilled. The *Blanche* was becoming an unlucky ship, it seems, as well as an unhappy one.[36]

Around Christmas 1870 the mood lightened, perhaps as the end of the tour of duty was approaching. The '*Blanche* Minstrels' put on a concert ashore to raise money for Albert Smith's mother and small steamers brought a regular flow of Wellingtonians to inspect and marvel at what one local paper called the 'finest specimen of naval architecture we have seen in these waters'.[37] The climax of the festivities was a cricket match: *HMS Blanche* v Wellington Cricket Club.

The match was more a fête than a sporting contest. Throughout the day bands played, stall-holders peddled their wares and bored children were diverted with donkey rides. His Excellency the Governor, a 'scientific player' of great local repute, honoured the local team with his presence and all government offices closed at noon so that his minions could see him in action.[38] Sport was close to New Zealanders' hearts even before they became an independent nation.

The two-innings' match started at ten o'clock sharp. Wellington batted first and swiftly notched up a handy 226 all out. The only disappointment was the Governor, who was bowled by Markham for six. The *Blanche*'s batting, like their marksmanship and navigation, was dire. In the first innings they were all out for 53, of which Sub-Lieutenant Simpson made six. In the second innings they did a little better, struggling 97 all out, thanks largely to a sterling last wicket partnership between Gunner Rawlings and Sub-Lieutenant Simpson who was left 17 not out. Now, at last, we have evidence that Bridgeman possessed at least one of the qualities likely to mark him out for promotion – he was a jolly good sport.

The local paper resisted the opportunity to gloat over the home side's victory by an innings and 76 runs, commenting generously 'the wonder is that they [the *Blanche*] shaped so well as they did' considering their lack of practice. As the proper match was over by 5.30 pm, two fresh teams were picked for an exhibition game. This turned out to be merely an opportunity for the governor to show off the talents that had let him down earlier. Opening his side's innings, he made 62 in a manner the local paper sycophantically described as 'in every respect admirable'.

Bridgeman's prowess with the bat clearly raised him in the sporting governor's estimation, for when shortly afterwards he went on an official visit to Whangarei, he was accompanied not only by Captain Montgomerie but also by a 'Mr Simpson'. The party stayed in colonial grandeur at the Whangarei Hotel and were greeted the next day by grateful 'settlers and many natives'.[39] The choice of Bridgeman to accompany the captain on the trip – the young sub-lieutenant's first official engagement – suggests that by the age of 22 he already demonstrated the civility, tact and geniality for which he would become universally respected in later life.

By Boxing Day 1870, the *Blanche* had made her way to Hobart Town, Tasmania, where her pronounced prow led to her being mistaken for a French warship.[40] The arrival of the Navy was a great event in the small colonial capital. The ship's officers were invited to several balls and reciprocated the kindness by sending the ship's fire engine (now recovered from the sea and cleaned up) to help extinguish a blaze in the town. There was, of course, the obligatory cricket match, this time against the Married Men of Hobart Town XI. The *Blanche* XI lost by over 100 runs.[41] Unfortunately, Bridgeman was not able to repeat the attention-attracting form he had shown in New Zealand. He made six and two not out and did not bowl.

Conscious of his duty to foster good relations with his colonial hosts, Montgomerie delayed the *Blanche*'s departure for Australia so that she could participate in Hobart's Twenty-Fourth Grand Anniversary Regatta. The day of games, entertainments, rowing races and a grand luncheon of interminable courses and even more interminable speeches was concluded with a dance and a display of night-time rocketry from an illuminated *Blanche*.[42]

By February 1871 the *Blanche* had moved on to Adelaide. There being no revolts to quell or lesser disturbances to sort out, the days passed in a tedious routine of drills and cleaning, punctuated only by a visit on the 8th by the energetic but otherwise undistinguished Governor of South Australia, Sir James Fergusson. Four days later, however, a sudden shaft of light fell on the young Bridgeman when his 32-year-old, globe-trotting brother Orlando steamed into Port Adelaide and foisted himself on Captain Montgomery and his crew for the next six months.

After dining with his father and brothers William and George at the New Falcon, Greenwich, on 29 August 1870 Orlando had boarded the *Paramatta* and set sail for Sydney. If there was a purpose to his journey other than pleasure, it is unclear. Having already undertaken a grand tour around the United States with his cousin Lord Milton (the future Earl Fitzwilliam), it seems that Orlando was bitten with an irrepressible quest for adventure and discovery. Now, in the company of two companions (Henry and Garbull, the latter usually referred to as 'the shrimp'), he was off to add Australia to his already lengthy tourist itinerary. He was no ordinary tourist, either. Oozing a Harrow-educated and well-connected confidence, he enquired, snooped, compared and marvelled with a surprising lack of prejudice, recording his thoughts and findings in a series of interesting diaries. The day after his arrival he bumped into 'an old shipmate of Francey's in the *Bellerophon*' who was now growing sugar in Fiji.[43] He soon picked up a string of acquaintances (noting how 'extraordinary' it was that 'one's Harrow friends turn up all over the world'), talked his way into honorary membership of Sydney's Union Club, hunted everything that moved, especially kangaroos, and expressed delighted surprise to find an *Illustrated London News* picture of Mary Fitzwilliam tacked up on the wall of a house in the outback.[44]

Our only regret is that, apart from a few incidental remarks, Orlando avoided giving intimate detail about his younger brother. That he was looking forward to seeing him is obvious. On 22 November he wrote that he was beginning 'to get into rather a state of excitement about ... whether Francey will be in Sydney,' and he was 'disgusted and disappointed' to find that the *Blanche* was in Auckland when he reached Sydney three weeks later.[45] Yet when they met, his only observation was that Francis was 'very much grown but otherwise not altered' and he had taken up smoking a pipe.[46]

Once Orlando had his leg over the gunwale, there was no denying him. After a warm welcome, he 'fairly took possession' of the ship, setting himself up in the Captain's lower cabin 'which he had kindly put at my disposal'.[47] When not prevented from doing so by his official duties, Francis followed his vigorous elder brother in a ceaseless whirl of sporting and social activities. They went on a kangaroo hunt with the governor, a dance at 'Mrs Hart's' and took opposite sides in a shooting match between the *Blanche* and the Harnley Gun Club.[48] 'Mr O Simpson', shooting for Harnley, came equal first with the Captain after the first round, hitting

Francis and Orlando in Sydney, 1871

five birds out of five released from the traps, and then went on to win the shoot-off. 'The whole business was great fun, so totally unlike Hurlingam,' commented the delighted Orlando.[49] His lowly opinion of the *Blanche*'s ability to shoot straight with any weapon was confirmed a couple of days later when he found its gunnery practice to be no more than 'pretty fair'.[50]

The brothers spent the rest of February in Adelaide before the ship moved on to Melbourne in March, from where they took a short vacation in Tasmania. Orlando loved the island and its people. Its shrimps, he declared, were 'capital' and he was tickled pink when he called at the Commonwealth Bank to withdraw some money – 'a commodity we could not get hold of in Melbourne' – and was told with disarming good humour, 'Oh, take the whole bank if you like'.[51] Significantly, perhaps, Francis was frequently too 'seedy' to share Orlando's wholehearted enjoyment of the colonial scene. He was too unwell to avail himself of a free ticket to the Melbourne Races, he was sick during the crossing to

Orlando dressed for the outback, 1871

Tasmania and he had sun-stroke during a sight-seeing trip up the Derwent River.[52]

At the end of the month the party received a telegram calling them back to the *Blanche*, which had been ordered to make another flag-showing foray into the Pacific. Although there was some urgency in the request, the crew hung around in Sydney for a further fortnight doing nothing in particular 'except the usual round of ... visits and dinner'.[53] By the middle of May they were at Upolu Island, Samoa, where the *Blanche* undertook some showy gunnery practice while Orlando went ashore to explore. Before long he had ingratiated himself with 'my friend Jim', been entertained in his hut and witnessed a war dance.[54] He announced the people of Savii 'as fine a race of men as it is possible to see' and delighted in their local concoction of cocoa-nut milk, claret and lime juice: 'One of the best drinks I know, ... so cool and refreshing'.[55] On Francis' day off he accompanied his brother to Jim's hut, where they both sat cross-legged on the floor and ate oranges before returning to the ship by canoe.[56] The image of the young Francis, his naval formality set aside for a few hours, seated on the ground and eating fruit with his Samoan host is one of the closest and most endearing we have of him.

For several days the *Blanche* continued its round of intimidating gunnery, formal landings 'for edification of chiefs' and 'savage' picnics.[57] Orlando was bowled over by the grace and beauty of a local Samoan chief's daughter who came on board on 25 May and was equally impressed by the dignity of the elderly King George of Tonga, who visited the ship dressed as a rear-admiral on 3 June.[58] From Tonga they proceeded to Fiji, where Orlando wandered too far from the ship and got caught up in a local battle between the shore people and their inland rivals, the 'Mountain Devils'. Francis was sent to find him and escorted him back to the safety of the ship.[59] An undated cutting from the *Fiji Times* suggests that the *Blanche's* visit was not altogether welcome. Her mission, it was reported, was to uphold British exploitation of local people.[60] At Levuke she seized the schooner *Challenge*, detained by the British consul for kidnapping natives to work 'against their wishes and consent', and supervised its return to Sydney in the hands of a prize crew.[61] By early July the *Blanche* herself was back in Sydney, from where Orlando sailed for San Francisco at the beginning of the following month. Sadly, his detailed written observations went with him, shutting off the valuable light that had illuminated his brother's career and returning him to the shadows of formal report and passing reference.

Whatever sorrow Francis may have felt at his brother's departure, it was tempered by the knowledge that his long tour on the Australia Station was almost at an end. The *Blanche* set sail for home in mid-September, arriving on 10 December 1871. On Monday 18 December Arthur Eyre wrote in his diary that he had heard from 'Carly' [Caroline Bridgeman] that 'Francey' had arrived in London on Saturday night. 'Aunt Fanny received telegram Sunday morning,' he continued, '& she & Uncle Wm. & Mary started off at once for London to see him'.[62] After almost four years' absence, the sailor was home from the sea.

Notes

1   Nelson's famous pre-Trafalgar message that England expected each man do his duty was more a signal for a general free-for-all rather than the vague patriotic exhortation which subsequent generations believed it to have been. See Gordon, *The Rules of the Game*, pp. 159-160.

2   Markham, *Scrapbook*, NMM MRK/8.

3   Markham, *Journal*, NMM MRK/7.

4   Markham's scrapbooks and journals are the principal source of information on the *Blanche* at this time. Although his career lurched from one disaster to the next, powerful patronage shielded him from the more severe consequences of his actions. See Gordon, *The Rules of the Game*.

5   Markham, *Journal*, NMM MRK/7.

6   Markham, M E & F A, *Sir Albert Hastings Markham*, p. 41.

7   1871, *Diaries*, Sheffield Archives, 1992/61.

8   2/4/1868, Markham, *Journal*, NMM MRK/7.

9   *Ibid.*

10 From an unspecified newspaper cutting in Markham, *Scrapbook*, NMM MRK/8.

11 11/2/1868, Markham, *Logbook*, NMM MRK/9.

12 14/8/1868, Markham, *Journal*, NMM MRK/7.

13 September 1868, Markham, *Journal*, NMM MRK/7 and *Scrapbook*, NMM MRK/8.

14 The information that follows has been taken from cuttings, some for the *Fiji Times*, collected in Markham, *Scrapbook*, NMM MRK/8; see also Markham, *Logbook*, NMM MRK/9 and *Journal*, NMM MRK/7.

15 Unspecified Sydney newspaper in Markham, *Scrapbook*, NMM MRK/8.

16 7/6/1871, Orlando Bridgeman, *Diaries*, Sheffield Archives, 1992/61.

17 3/9/1868, Markham, *Journal*, NMM MRK/7.

18 Markham, *Scrapbook*, NMM MRK/8.

19 Markham, *Journal*, NMM MRK/7.

20 Later, a retired admiral said a flogging he witnessed in 1869 was 'probably one of the last ... carried out in the service.' (Stokes-Rees, ed., William Stokes-Rees, *Yarns From An Admiral's Reminiscence*, unpublished mss in NMM STR/17, p. 7.) Obviously, Stokes-Rees didn't know what was going on aboard the *Blanche*.

21 Markham, *Journal*, NMM MRK/7.

22 15/12/1868, *ibid.*

23 Markham, *Scrapbook*, NMM MRK/8 and *Journal*, NMM MRK/7.

24 PRO ADM 196/39 (II).

25 *Navy List*, 1865.

26 *Ibid.*, 1871, records his having a grade 2 in seamanship.

27 3/7/1869, Markham, *Journal*, NMM MRK/7.

28 Markham, *Journal*, NMM MRK/7 and *Logbook*, NMM MRK/9.

29 8/10/1869, *Journal*, NMM MRK/7.

30 Cutting from an unspecified newspaper in Markham, *Scrapbook*, NMM MRK/8.

31 10/3/1870, Markham, *Journal*, NMM MRK/7.

32 *Ibid.*, which is the source of most information on the Campbell Reef incident.

33 Markham, M E & F A, *Sir Albert Hastings Markham*, p. 41.

34 Markham, *Scrapbook*, NMM MRK/8.

35 Cutting from *Taraniki Herald* in Markham, *ibid*.

36 *Ibid.*

37 *Ibid.*

38 *Ibid.*, from which all details of the cricket match are taken.

39 *Ibid.*

40 *Ibid.*

41 *Ibid.*

42 *Ibid.*

43 12/12/1870, Orlando Bridgeman, *Diaries*, Sheffield Archives, 1992/61.

44 *Ibid.*, December 1870 - January 1871.

45 *Ibid.*

46 12/2/1971, *ibid.*

47 *Ibid.*

48 February 1871, *ibid.*

49 22/2/1871, ibid. Markham, *Scrapbook*, NMM MRK/8.

50 24/2/1871, Orlando Bridgeman, *Diaries*, Sheffield Archives, 1992/61.

51 19/3/1871, 21/3/1871, *ibid.*

52 February - March, 1871, *ibid.*

53 1/3/1871, *ibid.*

54 18/5/1871, *ibid.*

55 24/5/1871, *ibid.*

56 20/5/1871, *ibid.*

57 25/5/71, 24/5/1871, Markham, *Journal*, NMM MRK/7.

58 Orlando Bridgeman, *Diaries*, Sheffield Archives, 1992/61.

59 6/6/1871, *ibid.*

60 Markham, *Scrapbook*, NMM MRK/8.

61 *Ibid.*; 7/6/1871, Markham, *Journal*, NMM MRK/7.

62 Eyre, *Diaries*, Sheffield Archives, 1992/61.

4 Last Chance

By the time he returned to England at Christmas 1871, Bridgeman had more experience of the world than most people see in a lifetime. He had sailed to the other side of the globe and back, visited the storm-swept Auckland Isles and the sunny havens of Samoa and come close to shipwreck on several occasions. He had witnessed death in many and horrible forms and seen both the best and the worst of human nature. Fêted, harassed and bullied, he had met exotic Pacific royalty, cheery colonial pioneers, pompous administrators, soldiers, slavers and sailors galore. Although his naval schooling, particularly regarding preparation for modern warfare, had left much to be desired, he could hardly have received a broader general education for whatever lay ahead.[1]

What lay ahead at the close of 1871, presumably, was the decision whether or not to remain in the Navy. We have no evidence that he contemplated leaving the Service either now or later but, as we shall see, at this stage his commitment to the Service was probably not as strong as it would become.

Surprising, even harsh though it may strike us today, Bridgeman had no official leave after his four-year Australasian tour.[2] He was still only an acting sub-lieutenant and needed to get the formal qualifications in gunnery and navigation before his promotion could be confirmed. To this end, on 19 December 1871 he was transferred to the Royal Navy's gunnery training school *Excellent*, where he remained until 13 April 1872.[3] Based on an old triple-decker launched in 1809 and an outdated turret ship, *Excellent* had been set up in 1830 in an effort to improve the Navy's gunnery. It had yet to fulfil the purpose for which it had been established. The very position of its hulks, moored head to stern on mud flats up a creek in Portsmouth Harbour and joined by a rotten wooden walkway, seemed to reflect the lack of importance which the Navy attached to them. Although they had been augmented in 1856 by the purchase of the adjoining Whale Island as a parade ground, this was no more than 100 acres of quagmire where convicts dumped clay and mud dredged from Portsmouth Harbour. 'Attitude is the art of gunnery – and whiskers make the man,' was the sort of mind-set reformers had to contend with and the *Excellent*'s staff began their instruction by apologising to their students for the poor quality of their out-of-date equipment. They need hardly have done so. The design of Naval gun mountings had changed little since Elizabethan times.[4]

The course began with theory – calculus, conic sections, chemistry, physics 'and a few other subjects with long names' – then advanced to the practical.[5] Target practice was carried out on ancient, unstable gunboats that rolled heavily in the slightest swell. The firer stood some two yards behind his weapon, clutching the piece of string that discharged his weapon. In theory, he yanked the lanyard when the two metal sights on the gun barrel were in line. In practice, because a ship was never at rest, he had to fire when the vessel was rolling upwards and just before the sights came into line. Good shooting required perfect eyesight and hand-eye co-ordination – and a fair measure of luck. Not surprisingly, less than 2% of gunners could place a ball within a foot of a flag 1,000 yards distant. 'The gunnery in those days was deplorable' commented Percy Scott in 1919, and officers who specialised in gunnery 'were laughed at as mere pedants and coiners of long words'.[6] The majority of captains still regarded their ships as either armed conveyors of fighting men or as platforms for encounters at close quarters, and inspecting admirals often left the ship at the time of the gunnery demonstration as they found the noise and dirt offensive. If we remember that this was a mere 44 years before the Battle of Jutland, fought between warships on the high seas scoring multiple hits on each other at ranges of several miles, then the inadequacy of the training afforded men of Bridgeman's generation is thrown into its true, alarming perspective.

Bridgeman's precise whereabouts and activities in the early months of 1872 are unclear. At some time he must have attended the Royal Naval College at Portsmouth as well as *Excellent*, for on 13 April his service record states that he 'passed college' and by June the *Navy List* is assigning him a third class in both gunnery and navigation.[7] He was now a full sub-lieutenant, albeit not a very distinguished or well qualified one.

The day after qualifying, Bridgeman joined the *Pembroke*, the Sheerness flagship of Vice-Admiral Charles Elliott. Perhaps bored by the dull routine of exercises and drills or fed up that the Navy had yet to grant him any leave since he joined the service, at his own request on 21 May he began two months' shore leave to which a further two months was added later.[8] What he did with his time ashore remains a mystery, although if his later pleasures are anything to go by he probably enjoyed a little shooting. It is doubtful that he read much and we have no evidence that he sought the pleasures of the opposite sex. Even if he did not, given his good looks and charming manner, the ladies probably sought him.

While still on leave, Bridgeman was assigned to the 51-gun wooden steam frigate *Narcissus*, the Plymouth flagship of Rear-Admiral Frederick Campbell.[9] The 3,500-ton vessel was still undergoing a major refit when Sub-Lieutenant Bridgeman joined her on 4 October and the ship's company remained cooped up in the adjoining hulk *Canopus* until 22 November.[10] Finally, in early December Captain Hopkins took the *Narcissus* into the Channel for post-refit trials. When the necessary adjustments had been made and a short break taken for Christmas, on 15 January 1873 they set sail for Vigo, Portugal, as the preliminary stage of Bridgeman's first crossing of the Atlantic.[11]

The voyage began in heavy seas. A sailor was lost in a fall from the rigging and an upset bogie caused a serious fire alert, so they had to put in at Vigo for a few days for repairs.[12] Then they were off across the ocean, sailing as part of a small squadron first to Madeira then on to Barbados and other British Caribbean possessions. The routine was much as it had been in the Southern Hemisphere, although on a rather grander scale. The dull rigmarole of cleaning, exercising and drill was punctuated by visits from island governors and formal displays of imperial power. The sun shone, the breeze was gentle and, as far as we can gather, the officers thoroughly enjoyed themselves. What the men confined below decks for long hours in tropical heat thought of it all, we can only imagine.

Barbados, Tobago, Trinidad, St Lucia, Antigua ... the *Narcissus'* itinerary reads like a modern cruise brochure. For Bridgeman there was the added pleasure of becoming a full lieutenant on 8 April. It was an automatic promotion for all who passed their exams. Nevertheless, having spent 3 years 266 days waiting for the moment, it was no doubt a sweet one. By this time the *Narcissus* had made her way to St Christopher, from where she went on to St Kitts and Jamaica on 15 April. In Jamaica Bridgeman left the *Narcissus* for a second stint in the fully-rigged *Topaze*, now serving as a training vessel.[13]

It is easy to mock the Navy's continued use of training ships like the *Topaze*, whose technology was dating by the day. But as long as the Service had vessels with masts and rigging, then it needed to train men to operate them. After all, only on the way out to the Caribbean the *Narcissus* had lost a man in a fall. The *Topaze* served other functions, too. As those who sail large vessels today understand very well, the key to the successful operation of such ships is teamwork, which life *Topaze* was designed to foster. Finally, several of Bridgeman's contemporaries spoke up for sail training for health reasons. As steam replaced sail, many officers were concerned at the decline in their men's fitness.[14] Where possible, they persevered with masts and rigging, at least in training, as a way of bucking the trend. Reginald Bacon believed the rigging a 'unique gymnasium'. Percy Scott agreed and felt that scampering about the spars and ropes was a 'fine training for a boy, although,' he added with no sense of irony apparent, 'it cost many lives'.[15]

We do not know whether any lives were lost in the *Topaze*'s airy gymnasium while Bridgeman was on board. He left the ship on 25 May and seems to have returned home in a mail steamer, arriving on 13 June 1873 for four months on half-pay.[16] A lot had been going on at home that year. On 28 March Uncle Henry had died, leaving Babworth Hall and his fortune for his wife's use, upon whose decease they should pass not to the family but to an outsider, Lieutenant-Colonel Henry Denison. Henry's other substantial property, Bilton Hall, went to his nephew Granville. William's family were left out of Henry's will altogether.[17]

A month later, on 30 April, Orlando married Catherine Cotes. It was by all accounts a happy union and their three daughters, Lilian (b. 1874), Evelyn (b.1877) and Olga (b.1878) grew up close companions of their distinguished Uncle Francey. We have only two clues as to what Bridgeman did when he returned that summer. We know that he was at the rectory in August, because Arthur Eyre baldly mentioned his presence there in his diary.[18] Beforehand, on 24 July, he had asked for his pay (four shillings a day when on board) to be forwarded to J A & W C Hallett & W H Dadge. The decision to have his affairs handled by his own firm of solicitors suggests not only a growing independence but also that he might have started to think more carefully about his future. A period on half-pay, Orlando's marriage and the (expected) cold shoulder in Uncle Henry's will may well have set the 25-year-old Bridgeman thinking. If he wished to remain in the Navy, which was now looking more certain, then to achieve a reasonable standard of living he had better succeed. And that meant doing rather better than third class in his exams, however charming and good at cricket he might be.

After a short spell at Devonport in the *Aurora*, in November Bridgeman was taken out in the paddle dispatch vessel *Helicon* to join Captain John Soady's *Invincible* in the Mediterranean.[19] It was significant move. Bridgeman's new ship, a Type 14 ironclad, was about as far removed from the *Topaze* as a ship could be at the time and quite unlike anything in which he had served before. Of 6,000 tons displacement, capable of 12.5 knots and armed with ten 9" and six 4" guns, the *Invincible* may well have been the vessel that fired Bridgeman's enthusiasm for the modern warship. It seems that this keenness attracted Captain Soady, too, for a couple of years later he reported to the Admiralty that he found Lieutenant Bridgeman a 'most promising officer'.[20] It is the opening entry in his Confidential Report and the first suggestion that he might, after all, have the makings of a distinguished sailor.

In July 1874 Bridgeman returned home in the *Helicon* for another spell on half-pay, before returning to the *Excellent* in September 'to qualify as a gunnery officer' on the 'long course'.[21] Here he would almost certainly have noticed the work being done on the development of torpedoes by one of the Navy's brightest young stars, the mercurial Jackie Fisher, who had recently been promoted to captain at the age of 33. Two future admirals,

May and Custance, were among Bridgeman's contemporaries. However, despite the inspirational presence of Fisher and the distinguished competition of May and Custance, Bridgeman made a mess of things. After only 17 days of the supposedly long course he left the *Excellent* and returned to sea.[22]

At this point a family story may be of relevance.[23] According to Charles Hingston, husband of Bridgeman's niece Mildred, over port one evening Bridgeman stated that around this time (the precise date is uncertain) he let himself down badly when attending a gunnery course at *Excellent*. Told that he was about to be posted to a menial position on a harbour guard ship, the certain graveyard of his career, he went to plead his case with his commanding officer (one would like to think he was Jackie Fisher, but he was more likely to have been Captain Thomas Bandreth). Bridgeman apologised for his slackness – he had apparently been treating his time at *Excellent* as an extension of leave – and asked to be given one last opportunity to redeem himself by serving in a major ship. The officer agreed, but warned the would-be playboy lieutenant that it was quite definitely his final chance. Bridgeman took it and the incident turned out to have been the major turning point in his career.

The ship that Bridgeman joined on 17 October 1874 was none other than the 10,500-ton *Northumberland*, captained by Thomas Lethbridge and flying the flag of the Channel Fleet Commander-in-Chief Admiral George Hancock.[24] During April 1875 Bridgeman was off sick for a fortnight.[25] This interlude apart, he obviously performed his duties on board satisfactorily, for after a summer on half-pay he was allowed to rejoin the *Excellent* on 29 September 1875. Over the next three years he divided his time between the gunnery school and the newly-established Royal Naval College at Greenwich (1 July 1876 - 7 June 1877), where he gathered the qualifications necessary for him to rise to the next rung on the naval ladder. In August 1876 he was awarded, in slightly mysterious circumstances, an Honorary Certificate from the Royal Naval College.[26] According to the *Navy List* of 1873 this distinguished qualification was 'given to Officers who are admitted as Students for a course of voluntary study, and who reach a certain standard at the examination on completing their course.'

By 1877, of the 22 officers raised to the rank of lieutenant at the same time as Bridgeman, only three could match his qualifications.[27] This, and Soady's laudatory observation, certainly suggests that his attitude had changed during the mid-1870s.[28] Not only had he volunteered for an academic course, but from somewhere he had found the interest and perseverance to shine at it. One assumes, nevertheless, that he took time off to attend the marriage of his 25-year-old sister Mary to the syphilitic bounder Walter Pleydell-Bouverie, which took place on 22 February 1876.

From Greenwich, Bridgeman moved back to the *Excellent*. Thanks largely to Fisher's dynamism and intelligence, the gunnery training school was changing fast. Though it was not yet the 'naval Mecca to which every ambitious young sailorman turned his eye' and some of the instruction was still dangerously haphazard (one officer recalled how a supposedly blank Hale's War Rocket was let off in the ammunition room, at which the entire class exited promptly through the portholes!), the school was far more efficient and forward-looking than when Bridgeman had first joined it.[29] Nevertheless, reverting to type, on 12 May 1877 he picked up only a Third-Class Certificate.[30] This entitled him to an allowance of five shillings a day. Such were the vagaries of the Royal Navy, however, that for the next nine months he was kept on half-pay and so had to manage on half-a-crown a day.

He returned to Portsmouth in February 1878 for the month-long Whitehead Torpedo Course at *Vernon*, an offshoot of *Excellent* established by Fisher in 1875.[31] Had someone with Fisher's imagination been around in the 1850s, when the Manchester inventor Robert Whitehead first approached the Navy with his idea for an underwater missile, a great deal of time and money might have been saved. The Service rejected his concept, only to buy it back ten years later under license from the Austrians. Fisher had immediately realised the torpedo's huge potential and turned *Vernon* into one of the Navy's most dynamic establishments.

We don't know what use Bridgeman made of his time there, but he remained a firm believer in torpedoes and torpedo craft for the rest of his career.[32]

After the *Vernon* Bridgeman spent a tedious few months in barracks while attached to the harbour-bound Sheerness flagship *Duncan*. The decrepit vessel was merged with the barracks two years later. In January 1879 he finally went back to sea. He joined the 2,000-ton corvette *Encounter* as senior lieutenant and first gunnery officer and left on his second extended overseas tour, this time to the China Station.[33] To begin with things did not go well. When the ship was inspected about six months after her arrival on station, Commander-in-Chief Admiral Robert Coote reported to the Admiralty that discipline on board the *Encounter* reflected 'discredit on [the] Captain [Hon Albert Denison] and Senior Lieutenant'.[34] Unfortunately, we do not know whether the disciplinary problems arose out of slackness or over-zealousness. If Bridgeman was still following the *Blanche* example, they may well have been the latter. Be that as it may, Denison took most of the blame and on 28 December he was replaced by Captain Charles Robinson, an officer of the favoured clique linked to the royal family, freemasonry and the powerful Culme-Seymours.[35] Even before his arrival, Bridgeman appears to have pulled himself together. His Service Record entry for 3 December reads: 'VGI, VG Gunnery, strongly recommended'.[36] Allied to the in-crowd and attracting favourable comment from his superiors, he was an officer very definitely on the way up. He was probably not harmed, either, by recent changes at the Admiralty. The First Lord in Gladstone's new administration was Francis Baring, Lord Northbrook, relative of Bridgeman's widowed aunt Frances.

Bridgeman continued to attract golden opinions throughout his stay in the Far East. 'VGI, VG Gunnery Lieutenant; an efficient officer and zealous First Lieutenant,' reads his Service Record for 20 March 1881, with the surprising postscript, 'Knows French'.[37] As all officers had to study French during their training, this presumably means that somehow he had acquired extra proficiency in the language. This may well have proved useful during his negotiations with Britain's *entente* partner,

1911-12.[38] By the end of 1881 Captain Robinson was 'strongly' recommending Bridgeman for promotion, repeating the sentiment two years later.[39] Weightier voices than Robinson's had also joined the chorus of approval of the 35-year-old lieutenant. Following Vice-Admiral Lord John Hall's inspection of the *Encounter* in the spring of 1883, which found the vessel 'a very creditable man of war', the inspecting officer recommended Bridgeman 'privately' to First Lord Northbrook.[40]

HMS Encounter *at anchor, 1879*

By the time Hall's words reached Britain, Bridgeman was on his way home. He had not been well. After three weeks' incapacitating illness in early 1882, on 13 November he was again taken unwell and remained off duties until 2 February 1883.[41] He was now tired and probably a little homesick and depressed. One cannot help wondering whether his ill-health was in some way related to his wish to see his family again.

Much had changed during his four-year absence. The ageing Willie and Fanny now had the Babworth Rectory almost to themselves. Of their children, only Francis' second sister Caroline, now 31, remained at home. The volatile Aunt Georgiana, whose distress had redoubled by the death in 1879 of her beloved and only son Arthur in the Ashanti Wars, stayed there from time to time. So too did the rector's remaining unmarried sister, Isabella. Otherwise, the rectory's long corridors and shaded rooms were cheered only by occasional visits from children and grandchildren.

Orlando, master of his own household, appears to have been serving in the West Yorkshire Yeomanry. The Rev William's second son, William, was away in Canada, while the third, George, may by this time have become Registrar of the District Probate Registry at Wakefield, a second Yorkshire connection. Their beautiful sister Mary had died tragically in childbirth in 1880 and her husband, Walter Pleydell-Bouverie, had married again and already started a second family.[42] In 1881, the third sister, Beatrice ('Bea'), had married Adolphus Duncombe, third son of the Dean of York. The marriage would remain childless. Three family connections with Yorkshire must have drawn Bridgeman north during his periods of leave from the mid-1880s onwards. On one of these visits he met Emily Shiffner, a charming spinster in her early forties, who lived with her mother at Copgrove Hall, Burton Leonard near Harrogate, an estate once owned by the Duncombes. The couple corresponded and the friendship blossomed. So began the longest and perhaps only deeply affectionate relationship of Bridgeman's life.

Copgrove Hall

He was on half-pay (4/3 a day) from 14 August to 29 October 1883.[43] He then went back to the *Excellent* for a third time 'to requalify'.[44] Things had moved on since he was last there, and he needed to catch up with both the advances in gunnery technology and the new professional attitudes emanating from the *Excellent*.[45] Fisher had recently become captain of the establishment and if Bridgeman had not had close contact with him previously, he must certainly have done so now. The straightforward, reliable Bridgeman was just the sort of man Fisher worked with best. Firebrand Fisher provided the inspiration and ideas, Bridgeman saw to the practicalities. Although he was never 'in the Fishpond' with Fisher's closest allies, during his time at *Excellent* he formed an alliance that did his career no harm. He also worked beside two other men who would feature prominently in his life in the years ahead, the gunnery expert Percy Scott and the bright young star of the next generation, John Jellicoe.

Incidentally, Bridgeman's 79-day stay at the gunnery school was some of the the last formal training he received.[46] Apart from one further gunnery course and a short spell at the *Vernon*, that was it. We have no record of his being given the opportunity to attend refresher courses or receive theoretical education in key areas such as signalling and strategy. Henceforward, he had to rely largely on instinct and experience to guide him through the profound changes in almost every aspect of naval practice that revolutionised the Service over the next 35 years. For an under-educated man who preferred the salt breeze to the still of the library, it would not be an easy path to negotiate.

NOTES

1 There is no way of telling what influence the harsh, incompetent Lieutenant Albert Markham exercised over the young Bridgeman. He may have been partly responsible for Bridgeman's attachment to strict discipline in later life. As far as seamanship goes, however, the pupil seems to have rejected his master's example. While Markham's propensity for nautical misjudgement continued unabated, culminating in the disastrous collision of the *Camperdown* and the *Victoria* in Malta harbour in 1891, by then Bridgeman had acquired a reputation as a first-class handler of warships of all types. See below, pp. 101-102.

2 He remained on full pay from 1864 to 1873. PRO PMG 15/78.

3 PRO ADM 196/17.

4 Bonnett, *The Price of Admiralty*, p. 131. Scott, *Fifty Years in the Navy*, p. 26.

5 Scott, *Fifty Years in the Navy*, p. 30.

6 *Ibid.* p. 26.

7 PRO ADM 196/39 (II)

8 PRO ADM 196/17; see also William Stokes-Rees, *Log of the Pembroke*, NMM STR/3.

9 PRO ADM 196/17.

10 *Ships and Service*, L.L.P.P.; Lieutenant Houston Stewart, *Log of the Narcissus*, NMM SWT/201.

11 *Ibid.* Stewart's *Log* is the chief source of information on the voyage of the *Narcissus*.

12 A bogie was a wrought iron cradle in which a heated cannon ball was placed to provide warmth, like a sort of storage heater.

13 PRO ADM 197/17.

14 Fitness for what? one wonders. Presumably, the concern was that unfit sailors would not perform well in hand-to-hand fighting, either on board or on shore. As both potentialities were now increasingly remote, the fitness question was largely irrelevant for anything other than general health reasons.

15 Bacon, *A Naval Scrapbook*, p. 40; Scott, *Fifty Years in the Navy*, p. 36.

16 *Ships and Service*, L.L.P.P.; PRO ADM 196/ 17; PRO PMG 15 78. The custom of putting men on half pay when not actually attached to a ship (meaning some officers spent almost half their naval careers on half-pay!) was incompatible with a fully professional Service and was eventually stopped early in the next century.

17 Nottinghamshire County Archives.

18 Eyre, *Diaries*, Sheffield Archives, 1992/61.

19 His movements between 27 October and 15 November, when he joined the *Invincible*, are unclear. *Ships and Service*, L.L.P.P.; PRO ADM 196/17.

20 PRO ADM 196/86.

21 PRO ADM 196/39 (II); *Ships and Service*, L.L.P.P.

22 PRO ADM 196/17.

23 See Chapter 1, note 2.

24 PRO ADM 196/17.

25 *Ships and Service*, L.L.P.P.

26 PRO ADM 196 39 (II). See also *Ships and Service*, L.L.P.P. The two sources do not quite tally.

27 *Navy List*, 1877.

28 In 1876 Soady was captain of the *Pembroke*, the flagship of the Admiral Superintendent of Chatham, Rear Admiral Charles Fellowes. It is unclear how he came across Bridgeman in this capacity.

29 Yexley, *The Inner Life of the Navy*, p. 117; Rowland Stokes-Rees, ed., William Stokes-Rees, *Yarns From An Admiral's Reminiscence*, unpublished mss in NMM, p. 10.

30 PRO ADM 196 39 (II).

31 *Ships and Service*, L.L.P.P.

32 See pp. 186, 190 for Bridgeman's support for flotilla craft in the Mediterranean.

33 PRO ADM 196/17.

34 PRO ADM 196/86.

35 See Gordon, *Rules of the Game*, pp. 337-339.

36 PRO ADM 196/86.

37 *Ibid.*

38 See pp. 184-185.

39 PRO ADM 196/86.

40 *Ibid.*

41 *Ships and Service*, L.L.P.P.

42 His second wife was Edith Lascelles (d. 1902), a granddaughter of the third Earl of Harewood. Their first child, Humphrey, was born in 1883. He was followed by Nancy, May ('Molly') and Elizabeth ('Betty'). Details of the family genealogy are taken from family trees and other papers in the private possession of Lady Loch, great-granddaughter of Mary Pleydell-Bouverie through her second daughter, Sybil.

43 PRO PMG 15/78.

44 PRO ADM 196/17.

45 Fisher played an important part in raising the status of gunnery in the Navy. As well as calling for heavier, quicker-firing and more accurate guns, he tried to see that they were used to good effect by modernising target practice and encouraging competitive shooting for prizes.

46 In his illuminating essay on Bridgeman as First Sea Lord, Nicholas A Lambert describes Bridgeman as not a 'gunnery expert' ('Bridgeman', p. 60). While strictly speaking this may be true – Bridgeman was never really 'expert' at anything – he was a gunnery officer and had received far more theoretical education in that speciality than any other.

5 In Sickness and in Health

Leaving *Excellent* in January 1884, Bridgeman went to the Mediterranean as first gunnery officer in the seven-year-old *Téméraire*.[1] Captain Henry Nicholson's fine-looking vessel, the last fully-masted British battleship to serve on the station, was a typical example of the transitional design of many ships of the time. By later standards she was tiny, only 5,400 tons; her hull was of wood but protected by massive armour plates; her main muzzle-loading armament was no longer poked angrily through ports but was arrayed in open-topped barbettes. She would have demolished a Nelsonian triple-decker as easily as she herself would have been demolished by a twentieth-century dreadnought.

It is a great shame that we do not know more of what Bridgeman got up to at this time, because his new station lay at the very heart of British overseas policy.[2] Three interrelated factors kept it there. The first was the parlous state of the Ottoman Empire and the consequential wish of the major powers at least to prevent others from expanding at Ottoman expense, if not actually doing so themselves. To this end Britain had joined the anti-Russian coalition to fight the Crimean War in the mid-1850s and come close to a second war with Russia in 1878, which resulted in Cyprus coming under British control. Secondly, with a growing proportion (one-third by 1911) of British food imports arriving from the Black Sea via the Mediterranean, it was vital for Britain to protect those busy seaways. Finally, the opening of the Suez Canal in 1869 had established a new and crucial route to India, the jewel in Britain's imperial crown.[3] Following an Egyptian nationalist uprising against growing European influence in 1882, the Navy had bombarded Alexandria prior to a British occupation of the country.

British military presence in the Mediterranean region was limited to a small garrison in Malta and never more than 55,000 soldiers in Egypt. The strategic role of the Navy, therefore, was of immense importance and in the last decade of the century she maintained ten first-class battleships and a host of smaller vessels at her bases in Gibraltar and Malta. Only days after Bridgeman's arrival, in response to a military scare in Egypt, the Malta fleet was called out in the middle of the night and set sail for Alexandria with an emergency landing force of several hundred sailors.[4] Three months after Bridgeman left the station – throughout his career he had an unfortunate knack of never being where the action was – the Sudan flared into the conflict that gave rise to the celebrated death of General Gordon (1884) and the imperialist slaughter at Omdurman (1898).

Though he saw no action, Bridgeman's diligence, common sense and practical good seamanship continued to attract attention. He mixed with officers who were to form part of the highly influential 'Malta clique' in the 1890s and in April was 'highly recommended for promotion', this time by the able Captain Henry Nicholson.[5] Nicholson's plea did not go unheeded, because on 30 June Bridgeman appears to have been promoted to the rank of commander.[6] This distanced him from the majority of those promoted to lieutenant in April 1873. However, it is not clear from the records whether he was given the full rank, 'the great fence where most of the field fall'. As things turned out, however, this did not matter: on 6 August his Service Record states baldly, 'Cancelled'.[7] It is not clear what was cancelled or why, but it seems to have been his promotion! Perhaps someone had noticed he did not have the paper qualifications requisite for his new rank and further training was required? Be that as it may, commander or not, after only 185 days in the Mediterranean Bridgeman returned home in a mail steamer in July and was on half-pay for the rest of the year.[8]

During the autumn Bridgeman attended two brief courses. The first was at the *Cambridge* school of gunnery at Devonport, commanded by Captain Cleveland, known affectionately as 'The Emu'. The second was the 'Lieutenants' short course on Torpedo'.[9] If, as seems likely, this was at the *Vernon* rather than the *Cambridge*, then Bridgeman found himself under the command of no less a figure than his sometime senior officer on the *Blanche*, the clumsy, ambitious Albert Markham, who commanded the *Vernon* from 1883-6.

By January 1885 the Admiralty's doubts over Bridgeman's qualifications were at an end. He left for the Pacific as commander of the *Triumph*, captained by Henry Rose and destined to replace the *Swiftsure* as flagship of the station commander, Rear-Admiral John Baird. First commissioned in 1873, the *Triumph* was hardly a shining example of modern naval technology, although recently, following an explosion on board, she had been refitted and re-armed with 9" and 5" breech loading guns. The vessel's antiquity, however, mattered little in the Pacific, where before the emergence of the USA and Japan as major naval powers any ship powerful enough to impose itself upon war canoes and junks without too much difficulty was sufficient to show the flag.

As far as Bridgeman's career was concerned, far more important than his ship (which was relegated to guard duty in 1890) was the replacement of Baird in July 1885 by Sir Michael Culme-Seymour. Small, tough, honest and slightly deaf, Culme-Seymour was one of the most influential naval figures of his generation and in many ways the epitome of the Service to which he devoted his life.[10] His family had close links with the House of Saxe-Coburg and had provided their monarch with no less than five admirals, some of whom we have already met. He was a fine seaman and stickler for efficiency and discipline. The ships and fleets that he commanded looked good and manoeuvred well; in all situations other than those requiring flexibility and spontaneity (i.e. wartime) they were certainly impressive.

Bridgeman and Culme-Seymour got on well. Where the commander-in-chief was sometimes a bit impulsive, Bridgeman was always calm yet firm. Nor was he afraid, we are told, to correct his senior if he believed him wrong.[11] Now in his late thirties, Bridgeman seemed to be developing qualities that not merely set him aside from his run-of-the-mill contemporaries, but suggested that, given his good connections and a little luck, one day he might rise to become a very senior officer indeed. There remained, however, a slight question mark over his health. Between 19 September and 26 October 1885 he had again been off sick.

Evidence of Culme-Seymour's approval of the commander of his flagship comes from two sources. The entry in Bridgeman's Confidential

Report for October 1887 reads, 'Satisfaction expressed at favourable report by Sir M Culme-Seymour of inspection of *Triumph*'. This is supported by a Service Record comment of 12 December the same year that concludes, 'Sir Michael Culme-Seymour calls special attention to him'.[12] Unfortunately, this was Sir Michael's parting recommendation. By the end of the year his position as commander-in-chief of the Pacific Station had been taken by an officer of an altogether different type.

The departure of Culme-Seymour probably left Bridgeman feeling a little isolated. His feelings cannot have been helped by news received earlier in the year of his mother's death on 23 March. As we have seen, the absence of any personal correspondence makes it impossible to say what Bridgeman's relationship with his mother had been. By all accounts she was an attractive, good and kindly woman, and the sentimentality engendered by absence and the harshness of his service life may well have magnified the icon-like image of her he carried in his emotionally-deprived sailor's heart. Although he had seen little of her since his childhood, her passing surely grieved him deeply. It may also have stoked still higher his growing affection for Emily Shiffner and made him all the

Lady Frances' grave at All Saints, Babworth

keener of finding a way of getting back to England to see her. The new commander-in-chief turned out to be just the catalyst he needed to galvanise him into action. Culme-Seymour he would never have deserted, but he had no such qualms about Heneage.

Sir Algernon Charles Fiesché Heneage, or 'Pompo' as he was commonly known, took over command of the Pacific Station on 20 September 1887. This extraordinary character, a sort of 'historical tourist attraction', appeared towards the end of a long line of highly eccentric Victorian admirals.[13] Lords of their own ships and showing scant regard for either regulations or shorebound superiors, they manifested their independence with appearance and behaviour that almost beggars belief. There were those who cluttered their quarters with wives, mistresses and pets, sported waist-length beards, exotic hats, and extraordinary mannerisms of speech, sentenced men to death for missing their ship, challenged offenders to boxing matches, punished boys by making them stare at a portrait of Nelson for hours on end and ordered soap and towel to be stored in white hat covers, 'but nothing else'![14]

Pompo was obsessed with his appearance. Each morning he broke two eggs over his head to hold his hair in elaborate curls. With his narcissism went a fetish for cleanliness. He went to sea with some 250 of his own immaculate white shirts and had them shipped back to England in batches for laundering. To inspect a ship or a station he wore spotless, lavender-scented white kid gloves, with an accompanying coxswain carrying a spare pair on a silver tray. The pristine fingers rubbed, delved and curled, seeking out the merest hint of filth. Once, finding dust on top of a pipe, he observed in his affected drawl,

> 'Dis is not de dirt of days. Nor de dirt of veeks, nor de dirt of months. It is de dirt of ages. Coxswain, gif me a clean pair of gloves.'

On another occasion, on being told that a mark on a lavatory pan was a flaw in the glaze, he replied sardonically, 'ven de Admiral says de pan's dirty, de pan is dirty'.[15] Yet, for all his affectation, Heneage was no mere fop. He could handle a fleet as well as any man and was capable of both kindness and extreme bravery.[16] Such an overbearing, contradictory character was quite beyond Bridgeman's comprehension and certainly beyond his liking. He did his duty for as long as he could stand it, even getting another 'Strongly recommended' for his Service Record, before the 'most zealous and able' officer 'retired to his cabin and remained there until the fleet surgeon, Thomas Bolster, invalided him home for a "slight rupture".'[17]

This story is frequently told as an amusing adjunct to Pompo's eccentricity. What has not been considered is the light it sheds on Bridgeman's personality. It occurred at a time when he was under considerable stress. He was coming to terms with his mother's death and, after an absence of more than three years, obviously wished to be with Emily. To make matters worse, the commander with whom he had been able to work very well had been replaced by the dominating, infuriating Heneage. From these trying circumstances Bridgeman was rescued by his hernia. It is perfectly possible that the young officer's illness was a sort of wish-fulfilment, an understandable reaction to the trying circumstances in which he found himself. As we have seen, something similar may have happened during his protracted tour of duty on the *Encounter*. He had been frequently 'seedy' while on the *Blanche*, too.[18] The symptoms of psychosomatically-induced illness are indistinguishable from those brought on by purely physical breakdown; indeed, the two commonly overlap.

Bridgeman's health failed him at other taxing moments during his exacting life. The most famous occasion occurred 25 years later when, overshadowed by the bulldozing personality of Winston Churchill, he was wrestling with the immense problems of the Admiralty at a time of extreme international tension. We cannot, of course, be certain that there are parallels to be drawn between the *Blanche*, *Encounter*, *Triumph* and Admiralty incidents, but it is worth considering. On the latter two occasions he made a swift and complete recovery as soon as the sources of his anxiety had been removed. A lot would be explained if we knew for certain that Bridgeman was prone to bouts of mild depression.

The invalided Bridgeman left the *Triumph* on 24 February and arrived home on 16 March 1888, reported unfit the following day but remained on half-pay only until 18 May.[19] Restored to full health, he moved to *Excellent* once more. The gunnery school was now commanded by Captain Compton Domvile with John Jellicoe among his staff. It is not clear what course Bridgeman followed at the *Excellent*, nor for how long. The *Navy List* records his uninterrupted presence there until early 1890. We know this to be not strictly accurate, for on 18 July 1889 he was seconded to a specially selected group of officers on board the brand new battleship *Howe* on manoeuvres. The Admiralty was keen to see how she performed.[20]

'The *Howe*,' wrote Captain O W Andrews many years later, 'was considered a very important ship'. Captained by Compton Domvile, who transferred from the *Excellent* at the same time as Bridgeman, it was crammed full of 'swells', most of whom knew each other well. As well as Commander Francis Bridgeman, this 'band of brothers' included Lieutenant-Commander John Jellicoe (also from *Excellent*), who would command the British fleet at Jutland, and Lieutenant Christopher Cradock, whose needless death in the battle of Coronel in the early days of World War I widened still further the rift between Bridgeman and First Lord Winston Churchill.[21] Prince George (the future George V was now a lieutenant in the Royal Navy) was an honorary member of the wardroom. During the prince's frequent visits to the ship Bridgeman had plenty of opportunity get to know the rather shy, unglamorous figure who 24 years later would set aside his liking for his old shipmate and handle the Bridgeman-Churchill crisis with exemplary tact. The distinguished Admiral Sir John Commerell VC, GCB, who famously disregarded dress regulations and saluting formalities and made no secret of his antipathy towards long-range gunnery, chose to fly his distinguished flag from the *Howe* for that year's Spithead Review.

Splendid though her crew might have been, the ship herself was a disappointment. She was one of the 10,300-ton Admiral Class battleships built as a result of the 1884 clamour for a more powerful Navy. In several respects they were a considerable improvement on previous battleships, being capable of an impressive 17 knots and carrying an equally impressive armament: four 13.5", 67-ton breech-loading guns in barbettes, backed by half-a-dozen 6" guns, torpedoes and a range smaller weapons. But the big guns were prone to exploding when fired and the bows were cut so low that in only moderate seas waves broke heavily over the decks, sweeping away the canvas coverings of the barbettes and sending tons of water sluicing down below. These and other defects, Admiral Sir Reginald Bacon concluded, made the Admiral Class 'really useless as seagoing fighting ships'.[22] The *Howe* was, if anything, worse than the others. She had been built in a hurry, as a consequence of which she was plagued with niggling faults. Leaking water and steam at an alarming rate and using proportionally more coal than any other ship in the Navy, she soon became known as the 'Anyhow' or 'Nohow'. Subsequently, after alterations and improvements, this changed to 'How D'you Do It?', but only until 1892, when she ran aground. She was refloated in March the following year and eventually sold in 1910.[23]

The review was followed by an elaborate war game between Fleet A and Fleet B. Ships were taken but greater significance was attached to the capture of Dublin, Waterford and Belfast. Clearly, the Navy was still

HMS Howe *at anchor, 1890*

thinking of itself as an adjunct to land operations. After the exercise Bridgeman and Domvile (accompanied at least nominally by Prince George) returned to the *Excellent* where Bridgeman's Service Record says he remained until January 1890. It is clear, however, that he had left the gunnery school at least two months earlier, for on 6 November 1889 he finally married Emily Shiffner.[24]

Bridgeman probably first met Emily on his return from the Far East in 1883 when he went to Yorkshire to visit his sister Beatrice, who had recently married Adolphus Duncombe. Henry Duncombe had built Copgrove, the imposing, beautifully situated mansion near Harrogate where Emily had long lived with her widowed mother, in the late eighteenth century. In 1861 the Duncombes had sold the Copgrove estate to the wealthy local bachelor James Brown. When he died 16 years later he left the property to his sister Mary, who had married Thomas Shiffner in 1841. Thomas was now dead. His younger daughter Anne had left home in 1876 to marry Sir Reginald Graham, leaving his widow Mary and elder daughter Emily (born in 1842) in possession of Copgrove. Her mother's death had left Emily an ageing and no doubt lonely heiress.

Mrs Walter Hingston believes Francis and Emily had known each other for 'a long time' before they married. The reason for the delay, she adds, was partly financial and partly his father's continued opposition to his sons marrying.[25] This may well have been so, though Emily may also have put off her marriage to be with her ailing mother.

Bridgeman had little money of his own and a commander's pay of 8/6 a day was hardly sufficient to maintain a single officer who mixed in circles close to the royal family and who was obliged by tradition to use his own funds to maintain his ship's appearance.[26] By the autumn of 1889, however, he knew that the long-awaited promotion to captain, raising his pay to 12/6 a day, was imminent.[27] The rational explanation for his not marrying until the age of 41, therefore, is that he simply could not afford to do so earlier. But human beings are rarely guided by reason alone. Had Bridgeman fallen hopelessly in love as a young man, no doubt he would have married in spite of everything (even paternal disapproval). His long

Copgrove, a perfect retreat from an imperfect world

years of bachelorhood support the view that, unless there was some secret love we do not know about, he was not a passionate man. In choosing a stout 47-year-old wife, six years older than himself and by whom he would have no children, he married for companionship. Family memories, passing references to Emily in correspondence and the fact that the couple were buried beneath the same gravestone all reflect a relationship that matured into one of deep affection.[28]

Bridgeman was of a practical frame of mind and Emily's estate and independent income must have been a contributory factor in his decision to marry. It is very likely that he had dreamed all his Service life of being able one day to settle in a place like Copgrove.

It was not as grand as Babworth Hall, with its painful memories of Uncle Henry lording it over his brother and his family in the rectory, but it had a more homely, comfortable feel than either of the mansions of his childhood. Approached down a long drive that wound gently upwards between ancient beeches and oaks, the rectangular, creeper-clad house was (and still is) an eloquent statement of upper-middle-class British confidence and comfort – the archetypal residence of a well-heeled country gentleman. Lawns, flower beds and fine trees were visible from every broad window. Beyond lay a tree-lined lake (even at home Bridgeman was never far from the water) where the lord of the manor liked to take his wife rowing on quiet summer evenings. Few buildings, other than the stables and a handful of estate workers' cottages, marred broad views of rolling Yorkshire countryside and distant Roecliffe Moor. Embraced by the tranquillity of Copgrove and surrounded by those who loved and admired him, all the horrors and disappointments, loneliness and wrangling of his Service life soon faded to become part of a distant, imperfect world.

In the graveyard of the tiny church of St Michael and All Angels, only a short walk from the estate gates, lay generations of Duncombes, Browns and their loyal, valued employees. Walking between the graves, Bridgeman would have noticed the grave of William Tuke, an estate worker who had died in 1871. On his headstone James Brown had gratefully inscribed these words: 'He entirely fulfilled the duties of his situation and was faithful and trustworthy'. The sentiments must have struck a chord in the sailor's heart. Duty, faithfulness and trust were qualities he understood and admired. They were what he strove for, what he gave his life to. And here they were, not in a smoky wardroom or on a freezing bridge, but deep in the Yorkshire countryside.

At the end of his career Bridgeman was criticised for spending too much time at Copgrove. It was not just the peace he sought in these retreats, nor the unquestioning support and love of Emily. It was what Copgrove stood for. Amid the hassle and political wrangling of the Admiralty, he found duty too often divided, faithfulness provisional and trust a sadly fragile gift. But in his pastoral Yorkshire stronghold he knew where he was and who he was. In a sense, after his marriage he was a divided soul, split between career and home. The former had priority, of course, because that was what he had been taught. But mingled with the anger and disappointment of his eventual dismissal, he must have experienced very genuine feelings of relief – even delight – that he was at last free to enjoy uninterrupted the gentle domestic pleasures that had been denied to him for so long.

In the spring of 1890 all this lay many years ahead. The Royal Navy was in the midst of great change and much needed the guidance of men with Bridgeman's wisdom and experience. After the mid-century reforms, for about 20 years the Service had carried out perfectly satisfactorily the multifarious tasks demanded by its parsimonious paymasters. Moreover, by 1884 it was doing so at a lower cost than in 1868. But as Bridgeman's own experiences have shown, the Navy was by no means the efficient, up-to-date war machine that complacent contemporaries believed it to be.

The problem was not that the Navy had deteriorated but that it had not kept pace with the changes going on around it. The Service's strategic role, for example, had not been clearly examined for decades. There was a general understanding that it was there to protect British interests: guarding trade, helping with colonial difficulties, defending Britain and Ireland against possible invasion and showing the flag with awe-inspiring dignity across the seven seas. But how could these many and sometimes contradictory tasks be best performed when not only the traditional enemy, France, boasted an increasingly powerful navy, but Russia, Austria, Italy, the US and, later, Japan and Germany were all building up their naval strength?[29] Which potential enemy, or alliance of enemies, posed the greatest threat, and what was the best disposition of ships to counter that threat? Should they be scattered around the world in small squadrons or gathered closer to home in large fleets? First Lord Sir Frederick Richards (1893-9) began to tackle such problems when he set up commerce protection squadrons, but they were never integrated into a broader strategic plan.

Naval officers were, for the most part, fine seamen. Most, however, like Bridgeman, had been trained in a sail-dominated service. Their battle thinking was dominated by wind direction and short-range gunnery followed by a general mêlée, not destruction of an enemy several miles away. As late as the 1890s warships were still training regularly to repel borders with hand-held weapons that included tomahawks.[30]

The perpetuation of such quaint, faintly ridiculous practices was not the fault of the junior officers or even of the captains. The blame lay with the Admiralty, which maintained out-dated regulations and gave officers little or no opportunity for re-education. Bridgeman, for example, attended several gunnery and torpedo courses but, as far as we know, no course that might enable him to integrate his updated gunnery skills into a modern battle plan. Moreover, given the narrow and generally conservative social circle from which all officers, high and low, were drawn and the unexacting academic standard required for entry into the service, they were predisposed to view with suspicion both independent thought and the radical change that it might suggest. As we shall see, the tragic accidental loss of the *Victoria* off Malta in 1893 would serve only to reinforce such attitudes.[31] The average naval officer thought of his job as practical and administrative. That it might also have been an intellectual exercise would, to the great majority, have been a concept as alien as female members of his crew. Moreover, even when an officer wished to go further into the theory of his profession, there was precious little material for him to draw on. The forward-thinking Reginald Bacon noted that before 1890 'there were no publications or standard works that were of much real value to the naval officer who wished to study either the war-time tactics or strategy of the modern Navy'.[32]

The Navy might not have changed its strategy or tactics much, but it had changed its ships. Yet it had done so according to no overall plan other than to incorporate new ideas more or less at random, while holding fast to the tried and tested as long as possible. This was not as unwise as it might sound. For many years it was not at all clear where warship design would end up. Wood and iron were tried in various combinations. There were sailing vessels with auxiliary engines and steam ships with some sail. In the later 1860s all-iron vessels designed for ramming were fashionable, while for a time some believed the future lay with slow, broad-beamed vessels armed with a few massive guns – little more than floating gun platforms. Only in the 1880s did modern warship design – steam powered and armed with powerful guns in turrets or barbettes – begin to win universal acceptance.

The result of all this change and experiment was a scattered rag-bag fleet of the obsolescent and the hesitantly modern, leading Admiral Hewell to dismiss most of the ships on show at the 1887 Naval Review as 'mere ullage'.[33] With hindsight, it is not difficult to see what Hewell meant: even the leaky *Howe* would have had little difficulty sinking the bulk of the fleet single-handed. That notwithstanding, given the scale of the Navy's global role, the sheer number of ships available to it was important. So too was the obsessive concern over appearance that so annoyed reformers like Percy Scott.[34] The mere appearance of the burnished *Blanche* among the remote islands of Fiji or off the coast of New Zealand had in its day served to deter all but the most determined malefactors.

The Navy's problem was one of priorities. Huge mastless battleships were necessary to counter the threat posed by growing European navies. But such vessels were hugely expensive and vulnerable to torpedo attack. Moreover, they were wholly unsuitable for the sort of long-range patrol work undertaken by the *Blanche*, for which sails were still considered a valuable asset. The argument about whether to do away with sails entirely rumbled on until the very end of the century. All new battleships were mastless after 1887, by when it had been shown that the drag of an idle screw, particularly a double screw, used up more coal than was saved by occasionally using only sail power. However, engineer officers were still looked down on by their seaman counterparts long after the sail-steam battle was over, and as late as 1892 Captain William Dyke could pronounce, 'I am certain that the only way of training officers and men to be sailors is in masted ships'.[35]

A long standing objection to steam was the dirt it produced, both from smoke and from coal dust. Similar cosmetic objections were levelled against gunnery practice, after which ship's officers might have to fork out up to £100 to restore their vessel to its previous brilliance.[36] This and the continued belief that gunnery was only a precursor to hand-to-hand fighting help explain why as late as 1890 the Navy's standard of gunnery had changed little from the time when Orlando Bridgeman had watched the *Blanche*'s projectiles bouncing off the waves a mere 15 yards from the side of the ship.[37] The Navy expended some 3,000 rounds during its bombardment of Alexandria in 1882 but scored only 10 hits on enemy guns. 'If the guns went off, the authorities were satisfied,' remarked Percy

Scott caustically after observing the Mediterranean fleet at gunnery practice in 1896, 'whether they could hit anything or not was regarded as a matter of no importance'.[38] Range-finding was haphazard, breech-loading guns were prone to explode and the variety of weapons made training in ordnance a nightmare. In 1888, 16 British battleships still sported muzzle-loading guns. When these were housed in barbettes, as was often the case, the barrels had to be kept short so that the guns could be withdrawn for cleaning and reloading. Short barrels inevitably meant short range and inaccurate shooting. It took an outsider to realise that all was not well with the Royal Navy. When faced with the likelihood of war with Russia in 1878, the country sang confidently,

'We don't want to fight, but, by Jingo!, if we do,
We've got the ships, we've got the men, we've got the money
too.'

But when W H Smith, the successful newsagent turned politician whom Disraeli had controversially appointed First Lord of the Admiralty the previous year, looked closely at the famous boast, he was shocked at its hollowness. The problem was not the men or the money, but the ships. There were lots of them, certainly, but whether they or those who commanded them were prepared to fight a major war was quite another question. Many were in a sorry state of repair. Those fit for sea were equipped with obsolete armament badly managed. The Admiralty itself Smith found proud, wasteful and unwilling to change.

Smith did what he could, but the crisis passed and with the election of Gladstone's cost-cutting Liberal government in 1880, the Navy was allowed to return to its old somnolence. But not for long. In September 1884, beginning with a sharp, well-informed article entitled 'What Is The Truth About the Navy?', the *Pall Mall Gazette* launched a campaign for reform that put the Senior Service at the centre of the political stage. It remained there for the rest of Bridgeman's career, moving aside only after the end of the First World War.

This development placed an extra burden on the shoulders of senior naval officers. They had not only to reform their Service, but they had to do it in the full glare of public scrutiny. To instinctive politicians such as Admirals Jackie Fisher and Lord Charles Beresford, this was no problem. Indeed, both were quite capable of manipulating popular opinion to serve their own ends.[39] But the majority of senior officers, Bridgeman included, were not political animals and had little or no experience in handling either MPs or the press. This did not matter much while they remained with their ships, but it created huge problems when they went to serve at the Admiralty. Bridgeman, brought up in a straightforward world of command-and-obey, simply did not know how to operate the innuendo, compromise and half truth that politics necessitated.

The naval scare of 1884 was followed by a second four years later. The thesis of *The Influence of Sea Power on History, 1660-1783* (1890) by the American naval historian A T Mahan lent academic respectability to the nation's fears. A powerful, efficient navy, Mahan argued, was the essential foundation for global power. With imperialism in full spate, his book was enormously influential both in Britain and around the world. It is said that the German Kaiser, eager to build up a navy capable of winning Germany a 'place in the sun', even tried to learn it by heart!

By 1900 the Royal Navy was second only to the monarchy in the list of the nation's favourite institutions. Beginning in 1890, 'Hurrah' trips were made around the coast to enhance the Service's public image. The 1891 Royal Naval Exhibition attracted $2^{1}/_{2}$ million visitors and in 1894 the Navy League was founded to aid recruitment and act as a pro-naval pressure group. There were sound economic grounds for maintaining naval expenditure, too. Hundreds of thousands of workers in the armaments, coal, iron and steel industries relied on naval expenditure for their jobs. It is estimated that the construction of a single large battleship kept over 2,000 men employed for three years. Against a background of international tension and competition, particularly the emergence of a brand new German navy, all these factors ensured that during the final years of Bridgeman's career the Navy occupied a more prominent position in the national consciousness than it had done since the age of Nelson.

In response to the crisis of 1884, the Liberals, who were loath to increase government expenditure but regarded a powerful Navy as essential for the protection of their other shibboleth, free trade, earmarked £3,100,000 for Lord Northbrook's five-year naval construction programme. The result was the Admiral Class 9,500-ton battleships, the Navy's first all-steel vessels. As we have seen in the case of the *Howe*, they were not a great success. With 45% of their waterline unarmoured, they were felt to be dangerously vulnerable to accurate gunnery and torpedo attack.[40] This led to the development of double hulls and the division of warships' interiors into watertight compartments.

The 1888 crisis spawned the Conservatives' 1889 Naval Defence Act, which allocated £21,500,000 for a 10-year building programme of eight new Sovereign Class battleships and dozens of smaller vessels, including 18 torpedo boats. The Act signalled the acceptance of a new yardstick of naval power. The Two-Power Standard stipulated that henceforward the Royal Navy, which previously had been content to remain superior to the French, should have more battleships than any other two navies combined. The standard, adhered to by both Conservatives and Liberals alike, was thought essential for a country that imported four-fifths of her food. 'It's not invasion we have to fear if our Navy is beaten,' trumpeted Fisher in 1904, 'IT'S STARVATION!'[41]

Pressure for reform came from within the Navy as well as from without. Fisher had reformed the *Excellent* during his period in command 1883-6 and lent powerful support to officers like Percy Scott who sought to carry a more professional attitude towards gunnery into the fleets. By 1904 the proportion of hits recorded at gunnery practice had risen to 43%. Three years later it was up to 79%. Each hit counted for more, too. The piercing power of a 12" shell fired by the *Nelson* in 1906 was almost three times that of the projectiles in use ten years earlier. Muzzle loading was phased out as quickly as practicable and a variety of quick-firing guns installed to counter the threat of torpedo boats.

Press interest helped bring about humanitarian reforms in the service. In 1903, following questions in parliament, sailors were for the first time issued with cutlery (previously they had provided their own).

Another campaign, in which George Bernard Shaw had played a prominent part, ended the 'disgusting debauch' of birching of cadets.[42] Not all the effects of the new interest in the Navy were necessarily beneficial. Very much aware that it was in the public eye, the Service became even more conscious of the image it presented. This tended to reinforce the tendency, growing over many years, towards uniformity, custom, obedience and appearance – doing things 'by the book'. As early as the 1890s there were complaints that the Navy had become over-regulated. An unfortunate incident from Bridgeman's own career illustrates the sort of thing that was going on.

While taking the *Camperdown* on a round-Britain hurrah trip, Admiral Culme-Seymour and Bridgeman, his flag captain, were invited by the mayor and corporation of Scarborough to attend a civic ball held in their honour.[43] During the evening the weather worsened and the battleship began to drag her anchors. The sensible course of action in such circumstances would have been to put to sea, but the commander was loath to break with tradition and leave with his senior officers ashore. He gave orders for more chain to be let out, which required men working on the open fo'c'sle. As the officers on the bridge watched, a mountainous wave rolled in from the North Sea and crashed over the deck. One man was swept away and drowned. A second suffered multiple injuries, including a fractured skull. Shortly afterwards, with his ship drifting perilously close to the shore, the commander finally took the decision to raise anchors and steam into deeper water. Rigid adherence to custom had resulted in unnecessary suffering and loss of life.

In his penetrating analysis of the Navy at this time, Andrew Gordon suggests that the Service's obsession with obeying the rules had even more profound consequences. Its 'most pernicious effect,' he ventures, 'was the confusion of warfare with ritualised team games'.[44] A good team man who played by the rules might have been an ideal partner at the crease, but his honour, courtesy and chivalry were patently inadequate in the kill-or-be-killed mayhem of a naval battle. They were also, one might add, hardly sufficient tools for the cut and thrust world of politics. As Bridgeman would discover to his cost.

NOTES

1   PRO ADM 196/17.

2   See Halpern, *The Mediterranean Naval Situation*.

3   At Disraeli's request, Victoria had accepted the title Empress of India in 1876.

4   Had they needed to go into action, they would have been of little use. Rigid adherence to some obscure regulation meant that the men carried neither rifles nor ammunition; Willis, *The Royal Navy as I Saw It*, p. 169.

5   PRO ADM 196/86.

6   PRO ADM 196/17.

7   Bacon, *A Naval Scrapbook*, p.140; PRO ADM 196/39 (II).

8   PRO ADM 196/17; PRO PMG 15/105.

9   PRO ADM 196/39 (II).

10 See Gordon, *Rules of the Game*, especially p. 251 et seq.

11 See p. 100.

12 PRO ADM 196/86; PRO ADM 196/39 (II).

13 Gordon, *The Rules of the Game*, p. 175.

14 Bonnett, *The Price of Admiralty*, p. 142. The book is a mine of scandalous information on naval incompetence. See also, Lowis, *Fabulous Admirals*.

15 Lowis, *Fabulous Admirals*, p. 35.

16 *Ibid.*, p. 32; Gordon, *The Rules of the Game*, p. 176. It may have been Heneage's kindness that had led him, when second in command of the Channel Fleet, to record a verdict of 'not guilty' on Albert Markham for running down the *SS Cheerful* in fog off Land's End in 1885.

17 PRO ADM 196/39 (II); Bonnett, *The Price of Admiralty*, p. 142.

18 See p. 61.

19 PRO ADM 196/86; PRO PMG 15/114 &123.

20 PRO ADM 196/39 (II); *Ships and Service*, L.L.P.P.

21 Andrews, *Seamarks and Landmarks*, p. 48.

22 *A Naval Scrapbook*, p. 174.

23 Andrews, *Seamarks and Landmarks*, p. 48.

24 PRO ADM 196/39 (II); *Ships and Service*, L.L.P.P. says he left *Excellent* on 12 February.

25 From a conversation with the author.

26 A ship required to be painted about eight times a year. The Admiralty paid for three coats, leaving the cost of the remaining five to be met out of the officers' pockets. (Gordon, *The Rules of the Game*, p.168.)

27 PRO ADM 196/39 (II).

28 This is certainly supported by the comments of Mrs Walter Hingston.

29 Reflecting later on the Navy's weakness in the later 1880s, Bacon reckoned, 'had we gone to war with France in those days we might well have been swept off the face of the globe'. (*A Naval Scrapbook*, p. 154.)

30 Andrews, *Seamarks and Landmarks*, p. 65. The majority of Victoria Crosses awarded to sailors in the nineteenth century were for bravery in action on land. (Gordon, *The Rules of the Game*, p. 169.)

31 See Gordon, *The Rules of the Game*, which examines these themes with wit and rare perspicacity.

32 *From 1900 Onwards*, p. 33.

33 Marder, *The Anatomy of Sea Power*.

34 *Fifty Years in the Navy*, p. 200.

35 Cited in Gordon, *The Rules of the Game*, p. 167.

36 *Ibid.*, p. 168.

37 See p. 61.

38 *Fifty Years in the Navy*, p. 93.

39 Fisher had talked at length with Hugh Arnold-Forster, the author of the seminal article in the *Pall Mall Gazette*, and Beresford, then Fourth Sea Lord, fuelled a second naval scare in 1888 by revealing the Navy's total unpreparedness for swift mobilisation.

40 Because of their lack of armour, the Admiral class battleships were known as 'soft-enders'. Beresford was prevented from testing their defensive effectiveness in case rumours of their vulnerability proved true! (Marder, *The Anatomy of British Sea Power*, p. 138.)

41 See Marder, *ibid.*, Chapter 8 and p. 65.

42 The words are Shaw's, cited in Bonnett, *The Price of Admiralty*, p. 132.

43 The story appears in Bacon, *A Naval Scrapbook*, pp. 177-8.

44 *The Rules of the Game*, p. 181.

6 'An Excellent Captain'

Bridgeman's elevation to the rank of captain took effect on 1 January 1890. Three days later he was officially 'superseded' in *Excellent*, from where Captain Domvile wrote to the Admiralty that he had proved 'an excellent and zealous officer', and remained on half-pay until late May'.[1] The extended leave must have been among the best months of his life. Marriage had brought him financial and emotional security and as a confirmed member of an elite band of senior officers in the world's most powerful navy his career prospects had never looked more rosy.

Bridgeman returned to duties on 22 May, when he joined his old colleague Sir Michael Culme-Seymour as Flag Captain in the *Camperdown*, flagship of a strengthened Channel Squadron. Like the *Howe*, the *Camperdown* was one of flawed Admiral Class 'soft-enders'. Culme-Seymour, whatever his faults as one of the 'definitive goosesteppers', was an excellent sailor with a 'first-class "eye" for manoeuvres', and the patent faults in his flagship's design and performance annoyed him intensely.[2] As well as the limitations noted in the previous chapter, the ship's Torpedo Lieutenant Reginald Bacon reported a wildly fluctuating electricity supply and such a plethora of safety devices on the guns that they often could not be fired at all.[3] When, after reporting the *Camperdown*'s shortcomings to a 'chief official' at the conclusion of a particularly rough voyage, the straight talking, irascible vice-admiral exploded with fury. 'Damn the man!' he shouted. 'He tells me a lie; turn him out of the ship!'[4] Life with Culme-Seymour was never dull.

Bridgeman's role, it seems, was to act as a counterweight or 'sedative' to the volatile vice-admiral. Perhaps because the flag captain was 'looked on as rather a hard man and a strict disciplinarian,' Culme-Seymour trusted and respected him, allowing him to get away with things he would never have tolerated from anyone else.[5] Reginald Bacon recalled a conversation between the vice-admiral and his captain on the subject of gunnery. Culme-Seymour, with his customary exaggeration, declared that the Navy's shooting had made no progress since his days as a midshipman. 'You have no right to make such a statement,' replied the younger man coolly.

'Oh, come Bridgeman,' bellowed Sir Michael. 'Surely I can say what I like?'

Bridgeman stuck to his guns. 'No, you can't. You as an Admiral have no right to make any statement that is not strictly correct.' Bacon concluded that although Sir Michael blustered on for a bit longer, Bridgeman's 'frigidity' eventually cooled him down.[6]

The reported incident, one of only a handful of examples of Bridgeman's actual conversation, brings out several aspects of the man: his strength, calmness and sense of justice, his interest in gunnery and the respect in which he was held, not only by Culme-Seymour but also by Bacon who 'admired him greatly' and regretted that 'he was too old to have an active command during the War'.[7] Bacon is the only person to have gone on record with such a comment and it may owe more to his friendship with Bridgeman than to objective judgement.

Bridgeman remained with Culme-Seymour in the unreliable *Camperdown* until May 1892. It is hard to tell what, if anything, he learned from the experience. The vice-admiral believed he was nearing the end of his seagoing career and through his lack of co-operation with the Admiralty seemed, 'too much given to imagining that the Service was made for his own convenience, and far too ready to manipulate it for his own comfort and advantage'.[8] Such comment, of course, worried him not one jot. But he did seem sorry to lose his 'VG' flag captain, whom he commended for his 'zealous and has a thorough knowledge of his profession'.[9]

It is not clear precisely what Bridgeman did on leaving the *Camperdown*. Over the summer he spent six weeks (11 July-18 August) as flag captain in the new, 20-knot, twin-screw, 3,600-ton protected cruiser *Iphigenia* ('for manoeuvres') and some time on half-pay, presumably at Copgrove. Emily's quiet gentleness must have come as welcome relief after months of Culme-Seymour's high-decibel tirades.[10]

Meanwhile, as Bridgeman was pottering about Copgrove acquainting himself with the staff and adjusting to the slow rhythms of country life, many hundreds of miles away an old comrade was helping to make naval history. And not in a manner he would have wished, either. Albert Markham, now a rear-admiral and second in command of the Mediterranean Fleet under the eccentric Sir George Tryon, had pursued an interesting career since the *Blanche*'s return from Australia in 1872. As well as surviving a court-martial under Pompo Heneage for ramming and sinking the steamer *Cheerful* in fog off Land's End, he had rounded up a few more slavers in the Pacific, had a go at exploring and written a book about it, attempted (unsuccessfully) to walk to the North Pole and commanded both the *Vernon* and the Training Squadron.[11]

Like many officers in the Mediterranean Fleet, 'Old Marco', now smitten with rigid religion, did not see eye to eye with his commanding officer. Contrary to the current fashion for uniformity, regularity and strict obedience at all times, Vice-Admiral Sir George Tryon believed there were occasions when authority was best devolved away from the centre. 'While an order should be implicitly obeyed,' he suggested,

> 'still circumstances may change and conditions may widely vary from those known or even from those that presented themselves at the time the orders were issued. In such cases the officer receiving orders, guided by the object that he knows his chief had in view, must act on his own responsibility.'[12]

As we saw with the *Camperdown* incident off Scarborough, acting on their own responsibility was not something to which naval officers were accustomed. So when on 22 June 1893 Tryon ordered his battleships to execute a clearly suicidal manoeuvre off the Syrian coast, his signal brought disbelief, panic and confusion in equal measure. Too late the bridges of the commander-in-chief's flagship *Victoria* and Markham's *Camperdown* ordered full astern. The *Camperdown*'s ram tore into the side of the *Victoria*. Shortly afterwards she turned turtle and sank to the bottom,

HMS Victoria *sinking with* HMS Nile *standing by, 22 June 1893*

National Maritime Museum, London

taking with her 358 officers and men, including Vice-Admiral Tryon.[13] Albert Markham had to face another court martial.

The sinking of the *Victoria* was more than just a naval disaster. It was a national embarrassment. To handle the crisis the Navy needed someone of experience, toughness and confidence; someone who would get the potentially divisive court-martial out of the way as painlessly as possible and then knock the Mediterranean Fleet swiftly back into shape. The task was given to a man from the very heart of the naval establishment, a relative of First Lord Spencer and a familiar figure at court – Sir Michael Culme-Seymour. It comes as little surprise, therefore, that in the autumn of 1893 Bridgeman found himself steaming out to the Mediterranean to join his old commander. To help him in his tricky command Sir Michael needed about him familiar officers of unquestioning loyalty and reliability.

By the time Bridgeman reached the Mediterranean to take up his post as flag captain in the brand new, 14,200-ton battleship *Ramillies* (a pre-dreadnought of the impressive Royal Sovereign Class), the court martial was over. It had been held in the hulk *Hibernia* in Valetta Harbour, far from the prying British press. Markham, Captain Johnstone of the *Camperdown* and other officers involved in the collision were exonerated from all blame, which fell, conveniently, on the deceased Tryon for signalling the fatal manoeuvre.[14] Given the circumstances and the obedience-before-initiative mind-set of the court, there could hardly have been any other conclusion. To have penalised Tryon's inferiors for obeying a command, however ridiculous, would have seriously undermined Service discipline and morale. Those who felt uneasy about the decision kept their own counsel.[15] There had been quite enough boat-rocking for the time being.

From a British point of view the *Victoria* disaster could hardly have come at a worse time. Colonial rivalry in North Africa, Persia, Afghanistan and Siam put Britain's relations with France and Russia under great strain, tempting her to abandon her international isolation, which at the time looked anything but splendid, and align herself with the Triple Alliance of Germany, Austria and Italy. Tension was at its highest in the Mediterranean, where, following Britain's 1889 naval expansion programme, the French had been steadily building up their Toulon Fleet. By 1893 the British presence of 11 battleships, seven cruisers and 12 torpedo boats (divided between Malta and Gibraltar) faced a French fleet of 17 battleships, 10 cruisers and 81 torpedo boats. Britain could, of course, call on reinforcements from the Channel. But as France and her new ally Russia (whose combined naval estimates outstripped Britain's by 1893) could be expected to act together in times of crisis, *The Times* declared contentiously on 31 October 1893 that Britain remained in the Mediterranean 'on sufferance' of the other two powers.[16]

In response to yet another naval scare, First Sea Lord Sir Frederick Richards drew up plans for a major hike in naval expenditure. He was backed by the Chancellor of the Exchequer but not by Prime Minister Gladstone, who resigned on 1 March 1894. His successor Lord Rosebery accepted the need for seven new battleships, many smaller vessels, five-year plans for the development of Malta and Gibraltar, an increase in naval personnel and the establishment of the Royal Naval Reserve.[17] By 1895 the naval estimates exceeded those for the Army for the first time in British budgetary history.

Within his limitations, Culme-Seymour did what was expected of him. To show he harboured no grudges, he incorporated many of the survivors from the *Victoria* (including Commander John Jellicoe) into the ship's company of the *Ramillies*. There was no further experiment with minimal signalling. All was done by the book, neatly, efficiently and on time. To the casual observer, the Mediterranean Fleet was soon in fine shape. It certainly created a good impression in Taranto and La Spezia, which it visited in October as part of British overtures towards Italy in response to the Franco-Russian threat. Jellicoe recalled his days under Culme-Seymour and Bridgeman with pride and affection.[18]

But looks were not everything. When Culme-Seymour took command in the Mediterranean he complained that the Admiralty provided him with no battle plan, 'beyond knowing the Channel Squadron is to join me in 10 days'.[19] The situation did not change. Nor was

HMS Ramillies *at anchor, late 1893*

National Maritime Museum, London

anything done about the division of the fleet between Gibraltar and Malta, which was little more than a bluff. If war had broken out, the Eastern Fleet would have been unable to keep the Suez Canal open, while the Gibraltar Fleet would not have been strong enough to match the Toulon Fleet without reinforcement.

Commenting on the practices of the Mediterranean Fleet in 1890, Admiral Dewar had observed that it was obsessed with 'quadrille-like movements ... which entirely ignored all questions of gun and torpedo fire'.[20] When Percy Scott arrived in the cruiser *Scylla* six years later, he 'expected to find great improvements in the routine in gunnery and signalling'. To his surprise, he found 'everything was just as it had been'. There had been no advance, except in 'housemaiding of the ships'. Target practice was just a matter of getting rid of ammunition as quickly as possible and there was no competition for heavy gun shooting.

> 'The state of the paintwork was the one and only idea. To be the cleanest ship in the fleet was still the objective for everyone; nothing else mattered.'[21]

Other observers made the same criticisms of Culme-Seymour's fleet. He trained his ships to work as a team, moving and acting together, 'without considering how these units should be used in time of war'.[22] But there was no war, and the gleaming fleet was impressive enough to prevent the French and Russians from risking one.

Tension, however, remained high. The death of the Sultan of Morocco in 1894 brought a stand-off between British, Italian, Spanish and French cruisers at Tangier. Later in the year, following Turkish massacres of Christian Armenians, Culme-Seymour was ordered to Beirut to put pressure on the Sultan. (Criticism of the Royal Navy pales into insignificance compared with the shambolic condition of the Ottoman Fleet at this time. Many ships were laid up without their screws, to prevent their being used in revolt against the Sultan!) Through all this Bridgeman seems to have behaved with impeccable correctness and zeal. Sir Michael reported favourably to the Admiralty on the condition of the

Ramillies, pronouncing his flag captain 'VGI', with a 'thorough knowledge of his profession in all its branches' and notable for his 'great tact and judgement'.[23]

Then, just before Christmas 1894, Bridgeman was suddenly invalided home with troublesome varicose veins. Once more his illness seems to have been more convenient than real. On releasing him, Culme-Seymour said he would be 'quite fit for any appointment at home,' and it wasn't too long before Bridgeman, veins miraculously restored to full working order, was back on the bridge of a sea-going warship.[24] So what was the varicose veins business all about? Like the hernia incident six years earlier, Bridgeman's complaint may have been simply an excuse to get away from an overbearing and exacting superior, or a genuine physical condition brought on by the stress of working for such a hard taskmaster. On this occasion, however, both are unlikely. Culme-Seymour not only went along with the varicose veins story but his relations with Bridgeman remained cordial for many years to come.

The third and perhaps most plausible explanation is that the varicose veins were a plot, concocted by Bridgeman and Sir Michael to get his flag captain home for compassionate leave.[25] Although we have no direct evidence, it seems likely that Bridgeman had heard of a sharp deterioration in his aged father's health and contrived with the help of his superior to get to see him before he died. Nevertheless, the shadow still remains over Bridgeman's mental and physical durability.

Official sources say that Bridgeman was with the *Ramillies* until January 1895, taking half-pay (7/3d a day) from 17 January until 16 December 1896.[26] It seems clear that he returned home before this, because on New Year's Eve 1894 'Francis Charles Bridgeman-Simpson of Copgrove Hall, Esq., a captain in Her Majesty's Navy' was appointed chairman of the newly formed Burton Leonard Parish Council.[27] Burton Leonard, the nearest sizeable community to the hamlet of Copgrove, had chosen its councillors before Christmas, when presumably Bridgeman had been present to offer himself for election. It is interesting that he chose to do this, for it shows not only that he returned from the Mediterranean with the intention of staying ashore for some time, but also that he was already putting down roots in his adopted community and following Emily's example of using his privileged position to help it.

The *Ripon Observer* reported the many occasions during the 1880s when 'Mrs and Miss Schiffner of Copgrove Hall' laid on outings and meals for poor children of the district. Earlier, in 1876, Emily had paid for a disused forge to be converted into a Reading and Coffee Room for the people of Burton Leonard, for which she was given an inkstand as a token of their gratitude.[28] Parish Council records show that the Copgrove estate traditionally helped the neighbourhood in several other ways, too, such as providing iron grilles to protect trees on the village green from damage by animals.[29] Beginning in 1889, Emily had paid for an extensive restoration of St Michael and All Angels, including installing new oak pews and using the wood from the old box pews for a dado around the walls, lowering the floor and relaying it with concrete, rebuilding the windows and adding two new porches. Her husband contributed a new organ costing £300.[30]

Bridgeman put in an appearance at Parish Council meetings throughout 1895 and early in 1896, being re-elected chairman in both years. His last recorded attendance at this time is on 15 April 1896, after which he does not appear again in the council minute book until 1919.[31] His father died on 1 April 1895, some three and a half months after his return from the Mediterranean. What Bridgeman's reaction was, we shall never know. But he was back in Burton Leonard two weeks later to chair a council meeting and at some time over the next year he changed his name by deed poll from his father's ostentatious Bridgeman Bridgeman Simpson to plain Bridgeman. The move looks very much like a long-awaited declaration of independence.

Bridgeman went back to sea on 16 December 1896, when he took up the post of flag captain with the Channel Fleet in the six-year-old protected cruiser *Blenheim*.[32] At this stage the German naval threat was no more than a smudge of smoke on the horizon and the Channel Fleet was still smaller and weaker than its Mediterranean counterpart, which it was expected to reinforce in time of crisis. Moreover, following Britain's recent

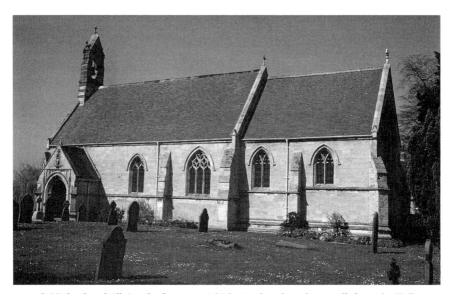

St Michael and All Angels, Copgrove, which stands only a short walk from the Hall

Copgrove Church organ, donated by Bridgeman c.1900

The grave of Rev William Bridgeman-Simpson at All Saints, Babworth

massive increase in naval expenditure, France had decided that as she could not match both Germany on land and Britain at sea, she would concentrate her resources on the Army. The self-belief of the Royal Navy riding high.

The Service's new-found confidence was displayed to the world in the Diamond Jubilee Naval Review which took place in the Solent on 26 June 1897. It was, according to *The Times*, a demonstration of naval power unparalleled in modern times. 165 warships were arrayed in five lines that stretched across 30 miles of sea. It was done, moreover, without withdrawing a single ship from an overseas station. (The Navy had 360 ships on its books, five times as many as any other country.) With much pomp and self-congratulation, the fleet was inspected by the Prince of Wales aboard the paddle-driven royal yacht *Victoria and Albert*.[33]

To help him celebrate the occasion Bridgeman invited a large family party to join him in the *Blenheim*. Emily (recorded affectionately as 'Aunt Emmy') was there, as were Orlando and his wife Catherine, their daughters Lilian (now 22) and Evelyn (19), Adolphus Duncombe and some of Emily's sister's family, the Grahams. The Review was followed by a large party at Copgrove in July.[34] As far as we can tell, they were both

National Maritime Museum, London

Diamond Jubilee Naval Review – Two lines of battleships with Magnificent, Royal Sovereign *and* Repulse *in the foreground*

strictly family gatherings to which he invited no well-connected, influential figures from either the political or military world. This reinforces family tradition that following his marriage Bridgeman was not a particularly ambitious man. His marriage and his new life at Copgrove had caused him to change his priorities. Home and family were now of great importance to him. Perhaps too, in conversation with Emily, he had begun to accept that, fine sailor though he undoubtedly was, he was no politician. He did not, therefore, strive for a promotion that might take him off the sea and into the alien world of the Admiralty.

Bridgeman left the *Blenheim* soon after the Review. In August he resumed his relationship with Culme-Seymour, who was now flying his flag in the *Victory* as Commander-in-Chief, Portsmouth. Bridgeman was flag captain in command of the *Duke of Wellington*, the *Victory's* tender that served as a general depot ship. He remained at this unexacting but no doubt socially enjoyable post until the end of the century. How he passed his days, we do not know, although in 1900 he had some sort of supervisory role over the Signal School.[35] From the evidence of family scrapbooks, it is clear that he was frequently at Copgrove where family gatherings now included his sister Mary's children, the Pleydell-Bouverie girls, and various relatives of Walter Pleydell-Bouverie's second wife, Edith Lascelles. After Edith's death in 1902, 'Aunt Emmy' and 'Uncle Francey' seem to have turned Copgrove into a refuge for all their orphaned nieces. Bridgeman also found time to deepen his ties with the local community by becoming a JP for the West Riding on 15 October 1900. He held the position until his death in 1929, when his name was deleted from the list.[36]

In the broader social sphere, which also had career implications, Bridgeman remained very much part of Culme-Seymour's favoured 'Malta Clique', with its close connections with the royal family and freemasonry.[37] He was a frequent guest at Culme-Seymour dinner parties but appears not to have reciprocated the hospitality by inviting his naval cronies (apart from Lord Stanhope Hawke) to the haven of Copgrove.[38] Home life and work were kept strictly apart.

The Portsmouth clique, 1898. Commander-in-Chief Sir Michael Culme-Seymour (second from right) with (left to right) Flag Captain Francis Bridgeman, Secretary H H Rickard and Flag Lieutenant E S Alexander-Sinclair

National Maritime Museum, London

NOTES

1   PRO ADM 196/39 (II); PRO PMG 15/114.

2   Gordon, *The Rules of the Game*, p. 567; Bacon, *A Naval Scrapbook*, p. 160.

3   *A Naval Scrapbook*, pp. 175-7.

4   Bacon, *ibid.*, pp. 174-5. Apparently, this was by no means the only occasion when the admiral raised his voice. Being rather deaf, he shouted most of the time and was the only person allowed to do so in the presence of Queen Victoria.

5   Evidence that Bridgeman was a strict, even harsh disciplinarian comes from the only adverse comment in the official records from this time. On 12 December 1890 the Admiralty expressed its disapproval that he had held in irons a man awaiting court martial. 'My Lords consider[ed] there was no necessity for such an action,' they concluded. (PRO ADM 196/39 (II).)

6   *Bacon: From 1900 Onwards*, p. 160.

7   *Ibid.*

8   From an unidentifiable newspaper report cited in Gordon, *The Rules of the Game*, p. 253. Sir Michael may indeed have used the Navy for his own 'comfort and advantage', but nowhere near as successfully as Sir Provo William Parry Wallis. Born in 1795 and given the rank of able seaman just after 4th birthday, Sir Provo had taken exceptional advantage of the order that officers who had served in the French wars would never be retired. He climbed steadily through the ranks to become an admiral of the fleet in 1877 and when he died in 1892, aged 101, he had been paid by the Admiralty for 97 years! (Bonnett, *The Price of Admiralty*, p. 100.)

9   PRO ADM 196/39 (II).

10   *Ibid.*; PRO PMG 15/144.

11   See above, p. 80.

12   Cited in Gordon, *The Rules of the Game*, p. 213.

13   The future Admiral of the Fleet John Jellicoe was one of those who managed to swim to safety.

14   After a convenient interval Markham was put on half-pay for seven years. He re-emerged to command the Nore and work on minesweepers in World War I. Knighted in 1904, he died 14 years later.

15   These included Fisher, who declared privately, 'If I were Markham, I would never hold my head up again'. (Cited in Gordon, *The Rules of the Game*, p. 289.)

16   Cited in Marder, *The Anatomy of British Sea Power*, p. 180.

17   To counter the threat of French torpedo boats the Royal Navy developed a new, fast vessel, the destroyer, the first of which had been laid down in 1892.

18   *Dictionary of National Biography*.

19   Cited in Marder, *The Anatomy of British Sea Power*, p. 177.

20   *Ibid.*, pp. 25-6.

21   Scott, *Fifty Years in the Navy*, p .73. Although vessels of the Royal Sovereign Class, like Culme-Seymour's flagship *Ramillies*, were a considerable improvement on previous battleships, they were still defective as gun platforms. They rolled heavily and their guns could be loaded in one position only.

22   Yexley, *The Inner Life of the Navy*, p. 54.

23   PRO ADM 196/86.

24 PRO ADM 196/86.

25 That spring Sir Michael had accepted spurious medical reasons for another of his officers, Hugh Evans-Thomas, returning to England to get engaged.

26 PRO ADM 196/86; PRO PMG 15/129 & 133.

27 *Minute Book of Burton Leonard Parish Council*, for information from which I am indebted to Mrs Barbara Wray.

28 Diggle, *Burton Leonard Past and Present*, pp. 92.

29 See note 26, above.

30 From a leaflet outlining the history of St Michael and All Angels, available in the church. Anon. ND.

31 See note 26, above.

32 Equipped with 9.2" and quick-firing 6" guns, as well as torpedoes, the 9,000-ton *Blenheim* still carried 118 pistols and 182 cutlasses – just in case!

33 The Naval Review was to some extent both a sham and a political *faux pas*. Some of the ships on display were little more than hulks that had to be towed into position and towed back to harbour again when the proceedings were over. The spectacle of a multitude of ships with white uppers and yellow masts might have been glorious, but it would have been difficult to have devised a colour scheme that presented an enemy with a better target. (Following the German example, naval warships were painted a universal battleship grey in 1904.) And the Navy's ostentation produced an understandable reaction from France, Russia and Germany, all of whom increased naval expenditure the following year.

34 Information based on photographs and captions in a family scrapbook in the private possession of Mrs Walter Hingston.

35 Gordon, *The Rules of the Game*, p. 321.

36 Wakefield Archives, QD1/124 & 151.

37 *Ibid.*, pp. 319-20, 337-9. Gordon understands Bridgeman, along with many in the Culme-Seymour circle, to have been a Freemason. This may have had some bearing on his subsequent promotions.

38 Family scrapbook, see note 26 above. The first recorded visit of the Culme-Seymours to Copgrove occurred in November 1901, after Sir Michael had retired.

7 'The Best Admiral we have'

In the autumn of 1901 Bridgeman was appointed Aide-de-Camp to the new king, Edward VII. A newspaper cutting (probably from the *Yorkshire Post*) says that he was given the position as a reward for his sterling work in the *Victory* at Portsmouth, but it was far more likely to have been at the recommendation of Sir Michael Culme-Seymour, who had ended his career in a similar position under Queen Victoria.[1] The king's links with freemasonry (he had been the Grand Master of England before his accession) cannot have done Bridgeman, a fellow mason, any harm. The position of ADC was largely honorary and required Bridgeman to do little more than attend certain formal functions.[2] The statement in his *Yorkshire Post* obituary, that he accompanied the king on visits to 'European Sovereigns', is unfounded. The only foreign trips undertaken by Edward at this time were to Germany and Denmark in August and September 1901 and there is no indication that Bridgeman accompanied him on either occasion.[3]

Captain Francis Charles Bridgman Bridgeman, the newly appointed Naval Aide-de-Camp to his Majesty, is fifty-three years of age. He received his present rank in 1890, and since that date his name has been associated with the *Victory* at Portsmouth. The King's message to the Navy still rings in the ears of the service, and by various acts and appointments he has since shown his unceasing interest in all that concerns its dignity and welfare. The appointment of Captain Bridgeman to be a Naval Aide-de-Camp is accepted by his friends as a compliment paid to an officer who had well deserved it.

Photo. Russell.

CAPTAIN F. C. B. BRIDGEMAN,
New Naval Aide-de-Camp to the King.

The Yorkshire Post's *announcement of Bridgeman's appointment as Aide-de-Camp to Edward VII, 1901*

In 1922 Bridgeman's links with the royal family would be strengthened by the spectacular wedding, which he probably attended, of Henry Lascelles, sixth Earl of Harewood and distant cousin of Bridgeman's step-nieces, to Princess Mary, only sister of George V.[4] There is a half-remembered family story that during a visit to London Bridgeman was taken seriously ill (health was never his strong suit) and confined to his bed in Brown's Hotel. The management was concerned that the ailing and apparently not especially well-off sailor might remain with them for weeks, running up debts he could not afford to pay.[5] Somehow, probably through the offices of Nancy Pleydell-Bouverie who had trained as a nurse at Salisbury Hospital and was now looking after him, Princess Mary got to hear of Bridgeman's plight and requested Brown's to ensure that he received the best possible care. This they duly did, and Bridgeman was soon well enough to return home. Tradition sets the story in the first decade of the century, but this does not seem possible. It is more likely to have taken place after Emily's death, which occurred nine months after the Lascelles-Windsor wedding.

Bridgeman ceased to be a royal ADC on 24 July 1902. He remained on half-pay until 13 January the following year, when he became captain of the 14,000-ton, 25-knot armoured cruiser *Drake*, attached to the newly-formed Cruiser Squadron under Admiral Fawkes.[6] It was his first sea-going appointment for six years and he returned to a Navy entering yet another period of radical change.

Naval development was never steady. As a consequence partly of the innate conservatism of its senior officers and partly of its tradition of eschewing technological change until it had been tested by other fleets, the Service progressed like a jellyfish on a piece of elastic – long periods of inactivity alternated with short, dramatic leaps forward. One such leap began when Lord Selborne, the gifted 43-year-old son-in-law of the Prime Minister, became First Lord of the Admiralty on 1 November 1900. It received greater impetus two years later when Fisher went to the Admiralty as Second Sea Lord and an even greater fillip when Fisher replaced Lord Walter Kerr as First Sea Lord on Trafalgar Day (21 October – a deliberate choice) 1904.

The 14,000 cruiser Drake, *which Bridgeman captained 1903-4*

At the turn of the century the Royal Navy was a vastly more effective and up-to-date service than it had been when Bridgeman had first joined almost 40 years previously. Even so, it remained 'in certain respects a drowsy, inefficient, moth-eaten organisation'.[7] Its shortcoming had been laid bare earlier in the year, when the country was shaken by one of the periodic invasion scares that captured the public's imagination from time to time in the years before the First World War. As the French assembled their Brest and Toulon Fleets in the Bay of Biscay and mobilised 150,000 men for manoeuvres, the Admiralty had done almost nothing.

Subsequent inquiry revealed that the naval estimates had been underspent for the last three years and the ships of the Reserve were so obsolete and broken down that, in the words of one Admiral, they posed no more threat to the enemy than so many Chinese junks.[8] All the old complaints about the Navy's deplorable gunnery came out, too. The new big guns might look daunting and sound even more so, but they were hardly put to best use when two out of every three shells fired in practice missed their target. Inspecting admirals were still in the habit of leaving ships before gunnery exercises to avoid the noise and dirt.[9]

The calibre of men at the top of the Service had not changed, either. There were few admirals of real intellect, causing Fisher to wonder unkindly how many of them actually had minds. However, he had the grace to admit that their shortcomings were hardly their fault as the Service had not chosen them for their brains, nor had it made much effort to educate those that had them. 'So long as an officer sings well or can get up a good set of theatricals,' observed one critic wryly in 1901, 'his most glaring exhibition of ignorance will be winked at'.[10] Even dangerously eccentric senior officers had not been entirely weeded out either. As late as 1906 Admiral Grenfell's cabin 'literally swarmed with Siamese cats'. He also,

> 'had glass tanks in his gun-ports full of frogs and strange fish.
> For these and for the cats the cabin was kept at a temperature
> of about 95° Fahrenheit, and was painfully odorous'.[11]

The most cogent reason for reform was the changing international situation. Bismarck's ruthless 'blood and iron' midwifery delivered a strong and healthy German Empire in the Palace of Versailles on 18 January 1871. For the next 20 years the primary military concern of the latest member of the family of nations was to maintain land forces sufficient to prevent its becoming a victim of French infanticidal wishes. Policy changed with the accession of Kaiser William II in 1888 and the dismissal of Bismarck two years later.

The emergence of the German Empire had, by and large, been welcomed in British military circles as a useful counterweight to the power of France. Doubts began to emerge in the mid-1890s, when the Kaiser voiced his support for the Boers in South Africa and Chancellor Bülow spoke of his country's new 'world policy' and of wanting her 'place in the sun'. In 1897, the German Minister of Marine, Admiral von Tirpitz, raised British naval hackles by saying that the trident had to be his country's fist and backed his remark up by announcing a massive seven-year naval expansion programme. This was revised upwards in

1899, projecting a German Navy of 38 modern battleships and hundreds of smaller craft by 1916. It was, he declared, a precautionary, defensive measure. Only by possessing a 'risk fleet' large enough to prevent Germany being dictated to by other powers would she be able to maintain her rightful position in the world.

Accustomed for nearly a century to regard the world's oceans as almost an extension of the Empire, the Royal Navy reacted to the German plans with a confused mix of incredulity, horror, condescension and rage. No fleet that threatened British naval superiority, they spluttered, could possibly be seen as defensive. How dare the German Emperor, a pompous little upstart, call himself (as he did) 'Admiral of the Atlantic'! It was a joke, and one in bad taste, too.

But beneath all the bluster and dismissive rhetoric lay very real concerns. Germany had a reputation for military efficiency and fine technology. The ships built would be neither technically second-rate nor poorly manned. Furthermore, as her projected battleships were comparatively small with short operating ranges, their obvious field of activity was the North Sea. This called into question the basis of British naval strategy, until now centred on the Mediterranean. Apart from Chatham, the Navy had no base that faced Continental Europe.

The construction of a large German Navy, together with those of the USA and Japan, would eventually make the maintenance of the Two-Power Standard if not irrelevant, then almost impossible to maintain. Nor did Britain's isolation, outside both the German-Austrian-Italian Triple Alliance and the Franco-Russian Dual Alliance, make things any easier. As a result, in January 1902, she finally came off the diplomatic fence and signed an alliance with Japan. Far more significant was the 1904 *Entente Cordiale* with France, Germany's sworn enemy. Although technically it was simply an agreement to settle outstanding colonial disputes, it soon led to co-operation in matters military as well as diplomatic. Britain drew up her first official plans for war with Germany the following year and by 1908 Fisher was telling the king, 'that we have eventually to fight Germany is just as sure as anything human can be'.[12]

If the growth of German naval power (and the relative decline in that of France) was the main force for naval reform in the early twentieth century, the nature of change was largely dictated by technology. Basic warship design, established by the time of the Royal Sovereign battleships, altered little, but two developments – watertube boilers and oil-fired, turbine engines – increased the ships' speed, range and efficiency. Torpedoes, which in 1898 operated erratically over about 1,000 yards, became effective over three times that distance. Wireless telegraphy revolutionised naval communications making it possible by 1914 to control, from London, fleets and squadrons ranged right across the world.

The appearance of reliable submarines at the turn of the century was potentially the most startling development. Fisher, always keen to espouse new ideas and thinking, believed they would revolutionise naval strategy and tactics, and he fumed mercilessly against more conservative-minded admirals who regarded them as dishonest, un-English weapons. (Admiral A K Wilson famously went as far as saying that he would hang all captured submarine crews as pirates![13]) As in many fields, France pioneered submarine development, but the Royal Navy ordered five craft in 1900 and five years later, thanks largely to Fisher's enthusiasm, had 39 either completed or on the slipway.

On the back of Naval Estimates that soared from £27.5 million in 1900 to £36.9 million in 1904, battleship construction continued apace. By the time Bridgeman was finding his feet on the bridge of the *Drake,* the Royal Navy's 42 capital ships outnumbered those of any three other navies combined. Improved battleships were allocated to the Reserve Squadron which, to counter the German threat, was elevated to the status of Home Fleet in 1902. The next year a new naval base was announced for the Firth of Forth. A Challenge Cup for heavy gunnery was set up, which led to an improvement in naval shooting that 'stunned' the French.[14] The Naval Intelligence Department was reformed and promising commanders and captains sent to a War Course at Greenwich for instruction in modern naval warfare and international law. In all these measures Selborne and his Naval Lords received the support of Edward VII, into whose receptive ear Fisher had for some time being pouring his bewitching aphorisms.

Jackie Fisher was everything the great majority of his naval contemporaries were not. Where they played by the rules, he played to win. At least, that's what the master of the memorable epithet said in public. 'If you rub it in both at home and abroad,' he declared,

> 'that you intend to be 'first in' and hit your enemy in the belly and kick him when he's down and boil your prisoners in oil (*if you take any*) and torture his women and children, then people will steer clear of you.'[15]

His secret of success in war was, 'Hit first! Hit hard! Keep on hitting!'[16] The same tactics – 'ruthless, relentless, remorseless' – applied to everything he did, 'regardless of everything and everybody'. To make the Royal Navy invincible and a lasting memorial to his genius was his enduring aim. And those who stood in his way, he warned, 'I crush, I crush'.[17]

Yet, for all his stark and startling rhetoric, Fisher was no cold-hearted tyrant. He could be as charming, as witty and as considerate as anyone – more so if the mood took him. He was a brilliant conversationalist, a tireless dancer and an inveterate reader of scripture. His pet project, the *Dreadnought*, was so named because the phrase 'Fear God and dread nought' appeared so frequently in the Bible. Boundless in energy, forceful to the point of mania and blessed with a computer-like memory, he was the most exciting and original admiral the Navy had seen since Nelson.

It goes without saying that so able and flamboyant a personality attracted almost as much hostility as admiration. Thick-brained admirals ('prehistoric' he called them) hated him for the way he bamboozled and out-manoeuvred them.[18] Snobs scorned his humble origins and his close, informal relations with the lower ranks. Conservatives disliked his radicalism, moralists his indiscretion, opponents his underhand ways. More serious critics pointed out that Fisher was not a particularly good fleet commander, nor did he concern himself enough with tactics. His sweeping statements certainly stirred things up, but as Admiral Richmond pointed out they hardly amounted to a 'logical and scientific system of war'.[19]

Bridgeman, as far as we can tell, liked and respected the extraordinary admiral without ever immersing himself totally in the fishpond. For his part, Fisher much appreciated Bridgeman's willingness to accept new ideas and his qualities as a fleet commander and seaman. Although Bridgeman was too staid for the two ever to become firm friends, Fisher trusted him and had more time for him than for most of his generation. And that, from Fisher, was quite a compliment.

Joining the Navy in 1854, aged 13, Fisher was a captain by the age of 33. He went on to found the *Vernon* torpedo school, distinguish himself by his ingenuity during the attack on Alexandria and reform the *Excellent*. Promoted rear admiral in 1890, he carried his reforming zeal to the Admiralty (1892-7) and the Mediterranean (1899-1902) before returning to the Admiralty as Second Sea Lord, in charge of personnel. Intent on bringing Naval education into line with modern requirements, he scrapped the *Britannia*, replacing it with Dartmouth College, and amalgamated the training of engineer and executive officers.

Vice-Admiral Jackie Fisher, the most influential
naval officer since Nelson

When he finally became First Sea Lord, Fisher was 63. At an age when most men are thinking of retirement, he launched himself with extraordinary energy into a programme of far-reaching reform. To achieve his Thatcherite aims of economy and efficiency he sought a 30% reduction in naval expenditure and a 30% rise in the Service's efficiency. To the delight of the Conservative government and the taxpayer, naval estimates fell by £3.5 million for 1905-6. Efficiency is less easily measured, but Fisher claimed that during his time at the Admiralty the Navy's strike power rose fourfold.[20]

He was responsible for four sweeping reforms. The 'abominable disgrace' of the Naval Reserves were completely overhauled by basing all ships capable of fighting effectively at Portsmouth, Plymouth and Sheerness and providing them with nucleus crews so that they could be ready for action at short notice.[21]

To take account of recent political and military developments – the alliance with Japan, the *Entente Cordiale* with France and the rapid growth of German naval power – the disposition of the Royal Navy was radically changed. Power was now focused on five key strategic points about the globe: Singapore, the Cape, Alexandria, Gibraltar and Dover. The independent squadrons that had patrolled the Pacific, the South Atlantic, North American and Caribbean waters were done away with and absorbed into new Cape and Eastern Fleets. Gone was much of the flag-showing, roving police work (or, as Fisher put it, 'shooting pheasants up Chinese rivers and giving tea parties to British consuls') of the kind undertaken by the *Blanche*.[22]

The change, although logical and certainly cost-cutting, attracted criticism on two fronts; one specific, one general. The new disposition of the Navy, it was pointed out, left British merchant vessels dangerously exposed to attack from rogue raiders that might manage to get away from the major fleets. On a less specific level, critics complained that by cutting flag-showing missions Fisher was damaging Britain's global prestige, from which incalculable commercial benefit had flowed over the past century. Their case received vociferous support when ships from the US Navy were first to reach Jamaica following a devastating earthquake there in 1907.

To bolster the Navy's presence nearer home, in February 1909 the Channel Fleet was absorbed into the powerful Home Fleet (the first to receive dreadnoughts), which had been established in October 1906. The Atlantic Fleet, reinforced with vessels from the Mediterranean, was moved to Gibraltar, from where it could move either east or west. These changes meant that three-quarters of the Navy's big battleships could be easily arrayed against Germany. The reduced Mediterranean Fleet was based solely on Malta.[23]

Out-of-date ships were ruthlessly scrapped or sold. In all 160 vessels considered too weak to fight and too slow to flee were done away with. They were replaced, in fire-power if not in number, by Fisher's favourite children: a new generation of all-big-gun battleships, of which the first was the famous *Dreadnought*.[24] The ship's speed (21 knots) and the long-range fire-power of her ten 12" guns were designed to enable her to destroy any enemy before they got close enough to return fire with either guns or torpedoes. The message was clear. The primary task of the Navy's capital ships was to sink enemy vessels. Boarding was out of the question and landing troops for operations ashore at best a secondary role.

The construction of the *Dreadnought* was the most controversial of all Fisher's innovations. It broke with the long tradition of learning from other navies' mistakes. As the First Sea Lord's great rival Lord Charles Beresford scornfully observed, all the Admiralty had achieved by constructing the vessel 'was to publish a new design just in time to enable other nations to profit by its defects'.[25] Moreover, the launching of the *Dreadnought* rendered every other battleship obsolete, ending Britain's naval supremacy at a stroke. As other countries were bound to come up with dreadnoughts of their own, the only way to restore the Navy's position was to build more than them, so fuelling a naval arms race. And the more powerful the Navy grew, the more apposite seemed Henry Labouchere's warning about military deterrents. 'What I fear,' he had quipped, 'is that, if we have a Navy so strong that we can crush all creation, we shall be inclined to try the experiment of using it.'

Things went well for Bridgeman in the *Drake*. Admirals Henderson and Fawkes reported favourably after inspecting his ship and in May 1903 he was made a Member of the Royal Victorian Order (4th class).[26] Better was to come, for on handing over his ship to Captain Jellicoe in August, he was promoted to the rank of rear admiral. His pay was now 25/- a day, although he received only half that amount until June the following year when he joined the 10-year-old *Victorious*, captained by Sackville Carden, as second-in-command of Lord Charles Beresford's Channel Fleet.

'Charlie B' (Admiral Lord Charles Beresford) and Kora, both in characteristic pose

Beresford was perhaps the most attractive of the trio of powerful, maverick figures with whom Bridgeman came into close contact during his time in the Navy.[27] Two years Bridgeman's senior, Lord Charles William de la Poer, Baron Beresford, had almost everything needed to rise to the very top of the Service. Well-connected, charming, dashing, fluent and immensely popular for his open manner and great kindness, 'Charlie B' lacked only the capacity for sustained analysis that a more academic education might have given him.[28] He was intelligent enough (though his mind deteriorated when he was in his fifties), but never showed the penetrating sharpness of a Fisher or a Churchill and was inclined to say whatever came into his head without thinking it through. This gave hostile wits a large target to aim at. In ungenerous mood, J L Garvin dismissed him as 'the biggest of all gasbags', while to Fisher he was little more than a 'boastful ass'. Churchill, ever the master of the witty put-down, believed Beresford had no brain at all, which meant that when he rose to his feet to make a speech he didn't know what he was going to say, when speaking he didn't know what he was saying, and when he sat down he didn't know what he had said.[29]

On leaving the *Britannia* in 1861, for a few years Beresford followed a round of postings similar to Bridgeman's. However, as we saw in *Britannia*, even as a cadet the flamboyant Irish peer had been regarded as someone rather special and in the 1860s he was chosen to serve in the Royal Yacht and accompany Prince Albert on his voyage in the *Galatea*.[30] In 1874 he entered the House of Commons as Conservative MP for Waterford, holding the seat until 1880. By all accounts he never allowed his political responsibilities to impinge too closely on his other interests, which were by no means restricted to matters maritime. Lord Charles, a close friend and companion of the Prince of Wales, had a reputation as an excellent sport – in the broadest sense of the term. The many stories of his sexual adventures are undoubtedly exaggerated, though it does appear that he did indeed have a pack of hounds in full cry tattooed on his back, with the object of their attention, a fox, entering a convenient hiding place lower down his lordship's torso. Bet he wouldn't walk naked from Hyde Park Corner to St James', he won the wager by making the journey in a floor-less carriage with its windows covered.

Beresford was appointed captain for the dashing part he played in the capture of Alexandria, an action that made him a popular hero. By the time he took over the Channel Fleet in 1903, he had seen further action in Egypt, served briefly and fractiously as Fourth Sea Lord, re-entered the Commons as a fierce critic of naval policy, published a book on the imminent break up of China and acted as Fisher's second-in-command in the Mediterranean. It was here, apparently, that bitter personal antipathy between the two men first arose. Seeing Beresford's ship, the *Ramillies*, make an untidy entry into Malta Harbour, Fisher ordered her to return to sea and 'come in again in a more seamanlike manner'. Beresford was not amused.[31] Relations remained cordial until it became clear that Fisher had no intention of retiring in January 1906 when he reached the age of 65.[32] Finding his path to the very top blocked, Beresford used every means at his disposal to discredit the man who stood in his way. The result was unedifying for both of them and deeply unsettling for the Royal Navy.

Before the creation of the Home Fleet, the Channel Fleet, with 12 battleships at its heart, was the principal defence against Germany. However, in October 1904 it was not the German Navy that Bridgeman and Beresford were concerned about, but the Russian. On 8 February Japan had provoked war with her Far Eastern rival by making a surprise attack on Russian-held Port Arthur. To make good early reversals, Russia ordered her Baltic Fleet to steam right round the world to join the conflict. On 22 October, having got as far as the Dogger Bank, it fired on Hull trawlers in the strangely mistaken belief that they were Japanese torpedo boats. Understandably, Britain's relations with Russia became even more strained than usual and the Channel Fleet was ordered to shadow the Russians as they made their way south.

In the Bay of Biscay the Russian Fleet divided, one half putting into the Tangier to take on coal. Beresford followed them there and waited off shore, watching. The crisis came to a head on 27-31 October, when the Channel Fleet cleared its decks and prepared for action. The situation was saved by last-minute negotiation, after which the Russians continued on

A postcard of Bridgeman printed in 1904 – the likeness, however, is dubious

their ill-fated journey to annihilation beneath Japanese guns in the Straits of Tsushima the following year.

During the Admiralty post-mortem Beresford revealed that if he had been ordered into action he would have sought to avoid what 'would more have represented a massacre than a fight' by giving the Russians time to get up steam and firing warning shots. The Admiralty, which now had Fisher as First Sea Lord, was flabbergasted at such outmoded, boxing-ring chivalry and Beresford was severely reprimanded for not being prepared to send the inferior Russian ships to the bottom without a second thought.[33]

What Bridgeman thought of all this, we do not know. Within his family there circulates a strange tale that his personal intervention during the Tangier incident prevented Beresford turning the crisis into full-scale conflict. The Channel Fleet commander was 'about to fire', the story goes, when 'Uncle Francey' told him that the enemy had to be given 'time to get up steam, or it will be war'.[34] If, as is possible, this is just a garbled version of the official story, it may be that Bridgeman endorsed Beresford's honourable but foolish intentions. There is, of course, just a chance that

Beresford really had contemplated engaging the Russians and had been dissuaded from doing so by the cool council of his second-in-command. If this was the case, then Britain owes a great deal more to Uncle Francey than it realises.[35]

Beresford left the Channel Fleet in March 1905 and after a two-month rest moved to the Mediterranean as Commander-in-Chief. Bridgeman remained with the *Victorious* until August, when he began a six-month spell on half-pay.[36] Before he left the ship, however, he underwent another hair-raising naval adventure – very nearly his last. This time his enemies were not Russians, but the tide, a lump of Scottish granite and the lure of a good dinner.

Sometime that summer the *Victorious* found herself in Loch Linnhe, a deep-water anchorage off the west coast of Scotland much favoured by the fleet for its social and sporting pleasures. The battleship entered the loch on the high tide, passed through the Corran Narrows and anchored securely in Inverscaddle Bay. Bridgeman was immediately taken ashore to fulfil a dinner invitation at Conaglen House, the grandiose hunting lodge of Lord and Lady Morton, old family friends.

The party was a white-glove Edwardian gathering of glittering formality and discrete ostentation. We can only guess what the rear-admiral thought of such occasions, to which he was certainly no stranger. He was neither a witty nor a flippant man – although his charm and fund of naval stories must have made him a pleasant dinner companion – and it is unlikely he took much pleasure from the scandal, repartee and mild flirtation that were the regular fare of such high-society gatherings. Judging by their homely, family-oriented lifestyle at Copgrove, both he and Emily regarded social set-pieces as something to be endured rather than enjoyed.

So there was Bridgeman, upright and spectacularly handsome in his full dress uniform, eating sparingly (unlike many illustrious Edwardians, including Beresford and the king himself, he never lost his figure) and chatting amiably to those around him, when a notably under-dressed figure entered the room and whispered something in Morton's ear. The earl nodded and the visitor moved down the table to where

Bridgeman sat. The ensuing conversation must have gone something like this:

'I beg your pardon, Admiral, but may I have a word with ye?'

'Of course.'

'Well sir, I've been his Lordship's gillie for many a year now and I reckon I ken the waters of the loch as well as any. Sailor or no.'

'No doubt,' Bridgeman replied, looking somewhat perplexed. 'And what of it?'

'I wouldna wish t'sound rude, sir, but d'y'know your fine ship's anchored over a rock that raises its head at low water?'

Bridgeman stiffened. 'Are you sure, gillie?'

'As sure as I'm standing here, sir.'

At this point something close to panic must have gripped Bridgeman. Painful memories flashed through his mind: the *Blanche*'s nightmare on the Barrier Reef, the avoidable tragedy in the *Camperdown* off Scarborough and the disastrous loss of the *Victoria* (how akin was that ship's name to that of his own!) in the Mediterranean. If, because he had used her as a taxi to take him to a dinner party, the *Victorious* went aground, or worse, the Royal Navy would be humiliated in the eyes of the

HMS Victorious, *eponymously remembered by a rock in Inverscaddle Bay, Loch Linnhe*

world and his career finished. Court martial, scandal in the press, gloating in Germany, distress for Emily ... the consequences were too dreadful to contemplate.

Bridgeman rose from the table, excused himself to his host and ran back to his launch moored at the quayside. Fortunately, it was a still night and he managed to get aboard his ship and take her into deeper waters before she settled onto the rock. It is not recorded whether he returned to the dinner party. Probably not. But he did reward the helpful gillie with a gold watch and the rock that had so nearly done for the *Victorious* carries her name to this day.[37]

The following March Bridgeman was appointed second-in-command to Beresford in the Mediterranean. He flew his flag in the *Venerable*, a 15,000-ton old-style battleship commanded by Captain Henry Pelly. Owing to improved relations with France and Russia (manifested in the Anglo-Russian entente of 1907) and the mounting suspicion of German intentions, the Mediterranean was no longer the crucial theatre of operations it had once been. Nevertheless, its strategic importance remained unchanged and the Navy was wary of the naval expansion being undertaken by Italy and Austro-Hungary, Germany's partners in the Triple Alliance.

Three pieces of evidence reflect how Bridgeman was now viewed in the service. On 23 October Fisher wrote to the king that he was 'about the best Admiral we have'.[38] As with so much that the paradoxical First Sea Lord said, the sub-text is more interesting than the words themselves. He obviously wished to talk Bridgeman up, as he had him in mind to command a much strengthened Home Fleet. Implicit in the remark is Fisher's belief that Bridgeman was abler, or at least more reliable and easier to work with than his commander-in-chief, Beresford. At the same time, Fisher was making it clear that he did not think much of any of the current crop of admirals. While maybe not damning Bridgeman with faint praise, he was at least shrinking him.

Three months later Beresford was committing to paper his own thoughts on his second-in-command. 'A delightful personality,' he extolled, 'and a most loyal and painstaking second. Knows the Service thoroughly and will make a brilliant C-in-C. Perfect knowledge of tactics'.[39] Beresford was a generous man. Even so, such high praise may have had as much to do with his desire for allies in his grumbling feud with Fisher as with Bridgeman's actual abilities. What both Fisher's and Beresford's remarks do bear out, however, is that although Bridgeman was highly regarded by both camps, he was perceived as belonging to neither (or both!). His 'delightful personality', it seems, captivated everyone he met. Except, as shall see, Winston Churchill.

The third reference to Bridgeman's abilities is a genuinely unsolicited testimonial. It comes from Reginald Bacon, the intelligent, 'technically progressive' captain of Bridgeman's flagship *Irresistible*, who left to take charge of the newly-launched *Dreadnought* in July.[40] Bacon was a high flyer and an unequivocal Fisher-ite who later got into deep trouble for passing on to the First Sea Lord unflattering observations about Beresford's behaviour in the Mediterranean. Beresford's increasingly rigid attitudes alarmed Bacon, one of those sharp enough to realise that the lesson of the *Victoria-Camperdown* collision was 'the necessity for every officer to cultivate belief in his own judgement, so as not to be afraid of acting correctly'.[41]

Bacon found no need to sneak on his immediate superior. He was impressed when, following discussion between himself, Bridgeman and Sir Hedworth Meux about whether the single or broken line was the better formation for engaging the enemy, Bridgeman put the matter to the test by arranging (and winning) a mock 'miniature battle' between his own battleships and Meux's cruisers.[42] While Lord Charles' mind was closing, Bridgeman's remained open. He did not espouse new thinking just because it was new, but his willingness to give it a try and adopt it if it proved successful shows a flexibility and wisdom rare among officers of his generation.

Meanwhile, as Bridgeman was manoeuvring his battleships about the Mediterranean, back in the Admiralty Fisher was engaged on even more momentous manoeuvres of his own. The announcement in July 1906 of his proposed alterations to the Navy's shipbuilding programme, consequential upon the successful launching of the *Dreadnought*, caused a great stir in the Tory press. In October he began tentatively to prepare for an even bigger change: the reorganisation and redistribution of the fleets.[43] The radical reform had to be brought in slowly, not just because of the inevitable opposition it would engender from his conservative opponents in the Navy and outside, but 'for fear of exciting the attention of the German Admiralty'.[44] At the heart of the proposals lay the amalgamation of the previously independent commands of Devonport, Nore and Portsmouth into a single Home Fleet. Reinforced with two battleships each from the Channel, Mediterranean and Atlantic Fleets, its task was to guard the North Sea, where, Fisher prophesied, 'the fight will be'.[45]

In Fisher's new scheme of things, Beresford, the senior fleet commander, would move to the Channel rather than to the new Home Fleet. Predictably, as soon as the plans were mooted, from the distant blue waters of the Mediterranean Beresford roared his disapproval. The Liberal First Lord of the Admiralty, Lord Tweedmouth, was eager to prevent the Beresford-Fisher hostilities from taking a turn for the worse and so wrote discreetly to Bridgeman, Beresford's second-in-command, asking him if he would try and find out exactly what Lord Beresford objected to and whether he had alternative plans of his own. It says much for Bridgeman's integrity and diplomatic skills that Tweedmouth felt able to entrust him with such a delicate undertaking.

Bridgeman did as he was requested and on 13 January 1907 had a private conversation with his commander-in-chief, trying to get him to say 'something definite as to his requirements'. Although reluctant, or unable, to be too specific, Beresford gave away enough to make it quite clear that a separate Home Fleet was an anathema to him. He would be 'content' with 14 'good battleships', six large cruisers and three divisions of destroyers under his own command with the Channel Fleet, and plans for a Home Fleet 'swept off'! Its place would be taken by an élite 'Home Division' of six or eight battleships, supported by a suitable number of smaller warships, commanded by a vice-admiral responsible to the commander-in-chief of the Channel Fleet – i.e. Beresford – who would oversee regular exercises between the Mediterranean and Channel Fleets, including the latter's proposed new Home Division. The scheme clashed head-on with Fisher's. When Bridgeman pointed out to his superior that the Board would find his plan difficult to meet, Lord Charles declared stubbornly that he would be satisfied with 'nothing less'. Bridgeman tactfully concluded his letter to Tweedmouth by purporting to agree with both sides: the reduction of the Channel Fleet gave his commander-in-chief 'real & solid grounds of complaint', yet if the Home Fleet was to be an effective force it had to be a powerful, independent command.[46]

In the event, Beresford's objections proved less inflexible than he had intimated. After a long interview with Fisher at the end of January 1907, he agreed to take over command of the Channel Fleet as long as it had more destroyers and from time to time could exercise, under his overall command, with either the Atlantic or the Home Fleet.[47] The agreement allowed Beresford to strut his stuff as the supreme commander in home waters, but it did not alter his hostile attitude towards Fisher's new creation. The position of Commander-in-Chief, Home Fleet, was not going to be an easy one to fill.

Fisher sought a man of broad talents. To gain acceptance within the service, he had to be a seaman of unquestioned ability. To help win over popular opinion, he needed tact and charm in abundance. To work with both Fisher and Beresford, he required patience, integrity and flexibility. In short, he had to be 'the best Admiral we have'.

NOTES

1   Family scrapbook, see Chapter 6 note 26; Gordon, *The Rules of the Game*, p. 320.
2   It would be nice to think that Bridgeman influenced the new king in his decision to hand over Osborne Palace to the Navy as a convalescent home for officers.
3   I am indebted to Miss Pamela Clark of the Royal Archives, Windsor Castle for this information.
4   4/3/1922, Sandars to Bridgeman, L.L.P.P.
5   At the time the incident probably took place, Bridgeman was in fact a very wealthy man. See p. 267.
6   PRO PMG 15/137; PRO ADM 196/86.
7   Marder, *From Dreadnought to Scapa Flow*, p. 6.
8   Marder, *The Anatomy of British Sea Power*, p. 383.
9   Marder, *From Dreadnought to Scapa Flow*, pp. 8 & 144.

10   Marder, *The Anatomy of British Sea Power*, pp. 389-90 & 386.

11   Lord Chatfield, *The Navy and Defence*, p. 71.

12   Marder, ed., *Fear God* ... , ii, p. 169.

13   Bacon, *Fisher*, I, p. 218.

14   Marder, *The Anatomy of British Sea Power*, p. 422.

15   Marder, ed., *Fear God* ..., ii, p. 51.

16   Cited *inter alia* in Bonnett, *The Price of Admiralty*, p. 182.

17   Marder, *The Anatomy of British Sea Power*, pp. 499 & 394.

18   Marder, *From Dreadnought to Scapa Flow*, p. 46.

19   Marder, *Portrait of an Admiral*, p. 49.

20   Marder, *The Anatomy of British Sea Power*, p. 487.

21   Marder, *From Dreadnought to Scapa Flow*, p. 10.

22   *Memories*, p. 42.

23   The ending of Britain's isolation and development of so many powerful navies around the world rendered the two-power standard unrealistic. During the years leading up to World War I it was replaced by a simple determination to keep the Royal Navy well ahead of its German counterpart.

24   See below, pp. 137-140.

25   Cited in Bonnett, *The Price of Admiralty*, p. 183. It was also argued that as in June 1905 Britain had twice as many battleships (46) as Germany and Russia combined, the Dreadnought was simply not necessary.

26   PRO ADM 196/86.

27   The other two being Fisher and Churchill.

28   His kindness and generosity made a deep impression on almost all who met him. Indeed, Andrews believed he was 'too kind' to his junior officers. *Seamarks and Landmarks*, p.73.

29   Marder, *From Dreadnought to Scapa Flow*, pp. 88-90.

30   See pp. 22 & 52. We have no record of Bridgeman and Beresford meeting in New Zealand.

31   Marder, *From Dreadnought to Scapa Flow*, p. 88.

32   He had side-stepped the problem by being made an additional admiral of the fleet in 1905, thereby gaining an extra five years on the active list.

33   Marder, *The Anatomy of British Sea Power*, p. 441.

34   7/1/1997, Elizabeth Hingston to Lady Loch, L.L.P.P.

35   When in 1912 Bridgeman fell out publicly and spectacularly with Winston Churchill, Beresford was in the van of those who sprang to the Admiral's defence. Pure politics, or was there a tinge of gratitude for services rendered? Bridgeman was a pall bearer at Beresford's funeral. See Chapter 13.

36   PRO PMG 14/141.

37   The Victorious Rock incident is another Bridgeman story that has come down to us through the Hingston family. It's veracity has been checked by Lady Loch and confirmed by the Morton factor Leonard Axelby.

38   Marder, ed., *Fear God*, ii, p. 104.

39   PRO ADM 196/86.

40   Gordon, *The Rules of the Game*, p. 167.

41 *A Naval Scrapbook*, p. 187.

42 *From 1900 Onwards*, p. 32.

43 See above, p. 123.

44 *Memories*, p. 246.

45 Marder, ed., *Fear God*, ii, p. 104.

46 Bridgeman to Tweedmouth, 14/1/1907; Tweedmouth correspondence, Admiralty Library, Portsmouth.

47 Tweedmouth to Bridgeman, 31/1/1907, *ibid*.

8 Dreadnought *and the Admiralty*

I n retirement Bridgeman is supposed to have said that he enjoyed his time in charge of the Home Fleet more than any other command. If he really did say that, then either he took a secret delight in controversy, or advancing years made his memory conveniently selective.

The creation of the Home Fleet was strongly criticised. Rear-Admiral Prince Louis Battenberg called the fleet reorganisation 'simply topsy-turveydom'. Beresford, clearly not mollified by Fisher's face-saving compromise, denounced the Home Fleet as 'a fraud on the public and a danger to the state'. Sticking to the position he had outlined to Bridgeman in January 1907, he told anyone prepared to listen that all ships allocated to the defence of Great Britain should always be under his command.[1] To ensure a ready audience for his invective, he used the fortune he had recently inherited from his brother to throw open his house in Grosvenor Street to almost any gossip monger in search of a good story. By June his

Prince Louis of Battenberg, who replaced Bridgeman as First Sea Lord in 1912

comments had become so out of order that the Admiralty felt it necessary to rebuke him officially.

The wisdom of appointing Bridgeman to command the new fleet was controversial too. Ignoring (or forgetting) the fact that the Home Fleet's freshly-appointed commander-in-chief was now a vice-admiral and that he himself had ventured, only a year previously, that Bridgeman would make a 'brilliant' commander-in-chief, Beresford objected that a man with no experience of independent command had been raised above full admirals and vice-admirals – 'men who have steadily gained experience' to fit them to high command. 'Where is the sense of this, even the sense of proportion?' he demanded.[2] At this stage he limited his attacks to matters of principle, avoiding direct public disparagement of the officer whom he had so recently praised to the skies. Bridgeman kept his mouth shut. He clearly liked both men and sought to keep at least a toe in both camps. But over the next few months the perceived snub rankled with the gouty and disillusioned commander-in-chief of the Channel Fleet, causing his opinion of Bridgeman to change markedly. When later in the year the Home Fleet came under his overall command for exercises, as planned, he had an excellent opportunity for a little back-stabbing.[3]

Meanwhile, Fisher skilfully rode out the storm without too much difficulty. He calmed the anxious Prince of Wales, who continued to take a keen if somewhat myopic and parochial interest in naval matters, and drew strength from the fact that Bridgeman had assured the First Sea Lord that in the event of war he would be quite prepared to be guided by men with sharper minds than his own.[4] The observation is interesting for the light it throws on the reasons for Fisher's promotion of Bridgeman and on the vice-admiral's own common sense and modesty.

For the first few months of his command Bridgeman flew his flag in the *Majestic*. He then transferred to the *Dreadnought* when she had finished her sea trials under Captain Reginald Bacon. Bacon stayed with the ship. He was joined by two men, Commander Charles Bartolomé and Bridgeman's secretary Charles Pollard, who moved from ship to ship with the admiral for many years. Bartolomé moved to the Admiralty to accompany him when he became First Sea Lord in 1911 and kept in close touch with him after his retirement.[5] Such loyalty was not exceptional, but it is further evidence that Bridgeman was well-liked and respected by those who worked with him and knew him best. When Lieutenant Barry Domvile, the son of Bridgeman's old captain at *Excellent* and in the *Howe*, heard from his mother the 'very welcome intelligence' that he was likely to be transferred to Bridgeman's staff, he was overjoyed: 'By Jove I hope it's true!' he wrote in his diary.[6] His pleasure was not just at the prospect of working in the finest ship in the world. Bridgeman was a popular man and one known to return loyalty with steadfast support.

When Bridgeman hoisted his flag in the *Dreadnought*, the men of Portsmouth dockyard presented him with a model of the ship that he kept all his life.[7] He grew fonder of the *Dreadnought* than any other ship in which he sailed and recalled her with such affection in his later years that on her behalf he ventured into print for the only time in his life. Although beautifully produced and printed, the 21-page *HMS Dreadnought Her Place in History*, which Bridgeman co-wrote with Captain W M James, is a more eulogistic pamphlet than serious history.[8] The building of the ship, it announced, had an effect without parallel 'in the history of warship

The launching of HMS Dreadnought, *Bridgeman's favourite command, rendered all other capital ships obsolete*

construction'.[9] Similar laudatory statements are accompanied by statistical tables and an outline of the ship's uneventful career.[10]

Built, remarkably, in only a year, the *Dreadnought* was indeed a splendid vessel. Pre-dreadnought battleships had thumped along at 18 knots; the *Dreadnought*'s turbines gave her a three-knot advantage over them. They carried 9" armour, she 11". Whereas their effective battle range was about 2,000 yards, the *Dreadnought* was a deadly foe at four times that distance. In the 1907 battle practice she scored 25 hits out of 40 rounds fired in eight minutes at 8,000 yards – a performance 75 per cent better than any other ship. The arrangement of her raked turrets allowed her to fire six 12" guns ahead or astern. The ships she replaced could fire only two. Her eight-gun broadsides were double those of her predecessors. She had, in Fisher's words, given the Royal Navy a 'substantial start' over all its rivals.[11]

Substantial though the start was, it was short-lived and costly. Five months after Bridgeman took up his command, Germany laid down her first dreadnought and began planning to widen the Kiel Canal to enable larger vessels to move in safety from the Baltic to the North Sea. Britain was forced to respond by laying down more dreadnoughts of her own, quickening the arms race and increasing the burden on the taxpayer. Fisher argued that as battleships of the dreadnought type were an inevitable development, Britain needed to get in first. This reversal of traditional naval thinking brought on several painful headaches.

Fine though the *Dreadnought* was, she was far from perfect. Part of the trouble stemmed from her being a compromise.[12] Fisher had wanted a faster, more lightly-armoured ship, while the prevailing naval demand was for a heavier and more densely armed one. The eventual outcome would be the construction of two types of warship, larger dreadnoughts and super-dreadnoughts, and battle cruisers, the first of which (*Indomitable*, *Inflexible* and *Invincible*) were completed in 1908-9. The original *Dreadnought* fell somewhere between the two. Her secondary armament, for example, consisted only of anti-torpedo guns, which limited the operations for which she was suited and left her vulnerable to attack from fast-moving smaller craft. Foreign navies that came later to dreadnought construction benefited from lessons learned by the Royal Navy.

There were difficulties of a more technical nature, too. Sea trials showed that in spite of her forward fire-power the *Dreadnought* was incapable of rapid chasing action because spray from the bow wave washed over the gunsights. With a strong wind blowing ahead, smoke from the forward guns made it very difficult for gunners in the aft turrets to aim properly. The problems would have been solved by adopting Percy Scott's Director Firing system, a step the authorities were reluctant to take for several years.[13] Similarly, fire control was poor. This was partly because the science of gun control had not kept up with the technological development of the guns themselves. When the Navy tackled the problem it opted for the low cost system developed by Captain Frederick Dreyer rather than the more expensive but much more effective system devised by Arthur Pollen, which incorporated an analogue computer.[14]

The second snag with the *Dreadnought*'s fire control was the position of the platform from which it was exercised – on a mast directly behind the leading funnel. As soon as the ship raised steam, the mast became so hot that observers could no longer enter or leave the control platform. They were obliged to sit there, gently roasting, while food and drink were hoisted up to them on a pulley! The mistake was repeated in the subsequent dreadnoughts *Colossus*, *Hercules*, *Orion*, *Thunderer*, *Monarch* and *Conqueror*. When Scott pointed out the problem to Winston Churchill, the masts were replaced at a cost of £50,000 each. Subsequently Scott discovered that the new masts were too slight to carry his much-vaunted Director Firing equipment and he was back again in the First Lord's office. This time Churchill was not prepared to intervene. Then, says Scott, 'I tried the First Sea Lord [Bridgeman], but met with no success'. When Director Firing was finally installed in all ships, every single mast had to be replaced, at enormous cost.[15]

By the summer of 1907, the new Home Fleet was in good order. Primary responsibility for this must rest with Bridgeman, although some credit is clearly due to his Flag Captain and Chief of Staff, Reginald Bacon, the confirmed Fisher-ite who had taken *Dreadnought* through the sea trials.

True to his policy of delegating responsibility to younger, more up-to-date officers, Bridgeman loaded Bacon with so much that he complained of being 'greatly over worked'.[16] Nevertheless, he enjoyed his job and found Bridgeman such a pleasure to work with that when Fisher invited Bacon move from the *Dreadnought* to become Director of Naval Ordnance, he declined. Fisher got his way in the end (he usually did) by speaking to Bridgeman and then deceiving Bacon into believing that his commanding officer had endorsed the transfer. Only later, when Bridgeman and Bacon got together, did they realise they had been tricked.

Bacon left the ship in August and his dual role was taken over by Captain Charles Madden, a man of equal calibre. A future First Sea Lord, he was described by Fisher, for whom he had worked as personal assistant, as 'one of five best brains in the Navy below the rank of Admiral'.[17] Whatever Bridgeman's limitations, Fisher made sure they were adequately compensated by the calibre of those around him.

Not all the bright sparks advising Bridgeman were Fisher-ites. Certainly not Lieutenant Barry Domvile. Despite opposition from Bacon, this intelligent, hedonistic young officer had got the transfer he wanted and was now assistant to Gunnery Commander Bartolomé.[18] While still in the Mediterranean, however, he had annoyed the First Sea Lord intensely for writing a prize essay on 'The Ideal Battleship' in which he had criticised *Dreadnought*'s lack of secondary armament. When Fisher discovered the traitor lurking in his pet ship, he vindictively arranged for him to be transferred to Beresford's Channel Fleet. The order was reversed when Bartolomé pointed out that this would be handing an able officer, conversant with all the defects of both *Dreadnought* and the Home Fleet, over to the enemy camp.

Domvile stayed where he was and found his initial 'very nice' impression of Bridgeman confirmed with interest.[19] As we have seen, Bridgeman was always prepared to stand by his staff if he felt they deserved his backing. Fisher's vendetta with Domvile did not go away and in 1909 he sought to have him invalided out of the Service for deafness. Bridgeman, then Second Sea Lord, took Domvile's side. The controversial lieutenant-commander was summoned to the Admiralty to meet First

Lord Reginald McKenna. McKenna had been surprised to find his First and Second Sea Lords at odds over so junior an officer and determined to sort the matter out himself. Calling Domvile into his office, he walked around him speaking in different tones. Domvile was having what was known in Edwardian medical parlance as 'a good day' and he picked up quite clearly everything McKenna said. Bridgeman had been vindicated. At the end of the interview Domvile was told he could remain in the Service and would be promoted at the end of the year, but he had to keep this secret.[20] Fisher liked being crossed no more than Beresford.

The work of Bridgeman and his officers in getting the Home Fleet operating satisfactorily culminated in a royal inspection during Cowes Week at the beginning of August. The ships were arrayed in the Solent, much as for the Jubilee Review ten years earlier. Bridgeman welcomed Edward VII on board *Dreadnought* and took him for short trip round the south-west corner of the Isle of Wight. His Majesty showed some interest in the ship and all its gadgetry. He was most pleased, however, to be in a warship 'flying all three of his flags for the first time: Admiral of the Fleet, Royal Standard, and the Admiralty flag'.[21] He showed his appreciation by making Bridgeman a Knight Commander of the Royal Victorian Order.

The Home Fleet might have looked good in review, but it had yet to be tested as a fighting force. The opportunity came in the combined fleet manoeuvres that took place in October under Beresford's overall command. He was not pleased with what he saw, or at least he pretended not to be, and on 11 December 1907 he circulated a memorandum throughout the entire fleet criticising the performance of the Home Fleet destroyers commanded by Commodore Bayly and declaring armoured cruisers to be 'unsound' as ships of war.[22] The Admiralty reacted swiftly and on 17 January 1908 ordered the memorandum to be withdrawn as Beresford's comments on armoured cruisers reflected badly on Admiralty policy and his criticism of Bayly implied criticism of 'the competence of the Commander-in-Chief of the Home Fleet'.[23] However justified Beresford's remarks — and there is not much evidence to suggest that they were anything other than sour grapes — Fisher was standing by his man.[24]

Beresford was stirring up trouble in other areas, too. On taking over the Channel Fleet he had complained, inaccurately, of the lack of war plans. When a new set arrived, he rejected them and drew up his own. As they were ill-thought-out and involved more ships than the Navy had in commission (a dig at Fisher's cost-cutting), the First Sea Lord was not impressed. In November 1907, Beresford went on to cross Percy Scott (not a difficult thing to do) when he ordered him to stop gunnery practice and paint the ships under his command for a visit from the German Kaiser. Scott objected that the order of priorities was wrong. Beresford gave him a public dressing down and the issue flared into a *cause célèbre*. Needless to say, in general the public considered gunnery practice more important than housemaiding to impress the man against whose navy the guns might one day be used in anger.

Fisher did not go out of his way to provoke Beresford. Indeed, when Bridgeman requested that one of the Channel Fleet captains, Hon Alexander Bethell, be moved to the Home Fleet as Chief of Staff, Fisher agreed but told Beresford only that Bethell was to be relieved of his command. Not a word of where he was going. Beresford was deeply suspicious and questioned Bethell's wife and even his nine-year-old daughter to try and find out what was happening![25]

This sort of thing could not go on much longer and Fisher determined to use Beresford's offensive December memorandum to put a stop to the 'incessant back-bitings' of a 'dangerous lunatic' against the Home Fleet.[26] He was afraid, he told Bridgeman in early January 1908, they might lead to some 'serious consequences'. So when Bridgeman complained to the First Sea Lord of Beresford's 'ill considered criticism' and 'offensive remarks', Fisher urged him to make a formal complaint. That was not Bridgeman's way of operating; instead, he wrote Beresford a personal letter. When Fisher showed a copy of it to Lord Tweedmouth, the First Lord was amazed at its moderate tone and declared that if he had been in Bridgeman's position he would have told the Commander of the Channel Fleet to 'go to hell'.[27] Perhaps those who objected to Bridgeman taking command of the Home Fleet were not so wide of the mark after all. Not because he lacked the necessary technical knowledge, but because he was simply too much of a gentleman.

The day after the Admiralty ordered Beresford's memorandum to be withdrawn, an article highly critical of him appeared in the *John Bull* magazine. It brought up his contretemps with Scott, mocked his 'swollen head' and ventured that he was unfit to succeed Fisher as First Sea Lord.[28] The article itself was bad enough, but when a copy of it was sent to every officer in the fleet, Beresford's fury knew no bounds. He was sure Fisher – 'that gentleman from Ceylon' – had been behind the article and its distribution. From this time forward the two men would not even shake hands in public and Beresford's supporters (the 'Syndicate of Discontent') did everything they could to undermine their chief's despised opponent.[29] The row rumbled on in every bar, wardroom and mess on land and at sea.

However ridiculous some of its antics may now seem, the Fisher-Beresford feud in which Bridgeman was fortuitously and almost certainly unwillingly involved was no joke. Beresford, for all his petty jealousy, was still a fine sailor and one capable of contributing to the development of the Navy. But because by now almost nothing he said was considered seriously at the Fisher-dominated Admiralty, sensible opportunities were let pass. A case in point was reform of the *Signal Book*.

In 1907-8 Captain Cuthbert Hunter suggested that the Royal Navy's *Signal Book* was in need of reform. After the *Camperdown-Victoria* collision great attention had been paid to signalling, to the point where, Hunter believed, it no longer facilitated battle tactics but actually hampered them by limiting individual initiative and restricting freedom of movement.[30] Like the unfortunate Tryon before him, Hunter wanted the system clarified and simplified. Beresford agreed, but rather than help the proposed reform, in Admiralty circles endorsement from the Commander-in-Chief of the Channel Fleet was the kiss of death. Hunter's proposals were turned down. Bridgeman remained true to his post-collision training under Culme-Seymour and was among those who defended the *status quo*. The Navy as it was suiting him nicely, too. He was made a Knight Commander of the Bath in the Birthday Honours and in December, following a state visit of Princess Christiana to Portsmouth, he was given special permission 'to accept and wear the Swedish Order of the Sword'.[31]

Bridgeman spent the summer trying out the new Invincible-class battlecruisers. He was disappointed with their performance and wanted them employed as cruisers rather than front-line ships. He also engaged in an elaborate war game, involving over 300 ships, with Beresford's Channel Fleet.[32] When this ended on 21 July both sides claimed victory and Admiral Sir A K Wilson was brought in to investigate. His report led to the Admiralty expressing appreciation at Bridgeman's performance and 'much satisfaction at the improvement in the results over those obtained in 1907'.[33]

All this took place against a background of yet another wave of public concern, fuelled by the Tory press, that the Royal Navy was too complacent in the face of German expansion. Following the Anglo-Russian Entente and the collapse of the Hague Conference on armaments, at the end of 1907 the Germans announced a radical revision of their 1900 Navy Law. Beginning in 1908-9, they planned to build three dreadnoughts and a battlecruiser for each of their next four years and two major ships each year thereafter.

The Admiralty Board did not panic and in December 1907 actually put forward a slightly reduced building programme for the following financial year. Although several of the Royal Navy's ships were showing their age, it was still much larger than Germany's and had a comfortable superiority in dreadnoughts.[34] The Kaiser's fleet was further hampered by a lack of large harbours. Wilhelmshaven was being enlarged but the alterations would not be finished until 1912 and the Kiel Canal would not be wide enough to take dreadnoughts until 1914.

The situation changed during the latter half of 1908. When Edward VII brought up the subject of naval expenditure during a visit to Cronberg in August, the Kaiser made it clear that the issue was not on the agenda. Two months later he made matters far worse by tactlessly calling the English as 'mad as March hares' in the *Daily Telegraph*.[35] In the outcry that followed the Navy League and a large section of the press demanded a massive increase in naval expenditure. *The Times* called for seven new dreadnoughts to be laid down and the Navy League for eight, the most British shipyards could handle.

Pledged to higher spending on social policies, this was not at all what the Liberal Prime Minister Asquith wanted to hear. Nor did the more radical members of his cabinet, of whom the most vociferous were Lloyd George and Churchill. After visiting Germany as a guest of the Kaiser the latter was convinced that the Triple Alliance posed no threat to Britain or her Empire. So when in December 1908 First Lord McKenna suggested the previously planned four dreadnoughts for 1909-10 be increased to six (two less than Fisher wanted), the cabinet split and Lloyd George hinted at resignation.

The eventual outcome was a compromise: four dreadnoughts for the upcoming financial year and, if it was deemed necessary, four more by April 1910. But when this proposal came before the Commons in March, MPs seized on the alarming estimation that if the proposed building programmes on either side of the North Sea were adhered to, by April 1912 Germany's dreadnoughts would outnumber Britain's.[36] So arose the famous cry, 'We want eight, and we won't wait'.[37] The government survived a censure motion but when the dreadnought-building plans of Italy and Austria-Hungary, Germany's allies, were revealed, McKenna finally announced an extra three dreadnoughts and a battlecruiser for the 1909-10 programme. Fears were further allayed when Australia and New Zealand offered to build a battlecruiser each.

In the middle of all this, Fisher was proceeding with the second phase of his reorganisation of the fleets. In March 1909 the Atlantic Fleet moved its headquarters to Dover and the Channel Fleet was absorbed into the Home Fleet, which now boasted 16 battleships and a further eight with nucleus crews. The Atlantic Fleet was left with six operational battleships. Given Fisher's certainty that the 'fight' would be in the North Sea against Germany, the changes were logical and they were supported by many serving officers as well as the King and the Liberal press. Needless to say, the Conservative press were less happy. As were certain admirals, led of course by Charlie B.

The abolition of the Channel Fleet meant that Beresford's command was at an end. Although he might theoretically have been given the job of commanding the enlarged Home Fleet, in the light of what had taken place over the last few years that was clearly impossible. In fact McKenna had decided as far back as May 1908 that Beresford had to go and the cabinet agreed shortly before Christmas. The Channel command ended formally in January 1908 and on 24 March Charlie B, still the darling of many ordinary sailors, hauled down his flag, symbolising his retirement from the Royal Navy. It was not the end of his career, nor of his trouble-making.

To 'diminish the sting' on Beresford, Bridgeman was also relieved of his command.[38] The sporting Second Sea Lord Sir William May (whom Fisher thought a 'cad') took over the enlarged Home Fleet and Bridgeman moved to the Admiralty to take up May's post there.[39] As he was no longer serving at sea, Bridgeman spent his time as Second Sea Lord (25 March 1909 to 24 March 1911) on half pay, supplemented by a London Allowance.[40] That such an anomaly still existed showed how much remained to be done to make the career of naval officer genuinely open to all men. In its obituary of Bridgeman the *Yorkshire Post* implies that he did not move readily to the Admiralty, but made it a condition of his going that eight dreadnoughts were laid down in the 1909-10 programme.[41] This does not appear to be strictly accurate, for Bridgeman certainly did not carry enough clout to alter government policy. But his was one of the voices, perhaps the most influential, that persuaded Fisher not to lay down all eight ships of the 1909-10 programme as battlecruisers.[42]

As Second Sea Lord Bridgeman was responsible for overseeing all matters to do with personnel, manning and mobilisation.[43] He was not by nature an administrator, nor had he been trained as one. He was essentially a practical man and although he had spent time ashore, notably with Culme-Seymour at Portsmouth, his real interest was in ships and sailing them. His spare time he spent hunting, not reading (although Copgrove boasted a library, he left almost no books in his will) and the hours he was now obliged to spend behind a desk, signing letters and ploughing through memoranda bored him rigid. Nor was he particularly interested in theoretical matters. In his mind the only way of seeing whether a new idea was any good or not was to give it a practical test. It was a difficult thing to do from behind a desk in London.

Bridgeman's life was not made any easier by the fact that his two immediate superiors, Fisher and the academically-inclined lawyer McKenna (First Lord 1908-11), excelled at the things he did not. Where Fisher was full of ideas and theories for improving the service, the Second Sea Lord was cautious and practical. Where McKenna thrived on briefs and the subtle cut and thrust of politics, Bridgeman wanted things tangible and straightforward. Besides, they were both Liberals (Fisher was often labelled a socialist for his egalitarian views) and Bridgeman was staunchly Conservative.

For a time the Second Sea Lord shared his frustrations with the energetic young man appointed to act as his Naval Assistant, Captain Robert Falcon Scott. Both were easily bored with desk work. But whereas the older man hankered after no more than the bridge of a battleship, the younger's dreams were far more exotic. Scott used his dull 10-5 Admiralty job as a means to an end, a way of paying the bills while he got the necessary approval and assembled the funds and men for a second Antarctic expedition. Its primary, obstensible purpose would be scientific research. However, a secondary, more spectacular ambition really fired Scott's heart – a desire to raise the Union flag before any other at the very heart of that bleak southern continent. The gallant sporting venture caught Bridgeman's imagination. Had he been 25 years younger ... With a wistful smile, he agreed to help Scott in whatever way he could, and Scott subsequently found working with him 'extraordinarily pleasant'.[44]

Fisher did not think much of his Second Lord's administrative work.[45] Lacking the sort of education that would have taught him to skim documents and précis their contents, he became hopelessly bogged down in details. He was irritatingly unrealistic about finance, too, and tended to assume there was more money to hand than there actually was. The civil service way was alien to him. When he had called for something to be done on board ship, it was done. When he tried the same at the Admiralty, he met with paperwork and prevarication. This annoyed and frustrated him and he got a reputation for threatening to resign when he did not get what he wanted. In short, he would much rather have been on the bridge of *Dreadnought*. It did not bode well for his return to the Admiralty two-and-a-half years later.

That said, Bridgeman did manage to oversee one or two useful innovations. One, the substitution of detention in barracks for detention in naval prisons, directly benefited all errant sailors and suggests that his penchant for strict discipline was tempered by genuine humanitarian concern. Had he discussed the reform with Emily? He also authorised tentative steps towards partnership between the Navy and private enterprise when he agreed that a pair of gunnery officers could be seconded to the firm developing an advanced fire-control table for the Navy.[46]

By the summer of 1909 Fisher was running out of steam. His reputation had been scarred by the latest naval scare, during which he had been subjected to a double-edged attack: he had been caught unawares by Germany's rapid naval expansion and had provoked that expansion by being 'too prone to make the pace' through pioneering dreadnoughts.[47] Meanwhile Beresford went on stirring and grumbling. He fed the Tory papers with an endless stream of anti-Fisher propaganda and told his party leader, Balfour, that Fisher had ruined the Navy. At home he chaired a 'shadow Board of Admiralty', where malcontents swapped dismal stories about the ruin of the Service they loved.

Bridgeman tried to keep clear of the cross-fire. Shortly after taking up his post at the Admiralty he went to call on Lord Charles, his old commander-in-chief, to show that whatever rumour might say he was still as fond of both the warring admirals as he had ever been. At Beresford's front door, his lordship's butler mistook Bridgeman for a 'mutineer recruit' to the Shadow Board and he was taken straight to the library where the Board was in full session, 'obviously plotting the downfall of the authorised and official Board installed at Whitehall'. The sudden appearance of the Second Sea Lord caused a flurry of activity as the Shadow Sea Lords did their best to hide their faces. One admiral turned and began furiously poking the fire. Another dropped a book and fell to all fours beneath the table to find it. A third stared intently out of the window at the London skyline, while a fourth 'buried his face in his papers with a unique absorption'. Beresford, abandoning his normally flawless suavity, hastily 'bundled Bridgeman out into another room'.[48]

At the end of March Asquith decided to sort our the Beresford-Fisher fiasco once and for all. With McKenna's consent he set up a private sub-committee of the Committee of Imperial Defence (CID) to investigate Beresford's charges against the harassed First Sea Lord. At first Fisher was furious at the inferred lack of confidence in him and he threatened to resign. He need not have worried. After four months the sub-committee reported that it was 'entirely satisfied with the readiness and complete efficiency of the fleet' and was convinced of Beresford's 'absolute incompetence'.[49]

Beresford, once so dashing and charismatic, declined into a seedy wind-bag, a self-professed expert on all matters maritime whose opinions were generally disregarded as too encrusted with bitterness to be of any value. Fisher, too, had had enough. He was disappointed the report had not been more positive in its support of him personally and after being created a peer, Lord Fisher of Kilverstone, in November, he retired on 25 January 1910.

The withdrawal of the First Sea Lord brought out an aspect of Bridgeman's personality that is rarely acknowledged. His ambition. Reporting (with embellishment, no doubt) on a conversation he had recently had with his 'awfully nice' Second Sea Lord, on 12 October 1910 Fisher wrote to McKenna that Bridgeman said when the First Sea Lordship became vacant he would refuse to serve under May or Fawkes as he had 'contempt for both of them'. But he would 'gladly remain as First Sea Lord himself with Callaghan as Second Sea Lord'.[50] The comment is strange. Bridgeman did not like Admiralty work and he must have known he was not particularly good at it. When he was offered the post of First Sea Lord two years later he accepted it only with great reluctance.[51] Moreover, remaining at the Admiralty would mean working with McKenna, who was not his cup of tea at all. And this, it seems, is one reason why he did not get the job.

Fisher's enigmatic letter continues by saying that he has already been to see Emily 'to oil the machine' – no doubt to tell her that her husband was likely to be disappointed in his ambition. He found her 'sweet but firm'. Fisher then turns reflective. 'I don't know why you should not have Bridgeman as First Sea Lord,' he muses,

> 'especially with such an excellent man as Callaghan as second. Bridgeman would carry more guns in the Navy than Fawkes by a long way, and a *persona gratissima* to the Tories, but the old couplet comes in here, and the First Lord is bound to have the man he loves!'

He then quotes 'I do not like you, Dr Fell ...'. Obviously, McKenna did not like Bridgeman and did not think him the right man to follow so distinguished a First Sea Lord as Fisher.

A short time later Fisher heard from Jellicoe, then coming to the end of a successful term as Third Sea Lord, that Bridgeman was 'fuming'.[52] It turned out that his anger arose not out of injured pride at being passed over, but at the candidate preferred to him. Sir Arthur Knyvet Wilson, VC had retired in 1907, aged 65. Now, having been made an Admiral of the Fleet when he stepped down and therefore eligible to five more years' active service, he was back on the active list and, to most people's surprise was chosen by McKenna to take over Fisher's desk. The appointment was a compromise. Wilson was by no means an outstanding admiral, but he was respected (the VC he won in the Sudan helped) and reliable. Furthermore, he was a proven administrator, a supporter of Fisher's reforms without being associated with either camp in the Fisher-Beresford debacle. He was also more experienced than either Bridgeman, Fawkes or May. Because of his age, he could be no more than a stop-gap. But at least, McKenna hoped, he would be a conciliatory one around whom the Service could once again unite.

Bridgeman was not so sure. 'I dare say that *under the circumstances* Wilson is the best solution,' he wrote to Fisher in a 'fire-eating letter' penned towards the end of November 1909, 'but I know from experience that there is no joy to be found in serving either with him or under him! Deadly dull! and uncompromising as you know! He will never consult anyone and is impatient in argument, even to being impossible!'

But Bridgeman was not one to let personal feelings get in the way of more important matters and he ended his letter with a cheery: 'Just off to hunt the fox, so please excuse more'.[53]

As it turned out, Bridgeman's fears about the appointment of Wilson proved well founded. It was not the new First Sea Lord's being 'deadly dull' that mattered, so much as his clam-like obstinacy and abrasive manner. He spoke rarely, and when he did as likely as not it was to offend someone. Bridgeman was particularly annoyed. He was treated, he complained, 'as if he were a second lieutenant on board a ship' and took strong exception when Wilson reminded him publicly that he was 'only his second'. When his superior took to interfering with his day-to-day work, Bridgeman got near the end of his tether and in one particularly trying week he threatened resignation three times! Controller Jellicoe and First Lord McKenna found Wilson equally frustrating.[54] He insisted on promoting only those known to him and he extended the same personal control even to fleet manoeuvres. When the fleet was exercising off the coast of Portugal, he had a bed moved into his room at the Admiralty and, according to Bridgeman, 'started them off by wireless telegraphy at a fixed hour'. Then, chattering away all night like a schoolboy with a new toy, he fixed the course and speed of every ship by remote control.[55] Any overall war plan that the Navy might possess was kept locked inside his head.[56]

One small but significant spark lit up Bridgeman's dull days at the Admiralty. His erstwhile Naval Assistant and protégé, Robert Scott, had realised his ambition and on the afternoon of 1 June 1910, amid much cheering and sounding of sirens, left London Docks bound for New Zealand and beyond in the 749-ton converted whaling barque *Terra Nova*. Thanks to Bridgeman's intervention, she flew the White Ensign, which Emily had formally broken from the mainmast at 5 pm. Earlier, the

Bridgemans had hosted a farewell dinner for Scott and leading members of his expedition. Pride, hope and perhaps a little envy mingled in the Second Sea Lord's breast as he stood watching *Terra Nova* slip slowly between the moored merchant men and make for the open sea. Later, these emotions were to change. On hearing that the Norwegian explorer Roald Amundsen had abandoned his attempt on the North Pole and moved his expedition to the South, Bridgeman is reported to have mused prophetically, 'Oh dear! I do believe that will mean a race and perhaps a tragedy.'[57]

Jellicoe got out of the Admiralty first. In December 1910 he was appointed a vice-admiral and put in charge of the Atlantic Fleet. Fisher, who was following (and heavily influencing) naval affairs almost as closely as he had done as First Sea Lord, was delighted at the move. He was convinced that in the coming war Jellicoe would be the ideal man to take charge of operations at sea. But as Jellicoe was ten years junior to his other favoured admiral, Bridgeman, he saw the need for the two to come to some sort of working arrangement. Having been together at *Excellent* and

Captain Scott and his wife, with the business manager to the expedition, Mr G F Whyatt, on the bridge of the Terra Nova *before she sailed for the Antarctic*

Popperfoto/Reuter

under Culme-Seymour in the Mediterranean, they were certainly used to each other's ways. Accordingly, as Fisher told Mrs Pamela McKenna, he spoke with Bridgeman (who displayed 'the inestimable gift' of being prepared to hand over command to 'a better man than himself' when in 'the forefront of battle') and declared him 'very happy' with the idea.[58]

In early January 1910 Fisher had Jellicoe to stay at Kilverstone. After he had gone, Fisher wrote to him that Bridgeman was 'prepared and wishes to lean wholly on you as regards war operations' and recognised that his role was only to come along and 'pick up the pieces' when the fight was over. To this end, Fisher went on, it was 'vitally important' for them to be 'on the closest terms and discuss every eventuality'. This was necessary because Bridgeman was not particularly forceful at getting his views across and hardly anyone but Jellicoe understood the 'immense change in tactics and strategy' that the new century had brought. He added with customary indiscreet asperity, 'I am quite certain A K Wilson don't realise it'. Fisher's request that Jellicoe meet Bridgeman 'more than half way' when they discussed strategy suggests the Second Sea Lord was probably not as aware of Fisher's Machiavellian proposal as his ex-chief made out. After all, he was still at the Admiralty, not in a sea-going command, and had not yet dropped his ambition of taking over as First Sea Lord.[59]

NOTES

1   Kerr, *Prince Louis of Battenberg*, p. 219; Gordon, *The Rules of the Game*, p. 367.
2   Kerr, *ibid*.
3   In July 1907 First Lord Tweedmouth arranged a conference between Fisher and Beresford to give them an opportunity to air their grievances and come to some sort of working agreement for the good of the service. It failed.
4   Lambert, 'Bridgeman', p. 56.
5   Jack Sandars mentions Bartolomé in his letters to Bridgeman during World War I, L.L.P.P.
6   6/11/1906, NMM DOM 11.
7   The model is mentioned in his will, L.L.P.P. See also Lombard-Hobson, *Never Go To Sea*, L.L.P.P.
8   Leeds, 1926.
9   p. 6.
10 Apart from ramming and sinking U29 in the Pentland Firth in August 1915, *Dreadnought* saw no action and was put up for sale in 1920, *ibid*., pp. 20-21.

11 Marder, *The Anatomy of British Sea Power*, p. 515.

12 See Gordon, *The Rules of the Game*, p. 10.

13 Scott, *Fifty Years in the Navy*, pp. 259 et seq. Director Firing (essentially firing in salvoes) was an attempt to solve the problems created by the enormous advances in gunnery – i.e. how to get 850 lb projectiles, travelling 13 miles and reaching heights of 22,000 ft, to hit a moving target from a moving ship when the projectiles took 12 seconds to reach their target.

14 The Navy switched to the Pollen system after the First World War.

15 Scott, *Fifty Years in the Navy*, pp. 263-7. See also Chapter 9.

16 *From 1900 Onwards*, p. 158.

17 *Dictionary of National Biography*.

18 5/2/1907, Domvile, *Diary*, NMM DOM 11.

19 18/3/1907, *ibid*.

20 Marder, *From Dreadnought to Scapa Flow*, pp. 86-7.

21 Bacon, *From 1900 Onwards*, p. 66.

22 Hough, *Admiral Lord Fisher*, p. 313.

23 Marder, *From Dreadnought to Scapa Flow*, p. 97.

24 Interestingly, when Admiral May took over Bridgeman's command his Flag Captain Herbert Richmond found the fleet full of unprofessional 'amateurisms'. He believed its commanders had devoted too much time to external appearance and not enough on the strategy to be followed in time of war. (Marder, *Portrait of an Admiral*, p. 19.) Old habits were clearly taking a long time to die.

25 Bennett, *Charlie B*, p. 305.

26 Marder, ed., *Fear God*, ii, p. 154; *From Dreadnought to Scapa Flow*, p. 91

27 Marder, ed., *ibid*.

28 Scott and Beresford clashed again in July when Scott gave his officers permission to disobey an order from Beresford that might well have resulted in collision. Beresford called in vain for Scott to be court martialled.

29 Marder, *From Dreadnought to Scapa Flow*, p. 99.

30 The whole issue is examined in depth in Gordon, *The Rules of the Game*.

31 PRO ADM 196/86.

32 Lambert, 'Bridgeman', p. 60.

33 *Ibid*.

34 It was estimated that by 1912 Germany would have 13 dreadnoughts to Britain's 18.

35 28 October.

36 Britain would have 20, Germany either 21 (the Conservative estimate) or 17 (the Liberal estimate).

37 Marder, *From Dreadnought to Scapa Flow*, p. 165.

38 Hough, *Admiral Lord Fisher*, p. 230.

39 Marder, ed., *Fear God*, ii, p. 337.

40 PRO PMG 15/145.

41 5/3/1929.

42 Lambert, 'Bridgeman', p. 60.

43   The Admiralty Board consisted of the First Lord, a cabinet member responsible for all naval matters to the crown and parliament (which, technically speaking, made all other members of the board subordinate to him), and three other civilians: the Civil Lord (responsible for buildings and works), the Parliamentary and Financial Secretary and the Permanent Secretary. They worked closely with with the four Sea Lords, all serving officers, of which the First Sea Lord (responsible for overall policy and the deployment, efficiency and strength of the fleets) was by far the most important. The Third Sea Lord (or Controller) looked after material and the Fourth supplies and transport. The Director of Naval Intelligence, head of the Naval Intelligence Department established in 1886, brought the Board's total to nine.

44   Scott to Bridgeman, March 1912. The letter is in the private possession of Sir James Graham, Bt, who most kindly made a transcript available to the author. See also pp. 187-188.

45   Marder, *Fear God*, ii, pp. 280 & 283; Lambert, 'Bridgeman', p. 58.

46   Lambert, *ibid.*, pp. 60-1.

47   Riddell, *More Pages From My Diary*, p. 17.

48   Bacon, *From 1900 Onwards*, p. 176.

49   Marder, *From Dreadnought to Scapa Flow*, p. 192.

50   Marder, ed., *Fear God*, ii, p. 272. Sir Wilmot Fawkes had been Commander-in-Chief Plymouth since 1908. The much respected Rear-Admiral Sir George Callaghan had been Second in Command of the Mediterranean Fleet for the same time.

51   See below, pp. 169-171.

52   Marder, ed., *Fear God*, ii, p. 282.

53   *Ibid.* Bridgeman had served under Wilson in the Channel Fleet.

54   Lambert, 'Wilson', p. 39-.

55   *Ibid.* p. 40.

56   Halpern, *A Naval History*, p.8.

57   A family story related by Mrs Walter Hingston.

58   Marder, ed., *Fear God*, ii, pp. 345 & 348.

59   *Ibid.*, pp. 349 & 337.

9 First Sea Lord

Bridgeman was finally released from Wilson's irritating overlordship on 25 March, 1911, when he boarded the *Bellerophon* and took back command of the Home Fleet.[1] The change was not universally welcomed. May, finding the fleet too unwieldy for traditional manoeuvres, had experimented with giving individual captains greater autonomy in battle situations. He had not stuck rigidly to the single line formation favoured by Fisher, Bridgeman, Wilson, Jellicoe and others but had practised breaking the fleet into semi-autonomous divisions, each responsible for working out how best to carry out the tasks allotted it in action.[2] On taking over, Bridgeman, whose ideas in Beatty's words 'were strictly limited to carrying on the old routine.' pulled back control to the centre and reverted to traditional tactics and formations.[3]

Later, Percy Scott also had harsh words to say about Bridgeman, as he did about everyone who did not think his Director Firing system the most important invention since gunpowder. With Jellicoe's support, Scott's system had been tested successfully in 1910 and he now wanted it immediately fitted to all ships. Bridgeman was cautious, as he was about all technological innovation. But he was by no means as hostile as Scott made out: we have seen how, as Second Sea Lord, he sent officers to work with the firm developing Scott's system. McKenna was also uncertain about the system. A ship using it, he believed, would expend all its ammunition in 30 minutes. Scott retorted that this did not matter one jot, as with Director Firing the enemy would be sunk in 30 seconds![4]

The case against Bridgeman's conservatism can easily be over-stated. He was not hostile to change *per se*, just insistent that it should not be made for its own sake. During his brief second period in command of the Home Fleet he developed its torpedo tactics and capacity for night action. Following his complaint to the Admiralty about the inadequate training of fire-control teams, a committee was set up to investigate the matter. He also carried out May's suggestion of widening the role given to submarines by allocating them to blockade as well as defensive duty.

On the broader question of how best to blockade Germany in wartime he strongly disagreed with the First Sea Lord's out-dated plans. Following the development of submarines (originally deployed solely in a defensive role) and mines, Fisher had moved away from the idea of a Nelsonian close blockade to what was known as a flotilla or distant blockade, which involved smaller ships patrolling the coast ready to alert the main fleet in case of an attempted break out. It was Wilson's reversal of this strategy, reverting to unrealistic and dangerous plans for a close blockade and even for landings on the enemy coast, that Bridgeman disputed. Finally, unlike Wilson, he did not insist on personally directing all fleet operations. On one occasion he criticised the up-and-coming Jellicoe for trying to do so. He 'does too much', he wrote to Fisher; 'he must trust his staff and captains, and if they don't fit, he must weed them out!'[5]

In his rather wild and unscrupulous *Memories* Fisher was to describe Bridgeman as an 'outstanding' personality to whom he owed 'eternal gratitude'. 'There are few people living,' he explained, 'to whom I am under a greater obligation than Admiral Sir Francis Bridgeman, GCB. This distinguished sailor aided me in the gradual building up of the Grand Fleet.'[6] Allowing for the customary hyperbole, it was still high praise and not necessarily unjustified. However much his detractors pointed to his lack of creativity, very few questioned Bridgeman's fine seamanship, steady judgement or the expert way he commanded a great fleet. As long as there were radicals like Fisher and, later, Churchill to move the Service forward, practical, experienced men like Bridgeman were essential to put their ideas into practice. The tragedy for Bridgeman was that while Fisher realised this, Churchill did not.

Saturday 24 June 1911 was probably the proudest day of Bridgeman's life. Now a full admiral and soon to be a Grand Commander of the Royal Victorian Order, he commanded the whole fleet at the spectacular Spithead Coronation Review (see plan, pages 160 to 161). This time it was not just the Royal Navy that was on show, but visiting ships from Britain's allies (France, Russia and Japan), a host of smaller European navies (Sweden,

Spain, Norway, Greece, Denmark and the Netherlands) and an exotic smattering from further afield – Chile, Argentina, China and Turkey – dominated by 20,000-ton *Delaware* from the USA. Most remarkably, in view of the fact that in barely two years' time they would be at war with the Royal Navy, there were also warships from the Triple Alliance, including Germany's first battlecruiser, the awesome 19,100-ton, 25-knot *Von der Tann*. Officers and officials attending the Review would have been better advised to study this splendid ship rather than crow about their own. Tougher armoured and sharper shooting than her Royal Naval counterparts, she sank the *Indefatigable* in the opening minutes of the Jutland engagement and survived more than 50 hits herself, only to end up on the bottom in Scapa Flow in June 1919.

On Wednesday 21 the senior officers went to London to sit with the German Crown prince at the Coronation of King George V, which took place on Thursday morning with all the customary splendour. That evening the 170 ships assembled for the Review were illuminated. On Friday the Mayor of Portsmouth entertained naval swells to a garden party

National Maritime Museum, London

*Edward VII (right) on board the Royal Yacht at Cowes, 1905, with Prince of Wales
(later George V, left) and his sons, the Princes Edward and Albert*

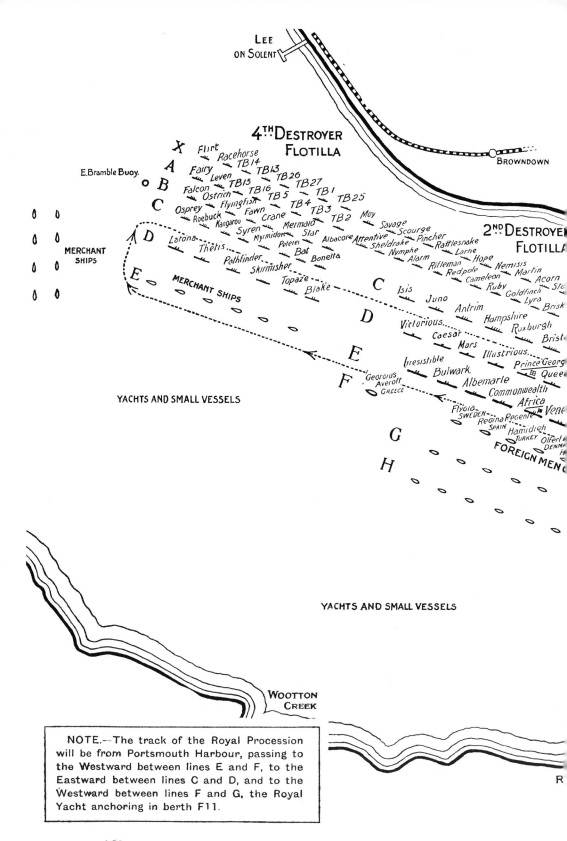

LEE ON SOLENT

BROWNDOWN

4TH DESTROYER FLOTILLA

2ND DESTROYER FLOTILLA

E. Bramble Buoy.

X
A Flirt
Racehorse
B Fairy TB 14
Leven TB 13
C Falcon TB 15 TB 26
Ostrich TB 16 TB 27
Osprey Flyingfish TB 5 TB 1 TB 25
Roebuck Fawn TB 4 TB 3 TB 2 Moy
D Kangaroo Crane Savage
Syren Mermaid Scourge
Larona Myrmidon Star Pincher
Thetis Petrel Albacore Attentive Rattlesnake
Pathfinder Bat Sheldrake Larne
Skirmisher Bonetta Nymphe Hope
E Topaze Alarm Nemisis
Blake Redpole Rifleman Martin
MERCHANT SHIPS Cameleon Acorn
C Isis Ruby Goldfinch Sta
Juno Lyra Brisk
D Antrim
Victorious Hampshire
Caesar Ruxburgh
MERCHANT SHIPS Mars Brist
E Illustrious
Irresistible Prince Georg
F Bulwark Queen
Georgius Albemarle
Averoff Commonwealth
GREECE Africa
Flyqia Vene
SWEDEN Regina Regente
G SPAIN Hamidieh
TURKEY Olferl
DENMA
H FOREIGN MEN O

YACHTS AND SMALL VESSELS

MERCHANT SHIPS

YACHTS AND SMALL VESSELS

WOOTTON CREEK

NOTE.—The track of the Royal Procession will be from Portsmouth Harbour, passing to the Westward between lines E and F, to the Eastward between lines C and D, and to the Westward between lines F and G, the Royal Yacht anchoring in berth F11.

R

REVIEW OF THE FLEET
BY
ESTY KING GEORGE V., on Saturday, June 24, 1911.

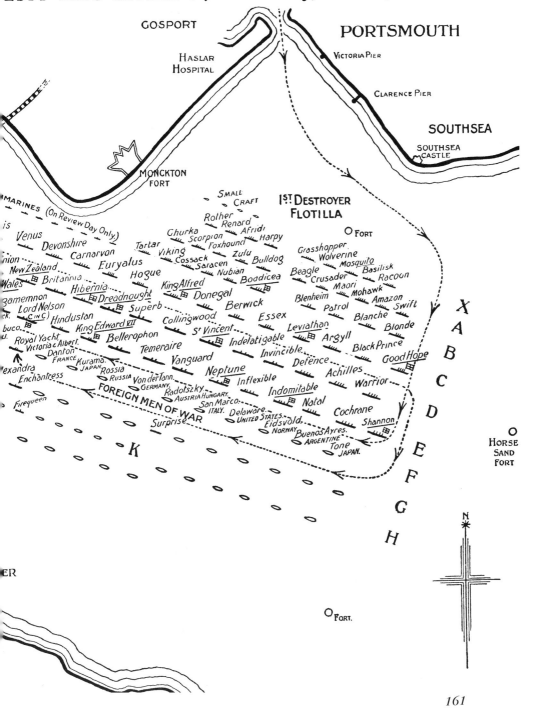

GOSPORT

PORTSMOUTH

HASLAR
HOSPITAL

VICTORIA PIER

CLARENCE PIER

SOUTHSEA

SOUTHSEA
CASTLE

MONCKTON
FORT

MARINES (On Review Day Only.)

SMALL
CRAFT

1ST DESTROYER
FLOTILLA

Rother
Renard
Ghurka   Afridi
Venus   Scorpion   Harpy
Devonshire   Tartar   Foxhound
Carnarvon   Viking   Zulu   FORT
New Zealand   Cossack   Saracen   Bulldog   Grasshopper
Euryalus   Nubian   Wolverine
Wales   Britannia   Hogue   Boadicea   Mosquito   Basilisk
Hibernia   King Alfred   Beagle   Crusader   Racoon
gamemnon   Dreadnought   Donegal   Maori   Mohawk   Amazon
Lord Nelson   Superb   Berwick   Blenheim   Swift
Hindustan   (CinC)   Patrol   Blanche
buco.   King Edward VII   Collingwood   Essex   Leviathan   Blonde
Royal Yacht   Bellerophon   St Vincent   Argyll   Black Prince
Victoria & Albert.   Temeraire   Indefatigable   Invincible   Good Hope
exandra   Danton   Vanguard   Defence   Achilles
Enchantress   FRANCE Kurama   Neptune   Indomitable   Warrior
FOREIGN MEN OF WAR   JAPAN Rossia   Inflexible   Natal
Firequeen   GERMANY.   Radotszky   Cochrane
San Marco.   AUSTRIA HUNGARY.   Shannon
Surprise   ITALY.   Delaware.
UNITED STATES.   Eidsvold.
NORWAY   Buenos Ayres.
ARGENTINE   Tone
JAPAN.

X
A
B
C
D
E
F
G
H

O
HORSE
SAND
FORT

O FORT.

K

N

ER

The Royal Yacht passing through the warships assembled for the Coronation Naval Review, 1911

Bridgeman coming aboard, greeted by (left to right) Mildred Hingston, Charles Hingston and Nancy Pleydell-Bouverie

Bridgeman and Rear-Admiral King Hall aboard the Neptune

and firework display. The new king reviewed the fleet the following afternoon, starting at 2 pm. After a few weeks with the fleet Bridgeman had transferred his flag from the *Bellerophon* to the 19,900-ton *Neptune*. With him had come the ever-loyal Bartolomé and Secretary Pollard. This splendid warship, identified by the white stripe on each funnel, took pride of place amid the awesome display of cold grey steel.

Bridgeman's naval career, past and present, was ominously woven into the surrounding pageant. The past was represented by Captain Michael Culme-Seymour, the son of his old protégé and now commanding the armoured cruiser *Argyll*. Sir George Callaghan, Bridgeman's second-in-command who would take over the Home Fleet on his superior's promotion to First Sea Lord at the end of the year, flew his flag in the *King Edward VII*. Bridgeman's successor at the Admiralty in 18 months time, Prince Louis of Battenberg, flew his in the *Africa*. The *Prince of Wales* displayed that of the commander-in-chief of the Atlantic Fleet, Vice-Admiral John Jellicoe, Bridgeman's old commander in the Mediterranean on whose shoulders the heaviest naval responsibility of the forthcoming war would fall.

'Never before, in the history of the world,' announced the official Review Programme,

> 'has one been privileged to see such a powerful and numerous array of warships as the mighty armada of British and Foreign vessels now gathered on the historic waters of Spithead.'

The multi-national make-up of the Review, it hoped, was a cause for optimism. The presence of German ships and those of her Triple Alliance partners seemed to suggest that the recent improvement in Anglo-German relations heralded an easier future. Furthermore, they believed that the freshly-concluded Anglo-American understanding would 'probably have an influence for good in the world'.[7] Sadly, in a matter of days events in Agadir showed how misplaced such optimism was.

In 1909, Germany had agreed that France had 'special political interests' in the unstable North African state of Morocco. There seemed nothing particularly out of order, therefore, when to protect the Sultan from an aggressive pretender and safeguard its interests there, France sent an armed force to Fez. On 1 July 1911 the issue was suddenly turned into an international crisis by the seizure of the Moroccan port of Agadir by the German gunboat *Panther*. The ostensible purpose of the action was to ensure that German interests in Morocco, such as they were, were not overridden. The real purpose appears to have been to force France to compensate Germany when, as now seemed certain, France took over the running of the country. But the move was heavy-handed and raised in the eyes of the entente nations the alarming prospect of a German naval base in North Africa. Britain and Russia hurried to France's side. On 21 July, without consulting his cabinet colleagues, Lloyd-George raised the stakes by declaring in his celebrated Mansion House speech that,

> '... if a situation were to be forced upon us, in which peace could only be preserved by the surrender of the great and beneficent position Britain has won by centuries of heroism

and achievement, by allowing Britain to be treated, where her interests were vitally affected, as if she were of no account in the Cabinet of nations, then I say emphatically that peace at that price would be a humiliation intolerable for a great country like ours to endure.'[8]

For several weeks, until an accord was signed on 11 October, an all-out European war seemed a very real possibility.

How did the Royal Navy react to this long-anticipated danger, when the Foreign Secretary, Sir Edward Grey, genuinely believed that the fleet might be attacked at any minute? In short the Admiralty – or, more specifically, First Sea Lord Wilson – displayed what the Assistant Secretary to the CID called 'extraordinary apathy'.[9] Wilson did not summon the Naval War Council or discuss the situation closely with his colleagues. He issued no War Plans. If there were any, they were either locked inside his head or in a safe to which only he had the key.[10] Worse still, he refused to press the cabinet for the 'warning telegram' that would have allowed him to put the fleet on alert. 'I was forbidden to take the fleet to sea,' Bridgeman wrote to Battenberg with unusual anger, 'or to take the necessary precautions while lying in harbour – exception being taken even to getting the [torpedo] nets out at night.'[11]

On the day of Lloyd George's Mansion House speech, when the German High Seas Fleet was exercising off the coast of Norway, Wilson was away shooting in Scotland and his Navy was scattered between Cromarty in Scotland, Berehaven in Ireland and Portsmouth and Portland on the south coast of England. The third and fourth divisions of the Home Fleet were in the process of paying off and handing their ships over to nucleus crews. On the last weekend in July, when the tension was at its height, Home Secretary Churchill found practically all senior naval staff on holiday and the Service's reserve supply of cordite unguarded. Acting on his own initiative (no one thrived on a crisis more than he), he sent 100 police to guard it.

The Agadir crisis uncovered an almost total lack of co-ordination between the Army and the Navy. McKenna and Wilson in particular came out of it badly. When asked at a meeting of the CID in August what he planned to do in the event of war, Wilson talked vaguely of tactics reminiscent of the Napoleonic era: close blockade, seizure of enemy bases and landings on a hostile coastline. Secretary for War Haldane and Sir Henry Wilson, the director of military operations, wanted the British Expeditionary Force escorted over to the Continent as soon as war was declared. Sir Arthur Wilson, adhering to Britain's traditional role in a European war, was sceptical about such large-scale land operations and reluctant to escort troops across the Channel before the German High Seas Fleet had been destroyed.

Asquith's cabinet was shocked by the Admiralty's lack of preparedness. Its unease deepened when, as a result of the Agadir climb-down, Admiral Tirpitz called for the German Fleet to be built up to the point where similar humiliation would be impossible.[12] When the much respected Haldane said he would resign unless the Navy were brought up to date and a Naval War Staff established, Asquith was forced to act. McKenna was opposed to the idea of formal War Plans and a Naval War Staff, so while on holiday in Scotland with Home Secretary Winston Churchill, Asquith decided that Churchill and McKenna should swap seats at the Cabinet table. McKenna reluctantly agreed and on 25 October Winston Churchill entered the Admiralty as its new First Lord.

Churchill needs little introduction. Nevertheless, it is worth pointing out that the man who took control of the Royal Navy in 1911 was very different from the widely-respected senior Conservative statesman of World War II. To begin with, he was a still a Liberal, dedicated to spending on social reform not armaments. In Bridgeman's words he was considered 'very strong on the economy line', not a trait the Admiralty appreciated.[13] Furthermore, he was only 37 and had a reputation (not wholly undeserved) of being a somewhat untrustworthy radical political maverick, a self-publicist who liked to have everything his own way. Finally, he was by instinct and training a soldier. Although a close friend of Fisher upon whom he relied heavily for advice, the Navy was a new experience to him.[14] It was rumoured that he thought Blake the famous seventeenth-century Admiral and Blake the poet responsible for

'Jerusalem' were one and the same man. That said, the qualities that were to make him a major world leader – his quick mind, boundless energy and determination, roaring self-confidence and, above all, his wonderful way with words, both written and spoken – were all in place. Wielding them to great effect, he took the Senior Service by storm.

If the Navy was not quite sure what it was getting, it soon found out. During his first 18 months as First Lord of the Admiralty, Churchill spent 182 days at sea to experience at first-hand how the Service operated. Everywhere he went he delved, questioned and challenged. He deliberately and infuriatingly courted the lower deck, frequently overrode the opinions of senior officers and welcomed or at least was prepared to consider most suggestions for change. He made many mistakes, as headlong reformers are bound to do, and trod on many salt-encrusted toes. He fell out with all but one of his First Sea Lords, including his close friend and ally Fisher, and when war came his strategic thinking, culminating in the ill-fated Dardanelles campaign, proved flawed. He took professional advice but tended to follow it only if it supported his own views – Jellicoe believed Churchill's failure to accept that someone of his experience and background could not possibly know all the answers was a 'fatal flaw'.[15] The weakness stemmed from his self-confidence, which was also one of his principal strengths: in the last resort he was convinced he knew best and could do almost anything he set his mind to. He was almost correct. For all his overbearing single-mindedness, Churchill was just the master the Navy needed to shake it out of its over-confident apathy. That it was far better prepared for war in 1914 than it had been two years earlier was largely due to his tireless efforts.

Sooner rather than later a clash between First Lord and First Sea Lord was inevitable. Wilson found Churchill overbearing and interfering; Churchill found Wilson stubborn, uncommunicative and unwilling to change. And because Wilson opposed plans for closer liaison with the British Expeditionary Force and the setting up of a Naval War Staff in particular, he had to go. That meant finding a new First Sea Lord.

Although several names were led into the stalls, the field was not strong and there was no clear favourite. Initially, Churchill himself wanted Fisher to return, but still feeling the bruises of his battle with Beresford, the ex-First Sea Lord was enjoying his role of *éminence grise* and preferred to stay where he was. Churchill, too, soon accepted that the old sea dog was better left lying low. To bring him back so soon would have reopened wounds that were even now only just healing over; besides, Churchill wanted the sort of free rein Fisher would never have allowed him. The Admiralty, like a warship, needed only one captain. The King was known to favour his friend Sir Hedworth Meux. When he was declared unsuitable, His Majesty switched his favours to Bridgeman's old friend Sir John Durnford, who was passed over only after Churchill had cabled him in the Mediterranean requesting he pack his bags and prepare to return home.

Fisher and Asquith leaned towards Battenberg, whom Fisher described as 'the most capable administrator in the Admirals List *by a long way*'.[16] Yet he was only a vice-admiral with no experience as a Sea Lord and when Lloyd George pointed out that his German name would not go down well with the public, Churchill compromised by making him Second Sea Lord. Sir William May believed he stood a chance of getting the job, a view he held in a minority of one. To Fisher, who disliked him strongly, he was 'a bit of wood painted to look like iron'.[17] So in the end Churchill wrote grandiloquently to Asquith that he had come down 'decidedly in favour' of Bridgeman, 'a fine sailor, with the full confidence of the Service afloat, and with the aptitude for working with and through a staff, well developed'.[18] The appointment, together with Wilson's premature retirement, was made public on 28 November 1911. There is no evidence that either Churchill or his staff had looked closely into the new First Sea Lord's health record.

Although tangible evidence of his practical gifts was sadly lacking, Bridgeman was clearly a capable, talented man. Nevertheless, he was chosen to succeed Wilson more for what he was not than for what he was. He was not closely associated with either the Fisher or the Beresford camps; he was not a popular figure of strong views likely to oppose Churchill's reforms; he was not of German descent; he was not awkward and uncommunicative; and he was not likely to be in office in 1914 when

Fisher was convinced war would begin. He was to be a convenient stop-gap between the awkward Wilson and the dream ticket of Battenberg-Jellicoe. 'The sweetest thing about the Admiralty revolution,' Fisher wrote to Gerald Fiennes from Naples at the end of the year,

> 'is that not a soul has yet discovered what it all *absolutely* and *solely* pivoted on! ... Jellicoe to be Admiralissimo on October 21st 1914 when the Battle of Armageddon comes along! He automatically becomes Commander-in-Chief of the Home Fleet in two years' time! ... [He will be] about the same age as Nelson at Trafalgar and possesses all Nelson's attributes except Lady Hamilton and there I sympathise with him'.[19]

Bridgeman may well have noticed more than a suggestion of this sub-text in Churchill's cool letter of 17 November inviting him to take over Wilson's position. Penned on board the Admiralty yacht *Enchantress* at Devonport, it began with a lengthy preamble about the need for the new Board of Admiralty to support him at a time when the estimates were going through Parliament. It went on to say that Churchill sought a First Sea Lord who would ensure that the

> 'opinion of the Sea Service shall be effectively represented at the Admiralty, & that their confidence shall be sustained by the appointment of a First Sea Lord fresh from the handling of great fleets & in the closest touch with actual operations'.

Then, believing ('you will correct me if I am wrong') Bridgeman and he were 'in general agreement upon the broad principles of naval policy, including among other things the creation of a Naval War Staff,' he asked the 63-year-old Commander-in-Chief of the Home Fleet if he might submit his name to the King for appointment as First Sea Lord. No effusive praise, not even a laudatory adjective. From the outset Churchill made it plain that what he needed was a link between the Admiralty and 'actual operations'. That was all.

The lukewarm tone of the invitation was made the more apparent by later reference to Battenberg as a 'brilliant officer'. The letter also affords plenty of evidence of the no-nonsense manner in which Churchill wished to operate. Whatever Bridgeman thought of the idea, he was told that Battenberg had already accepted the post of Second Sea Lord. He was also told how the rest of the Board and the high commands had been re-arranged: Callaghan would take over command of the Fleet, with Jellicoe as his second-in-command, where he would have 'his chance of displaying the necessary qualities & acquiring the necessary experience to fit him for the succession'. Churchill concluded with the brusqueness that is the hallmark of a man used to command, 'I have decided that these changes shall operate at once'.[20]

There was no hint of Churchill's intention of turning to his Second Sea Lord, not his First, for advice on important matters. Nor was there mention of the promotion of Beatty, whose 'mind had been rendered quick and supple by the situations of polo and the hunting-field,' to become Churchill's 'principal counsellor' as head of the Naval Secretariat.[21] Figureheads might have ceased to feature in sea-going ships, but Churchill still had need for one at the Admiralty.

Not long previously Bridgeman had been very keen to take on the job of First Sea Lord. By the autumn of 1911 his attitude had changed completely. We don't know for certain why, but several factors must have come into play. He had angled for the top job while Second Sea Lord. Now back with the fleet, he realised that his heart was with the ships at sea not behind a desk at the Admiralty. He still had work to do, too, and after bowing to Churchill's insistence he wrote to Fisher: '[I am] ... *very* sorry to give up the Fleet with all its splendid officers and men. We were getting on famously with internal reforms, etc., much needed!'

Emily shared in his distress and wept when she heard he was returning to the Admiralty.[22] Knowing her husband better than anyone, she realised he was being called into a world he neither fully understood nor particularly cared for. Perhaps she feared for his health, too. Twice during his career he had been invalided home and recently he had been operated on for appendicitis. Did she sense something even her husband did not recognise – that under his tough, breezy exterior lay a sensitive core liable to crack under great strain?

There were other reasons for Bridgeman's reluctance. He wished the top Admiralty job to go to a younger man, one who would better understand the new First Lord. A cost-cutting, radical, Liberal ex-soldier like Churchill was not Bridgeman's cup of tea at all. Finally, he realised he was a short-term, compromise candidate and he did not like it. Although Fisher made a lot of Bridgeman's willingness always to follow rather than lead, for his own purposes the ex-First Sea Lord exaggerated his protégé's docility. As we saw in the way he stood up to Culme-Seymour, Bridgeman might be unfailingly courteous but he was certainly no moral coward. Against his better judgement he accepted his token appointment only because all his life he had been taught to do one thing above all others. His duty to the Royal Navy.

So when Bridgeman had got over the surprise of Churchill's approach, his instinct was to decline the offer. And when he was eventually persuaded to accept, he did so 'much against the grain'.[23] His close friend Jack Sandars, Balfour's confidential secretary with whom Bridgeman shared, perhaps unwisely, many of his closest thoughts, told the Conservative leader that Bridgeman's reluctance to take up the post had been extreme. He had 'begged and begged to be excused,' yielding only when Churchill insisted and then 'sorely against his own wishes'.[24]

Apart from a sound, scholarly article from Nicholas Lambert, Bridgeman's work as First Sea Lord has attracted little attention from historians.[25] He is usually dismissed as a colourless character who was swallowed up and cast aside by the sweep of the Churchillian tide. This is partly explained by the absence of his personal papers, which makes it very difficult to reach the real man behind the bold, confident handwriting. He also suffers from having lived within the same timeframe as Fisher and Churchill, whose towering personalities dwarf all other features in the landscape. His lack of intellectual training and interest in theory has counted against him, too; academic researchers are inevitably inclined towards men and women of their own kind rather than those of a practical bent. Certainly, it would have been better for Bridgeman's reputation if he had rejected Churchill's pleading and the nudge of his own conscience and remained with the Fleet where he commanded 'immense confidence'.[26]

As it was, during his year at the Admiralty Bridgeman turned out to be the wrong man in the wrong place at the wrong time. He had, as Fisher warned Churchill, 'no genius whatever for administration' and made no secret of the fact that he found being confined to an office distasteful.[27] Although he 'certainly possessed greater intellectual ability' than Wilson and undoubtedly had reliable judgement and a deep knowledge of the practical aspects of the Service, he could not match Churchill for confidence or speed of thought.[28] His slowness and caution easily gave the wrong impression. In 1915, when the junior Sir Michael Culme-Seymour wrote critically of Bridgeman to his venerable father and was challenged to justify his remarks, he explained:

> 'He is no doubt not quick in pushing a point, & requires a lot of explanation before he gets to the bottom of it, & Winston & his school cannot put up with that & do not appreciate how valuable his opinion is when he has ultimately mastered the subject in question'.[29]

Moreover, having spent much of his life in the shadow of a series of domineering characters — his father, Markham, his brother Orlando, Heneage, Culme-Seymour, Fisher — Bridgeman lacked the confidence to press his views in the company of extroverts and skilled debaters. When asked to make a swift decision, he retreated into caution or, in extreme cases, stubbornness. This made him appear less intelligent and open-minded than he was. Like Wilson before him, he was at his most vulnerable in situations most alien to him — defending the Navy's corner against politicians, especially on the Committee for Imperial Defence.[30] In the end though, as Arthur J Marder wisely concluded, his real tragedy was being at the Admiralty at the same time as Churchill:

'Although not a particularly forceful person, and more a follower than a leader, Bridgeman ... might have made a moderately successful First Sea Lord, had he served under anybody but Churchill. The two simply did not get along, the root of the trouble being Bridgeman's resentment against the First Lord's interference in everything.' [31]

In the eyes of the press Bridgeman was a man who had risen without trace. From the outset they saw through Churchill's appointment of an uncharismatic admiral to act as a front man for Battenberg. Bridgeman collected unfavourable cuttings and sent them to Fisher, commenting wryly, 'That's what comes of being modest'. Fisher's reply from the Grand Hotel National in Lucerne was both overblown and patronising:

'I have labelled your letter, which came a few minutes ago, *"The letter of a Patriot"* for my memoirs ...

Seriously, it is a splendid act your coming as First Sea Lord, and I don't wonder that Lady Bridgeman weeps!

... I need not also tell you, who are as fully aware as I am, that Jellicoe is head and shoulders beyond all competitors (not excluding Battenberg), that your self-sacrifice in getting him as second-in-command of the Home Fleet is the most patriotic act ever performed by anyone! ... *no wonder that he* [Churchill] *thanks you profusely!*'

Fisher knew perfectly well that Bridgeman had had no say in Jellicoe's appointment. Bridgeman must have been aware of this and Fisher's letter, for all its effusive praise of his patriotic duty, merely confirmed his worst fears – he was regarded by Churchill and Fisher as little more than an ornate pawn in a game over which he had little control. The ex-First Sea Lord even said that in the event of 'any big business like war' he would return home to support Bridgeman, implying astutely that the new First Sea Lord might not be able to stand the strain on his own. In the light of this, what was Bridgeman to make of Fisher's concluding reassurance?

'You may be perfectly sure of one thing and that is that Winston will stick to you like a limpet – I know him very intimately indeed and he has given me his entire confidence...' [32]

Only time would show whether this was just another bit of Fisher hype. But for the moment the omens were not propitious.

Bridgeman would have regarded the future even more gloomily had he known that Fisher was less interested in the detail of the new appointments than in the fact that they represented an 'immense' personal triumph: 'I almost think my greatest satisfaction at the present moment is the delightful *"smash up"* for Beresford ... and others' at their failure to get a single member of their clique onto the Board of Admiralty. As for Bridgeman, he would cast 'a halo of integrity and firmness round the board,' while real power and influence rested elsewhere. Writing to congratulate Churchill on the splendid way (Fisher's way!) he had arranged things, Fisher said cynically he was sure 'No. 2' would 'run No. 1'.[33]

The success of the plan depended on Fisher's evaluation of Bridgeman as little more than a willing cipher. Tragically, he got it wrong. Bridgeman was an experienced and able commander and while prepared to listen and take advice, in the last resort he would not be 'run' by anyone.

NOTES

1   May moved to Devonport as Commander-in-Chief and remained there until his retirement in March 1913.
2   See Dewar, *The Navy From Within*, p. 124.
3   Roskill, *Earl Beatty*, p. 71.
4   *Fifty Years In the Navy*, p. 241 et seq. Director Firing was taken up by Churchill and given new trials in 1912. When these proved satisfactory, it was fitted to all major warships and proved its worth in the First World War.
5   Marder, ed., *Fear God*, ii, p. 418.
6   p. 246.
7   Official Programme, Gale & Polden Ltd, London [1911].
8   Cited, *inter alia*, in Ensor, England 1870-1914, pp. 434-5.
9   Marder, *From Dreadnought to Scapa Flow*, p. 242.
10 *Ibid.*, p. 244.
11 30/9/1911, cited in Lambert, 'Wilson', p. 47.

12 He wanted Germany to match Britain (the first time he had mentioned the potential enemy by name) 2:3 in capital ships.

13 4/12/1911, Marder, ed., *Fear God*, ii, pp. 418-9.

14 Churchill's switch from the Home Office to the Admiralty was technically a demotion and nine years earlier he had poured scorn on Austen Chamberlain's stated ambition of becoming First Lord.

15 Cited in Marder, *From Dreadnought to Scapa Flow*, p. 255.

16 Marder, ed., *Fear God*, ii, p. 398.

17 *Ibid.*, p. 439.

18 *World Crisis*, i, p. 61.

19 Cited in Hough, *Admiral Lord Fisher*, p. 314.

20 L.L.P.P.

21 Churchill, *World Crisis*, i, pp. 65-6.

22 Marder, *Fear God*, ii, p. 418.

23 Randolph Churchill, *Churchill*, ii, p. 541.

24 5/12/11, Sandars mss. 765, f. 20.

25 Lambert, 'Bridgeman'.

26 10/11/1911, Fisher to Churchill, cited in Lambert, *ibid.*, p. 58.

27 *Ibid*; 11/12/1912, *Lord Lytton to Bridgeman*, L.L.P.P.

28 Roskill, *Churchill and the Admirals*, pp. 20-1.

29 4/1915, S.W.P.C.

30 See Lambert, 'Bridgeman', p. 38 & Marder, *From Dreadnought to Scapa Flow*, p. 258.

31 *Ibid.*

32 8/12/1911, L.L.P.P.

33 Lambert, 'Bridgeman', p. 56; Hough, *Admiral Lord Fisher*, pp. 313 & 247.

Admiral Bridgeman – A fine sailor, with the full confidence of the Service afloat

10 'Unable to concur'

Bridgeman got a taste of his youthful superior's unusual way of doing things even before he had officially begun his 383 days as First Sea Lord.[1] Instead of seeing Admiral Wilson personally, Churchill asked Bridgeman to take him a letter requesting his resignation and saying 'he might have a peerage if he liked'. Bridgeman thought the letter 'a fine example of what a letter ought not to be under the circumstances' and Wilson, 'without any grace whatever,' rejected the offer of a seat in the Lords.[2] Beresford, ever alert to chinks in the armour of the Fisher-Churchill axis, demanded the public be told whether Wilson had resigned or been sacked.[3] It was not an auspicious start.

Nevertheless, while not appreciating Churchill's tactless handling of Wilson's resignation, Bridgeman could not but be impressed by the 'very clever' First Lord's dynamism, originality and charm. He was, he told Fisher, not only 'very pleasant' but he also seemed 'determined to get on with his Board'. As for new ideas, Bridgeman went on, his mind was 'full of new schemes of strategy, which are almost too bold to be believed!'[4] This was just what Fisher wanted to hear and he reported back to Churchill that 'dear old Bridgeman' was like the Roman pro-consul Gallio, willing and easy-going.[5] This patronising attitude towards Bridgeman, which Fisher showed time and again, gave a misleading impression of the man. Consequently, he must be held indirectly responsible for Churchill's angry disillusionment when the First Sea Lord turned out to be no mere stool pigeon. Fisher would have helped his young friend more by passing on what Bridgeman said in a letter written two days later: all was going well at the Admiralty and he had no intention of playing second fiddle to anyone.[6]

Although by inclination a listener and mediator, Bridgeman was not, as we have seen, instinctively hostile to change. He was just cautious about introducing it. Indeed, in Nicholas Lambert's words, he showed a 'willingness to consider questions of policy afresh, unhindered by traditional ways of doing things'. Lambert also notes that the new First Sea Lord,

> 'displayed an unusual willingness to listen and take advice from almost any quarter. He consulted widely on nearly every question involving a change in policy ...' .[7]

Once Percy Scott's Director Firing had proved itself in competition with existing technology, for example, he gladly endorsed it.[8] He was quite prepared to delegate, too, although he did not always do so wisely. Sometimes it was simply an exercise in buck-passing. Bridgeman's reluctance to put forward his own opinions annoyed the forthright Churchill. On one occasion he reminded Bridgeman that as he was the First Lord's 'principal naval authority in the state' he had to stick his neck out sometimes. 'What is your opinion?' demanded the frustrated Churchill.[9]

In 1911 Bridgeman set up a committee to enquire into the training of fire-control teams but left it to others to implement its recommendations.[10] The following year, when considering how best to amend Wilson's unrealistic plans for a close blockade by large surface ships, he drew up a general outline of what he wanted and entrusted the War Staff to work out the details.[11] He worked hard, often staying at his desk seven days a week, but he did not have the stamina for the sort of all-night discussions that Churchill and Fisher liked to share.[12] He would not have enjoyed them much, either; while he wrote a good letter, words were not his forte. There was also the vexed question of his health.

After Bridgeman had been at the Admiralty a few months he began to suffer from bouts of illness that kept him away from his post for short periods during April, September and November 1912. He missed three Admiralty Board meetings and half of the six CID meetings which he might have attended.[13] However, in the light of his record for contracting dubious ailments at convenient times (for example, the 'hernia' that rescued him from Heneage and the 'varicose veins' that got him back from the Mediterranean) it is possible that the 'bronchitis' he suffered from while at the Admiralty was of similarly questionable seriousness. After six months of working with Churchill he was clearly unhappy with his situation. It is well within the bounds of possibility that his anxiety, or even mild depression, manifested itself in physical symptoms. It is significant that he missed Board and CID meetings, as it was at these that his weakness in debate made him feel most uncomfortable.

It was not straightforward disagreement with the First Lord that Bridgeman found difficult to handle so much as the manner in which he was treated. Sometimes Churchill was blunt to the point of rudeness. In January 1912 he was worried at the Navy's lack of contingency plans for coaling the Fleet in the event of a national miners' strike. 'You should prepare a plan ...' he told Bridgeman, and then went on to outline what that plan should contain.[14] On other occasions Churchill plainly did not trust his First Sea Lord's judgement. Also in January 1912, a report from the British consul in Stettin on Germany's new and very fast V1 destroyers was circulated round the Admiralty. 'Our policy of slow destroyers has never been explained to me,' noted Churchill tersely, implying that he had not been briefed properly. Bridgeman explained that the difference in speed between British and German destroyers was not really significant and the Navy's ships were better armed and more seaworthy. Despite this reassurance from his senior advisor, Churchill's misgivings remained. 'I am glad to find grounds for being reassured,' he wrote, '& shall be quite ready to be convinced by sound reasons.'[15] He had obviously not thought Bridgeman's reasons sound enough.

By March 1912 Churchill felt sufficiently confident to cancel at the last minute the new War Plans that had been drawn up by the War Staff and, apparently, accepted by Bridgeman.[16] Ernest Troubridge in vain asked his First Sea Lord to stop this civilian intervention in strictly naval affairs. Although Bridgeman probably thought no more of the new plans (calling for a huge number of cruisers and destroyers to watch the coast of Northern Europe) than he did the old, he cannot have liked the First Lord's overriding them without his consent. They were, after all, the product of the War Staff which was answerable to him (see over). He did not appear to have had much say, either, in the fresh set of war plans issued in November 1912. Had he had more input, the plans would probably have made more use of submarines of which he was cautiously approving. They owed most not to the Admiralty at all but to the Home Fleet Commander, Admiral Callaghan, whose advice on planning Churchill placed above Bridgeman's.

Churchill had come to the Admiralty with the specific intention of establishing a Naval War Staff. Bridgeman knew this and his open support for the proposal helped incline the First Lord towards him when he was seeking a suitable successor to Wilson. Yet it was not Bridgeman but Churchill's man of the future, Battenberg, who was officially given the job of setting the War Staff up.[17] And once in operation Bridgeman soon discovered that its controlling reins led directly to the hands of the First Lord instead of to his own. It was arrangements of this sort that led even the German Naval Attaché to tell Berlin that the First Sea Lord was 'only a "placeholder" for Prince Louis of Battenberg'.[18]

The Navy War Council became the Navy War Staff on 8 January 1912 and the Royal Naval Staff College set up at the Naval War College, Portsmouth, to support it.[19] Bridgeman insisted, against Churchill's wishes, that the head of the new body be responsible to the First Sea Lord, not the First Lord of the Admiralty. It made little difference. Rear Admiral Ernest Troubridge, the first officer to fill the post, was appointed by Churchill without consulting Bridgeman. At this stage of his career Troubridge had little respect for Bridgeman, and to his superior's annoyance and frustration he tended to report directly to the First Lord.[20]

The other Admiralty officer who got under Bridgeman's skin for precisely the same reason was Battenberg, the Second Sea Lord. He was permitted to attend meetings of the CID and in close consultation and co-operation with Churchill appeared to usurp the First Sea Lord's role as principal formulator of strategic policy. His behaviour was all the more irksome to Bridgeman because whereas he respected Troubridge's ability but disliked his methods, he had no time at all for Battenberg as a professional sailor. He conceded that the Second Sea Lord, like Churchill, used 'well chosen language' and could 'write voluminously'; but he scorned his understanding as 'superficial' and believed him 'utterly deficient in technical knowledge'.[21]

Churchill faced difficult decisions regarding Germany. As a radical Liberal he was pledged to shaving government expenditure on armaments wherever possible, but he took over the Admiralty when, following its Moroccan humiliation, Germany was intent on a further round of naval expansion. Lack of evidence makes it impossible for us to know precisely what Bridgeman thought of the situation. He had always argued for the strongest possible Navy, for example preferring full battleships to battlecruisers. Yet, unlike some of his colleagues, he does not appear to have been inflexibly opposed to the pivotal power in the Triple Alliance. In a note to the Foreign Office written on 12 December 1911 he said he saw no 'insuperable' difficulties with the idea of exchanging naval information with Germany. The suggestion was not followed up.[22]

A more positive move was made the following February when Lord Haldane, a skilled negotiator and fluent German-speaker, visited Germany with all-party backing to explore how the naval escalation might be prevented from getting out of hand. Although his mission had little hope of success, its chances became even slimmer after a tactless outburst back home from his First Lord. Speaking at Glasgow on 9 February, Churchill compared the importance of the Royal Navy to the British Empire with that of the High Seas Fleet to the essentially European German Empire. Whereas a powerful Navy was essential to Britain, he reasoned, 'from some points of view the German Navy is to them more in the nature of a luxury'.[23] The remark sent ripples of dismay through the political establishment in Britain; in Germany the response to the idea of a *Luxusflotte* was furious. The Haldane mission was doomed and he returned home on 12 February bearing a copy of Tirpitz's latest proposals. They called for even heavier spending than had been previously feared.

Two days later Churchill circulated a draft of the new German Navy Law to his Admiralty colleagues. Its main feature, he pointed out, was 'the extraordinary increase in the striking force of ships of all classes'.[24] There could be but one response. The March Estimates, put forward with Bridgeman's full support, made no attempt to disguise the fact that the Royal Navy was building against Germany, head to head, with the aim of retaining a 60% superiority in dreadnoughts. Starting in 1912-13,

Britain's annual capital ship programme would be 4-5-4-4-4-4. The German plan was for 2-3-2-2-3-2.[25] Shortly afterwards Churchill tried to make up for his earlier *faux pas* by proposing a 'Naval Holiday' with Germany. It was dismissed as English arrogance. Tirpitz's Navy Law was officially published in late March and became law in May.

Churchill was not content with just more ships. He wanted them to be of the right type and in the right place. The latter consideration led to yet another proposal for reorganising the fleets. As 'we cannot have everything or be strong everywhere,' he wrote to Fisher, the Navy needed to be 'overwhelmingly supreme in the decisive theatre,' the North Sea.[26] To this end he proposed that as from 1 May the Home Fleet should be enlarged to 33 ships (including the flagship) by amalgamation with the Atlantic Fleet and by withdrawing ships from the Mediterranean. The principal fleet would then consist of four battle squadrons, each of eight dreadnoughts. A second fleet of two battle squadrons would be manned by nucleus crews and a third of similar size kept operational by maintenance parties.

Since 1905 the Navy had been laying down both battleships and battlecruisers. Strongly supported by Bridgeman, who had never been keen on the hybrid battlecruisers, from 1912 onwards all new dreadnoughts were to be laid down as full battleships (or 'super-dreadnoughts'). These vessels would not only be better able to hold their own in a large-scale naval engagement, it was argued, but by opting for battleships Britain might discourage Germany from laying down further battlecruisers, which were perceived as a potent threat to commercial shipping. At the same time the role of existing battlecruisers was changed.[27] Fisher had defended their comparatively light armour by arguing that speed was their protection. This may well have been true, but they could be effective against larger warships only if they could shoot rapidly and accurately while steaming at high speed, something that was not possible until the Pollen system was installed after the war. Consequently, the battlecruiser squadrons were arrayed in a mini-fleet of their own and given the task of scouting for the main fleet and, if necessary, engaging enemy battleships. It was a task for which they had not been designed. Even their new role was envisaged as temporary: a plan to disband the battlecruiser squadrons in 1915 when the new Queen Elizabeth-class battleships were ready was shelved on the outbreak of war. Bridgeman's doubts about battlecruisers, particularly as front-line ships, were largely justified by the experience of war. While quite able to hold their own in small-scale engagements, such as the Battle of the Falkland Islands, their inadequate armour proved a liability at Jutland, where three were sunk.

The new Queen Elizabeth-class battleships laid down in 1912 turned out to be among the most successful warships Britain ever produced. Their design owed something to Bridgeman's input but more to Churchill's. With notable insight, Bridgeman wanted the Navy to re-think its attitude towards torpedoes. The weapon had advanced so far, he believed, that it was virtually impossible to prevent at least one getting through to its target. Future warship design, therefore, ought to concentrate not on loading a ship with anti-torpedo secondary armament, but on strengthening armour below the waterline and dividing the interior of the ship into as many watertight compartments as practicable to ensure minimum damage from a torpedo hit. These ideas were incorporated into the design of the Queen Elizabeths.[28]

Over armament and means of propulsion, as in most matters, Churchill got his way. The Admiralty was unsure whether the fast battleships should carry new 15" guns in one less turret than hitherto or tried and tested weapons of smaller calibre. Bridgeman took the advice of Controller Rear Admiral Charles Briggs (whom Fisher considered a 'second-rate man') and opted for the latter, arguing that the larger guns had not yet proved their superiority.[29] Churchill, egged on by Fisher, overrode him. History proved him right.[30] The Queen Elizabeths' eight 15" guns could each fire a 1,920 lb. shell over 35,000 yards, giving a heavier broadside than 10 guns of only 1½" less calibre. The extra space provided by the removal of a turret was used as additional engine space, enabling the ships to reach a lively 25 knots.

Churchill's second innovation was to insist that the Queen Elizabeths' boilers were oil-fired, the first capital ships to be so powered. The benefits of efficiency, endurance and cleanliness were clear but given

Britain's ample coal supplies and need to import all its oil, it was a risky move. In 1912 Churchill got Fisher to head a Royal Commission on Fuel Oil to examine the issue and lessened the chances of a fuel shortage by persuading the government to buy a controlling interest in the Anglo-Persian Oil Company.

The proposal to withdraw ships from the Mediterranean to make more resources available for service in the North Sea had been under consideration even before Germany's latest spurt of warship building. Nevertheless, the plan to move the Malta battle squadron to Gibraltar and the latter to Portland ran into a storm of protest.[31] The Tory press castigated it as abandoning the Empire and leaving Britain's vital trade artery at the mercy of any second-rate power capable of wielding a knife. Furthermore, it involved closer co-operation with and reliance on France, a change in thinking that many, particularly those of the older generation, simply could not accept. Even the Navy War Staff preferred higher expenditure to reliance on 'country of unstable politics'.[32]

Bridgeman was not of this school.[33] The scantiest of evidence – an Admiralty record of Bridgeman speaking French and a passing reference to the possibility of his father moving to Boulogne – suggests that a sniff of Francophilia may have scented the air of Babworth Rectory. The First Sea Lord's relations with France while at the Admiralty bear this out. One of his first official duties was to receive the new French naval attaché, the grand-sounding Commander Count Christian-Marie Le Gouze de Saint-Seine. The two got on well and Bridgeman told his visitor that he 'completely approved' of the way the French Navy was disposed, with main battle squadrons in the Mediterranean and smaller ('flotilla') craft and submarines protecting the Channel.[34] Seeking to clarify the vague arrangements left by Fisher and Wilson, he went on to hint that the Admiralty would welcome closer co-operation against a 'common enemy', perhaps dividing the Channel into spheres of operation for flotilla craft.[35] Saint-Seine reported optimistically back to Paris, urging that Bridgeman's offer be followed up with formal talks towards a written agreement covering such matters as signals and strategic co-ordination. It was all a bit bold for the French government, which contemplated little more than an exchange of ideas. Despite another request from Saint-Seine that France 'seize Bridgeman's offer', the cordial and constructive discussions came to nothing.[36]

Naval opposition to the proposed partial withdrawal from the Mediterranean (with Beresford in the van, of course) was endorsed by diplomats who feared it would be interpreted by the Triple Alliance as a sign of weakness. That, they argued, might incline Italy and Spain more favourably towards the Berlin-Vienna axis. The problem was discussed by the CID and then in May at a top-level conference held on board the *Enchantress* in Malta Harbour. Churchill and the Prime Minister were there, so were Field Marshal Lord Kitchener (Viceroy of Egypt and bitterly opposed to Churchill's proposals), Battenberg and Beatty. But not the First Sea Lord. Presumably Churchill wanted around him only those naval men who would approve his every word.

The Malta discussions produced a compromise proposal: a powerful cruiser presence in the Mediterranean, divided between Malta and Gibraltar, where a pair of battlecruisers from the North Sea would henceforward be based. In presenting the revised plan to the cabinet Churchill exaggerated the strength of Bridgeman's support for it and cited (cleverly out of context) the First Sea Lord's equivocal observations on the usefulness of battlecruisers. 'At present the British battle cruisers have immense prestige in themselves,' Churchill quoted;

> 'no one really knows their full value; it is undoubtedly great
> – it may be even more than we imagine. In the
> Mediterranean they could operate with great effect ... even
> their appearance has a sobering effect.'[37]

Bridgeman had not been consulted over the Malta compromise. He did not like it and agreed to it only reluctantly. He objected in particular to the weakening of the North Sea Fleet by two battlecruisers and demanded that they be replaced at once by two new ships.[38] Following Fisher, he believed British interests in the land-locked sea could be perfectly well served by a large number of flotilla craft and submarines.[39] He probably also recognised that the compromise reflected an insensitive lack of confidence in French naval power, a prejudice which he had earlier worked to overcome. Significantly, Churchill did not pass on to him what went on in Cabinet, nor was he honest to his Cabinet colleagues about the First Sea Lord's reservations and requests for new construction.[40] In July the Mediterranean compromise was rejected by the CID, which called for the British presence at Malta to be equal to that of any other single power, excluding France. Again without consulting Bridgeman, Churchill accepted this. However, he did extract the significant proviso that no battleships be sent until new ones were available in 1915; until then the Malta Squadron would have to make do with four battlecruisers.

Fisher's proposal for the Navy to patrol the Mediterranean with flotilla craft and submarines only was also discussed and turned down. Churchill, claiming that he had the full support of the Board, endorsed the rejection. Once more, he was not being quite honest. Battenberg's and Troubridge's backing he may have had, but not that of the First Sea Lord whose views he considered either irrelevant or too contrary to be mentioned.[41] Bridgeman, edged towards the sidelines during his first few months at the Admiralty, was now somewhere at the back of the stands.

Two other points are worth making about the Mediterranean controversy. It showed that in some areas Bridgeman's thinking was ahead of the field. His faith in submarines, which shortly before he left office he was suggesting might be sufficient to blockade German ports, is a case in point. Given that during the war Germany's submarine blockade came close to bringing Britain to her knees, it was not such an unrealistic idea. Secondly, the Mediterranean compromise was just that – as Troubridge would discover to his cost in 1914, it left the Royal Navy dangerously vulnerable and with no clear view what it was supposed to do. For this 'mess' Bridgeman held Churchill entirely responsible.[42]

There is no evidence before 1912 of Bridgeman being a difficult man. Indeed, he impressed everyone with his good manners, sense of fair play and courtesy.[43] Duty, not ambition, had taken him to the highest active post the Navy could offer and when he expected his colleagues to play by the rules, as he had done all his life. Churchill, ruthless, scheming, nakedly ambitious, was an anathema to him. When Bridgeman had met men like this at sea there had always been a higher authority to turn to, a code of procedure or regulations he could point to. Now there was no higher authority than himself. In the devil-take-the-hindmost world of politics there was no standard code of practice, either. He was alone, naked and owing to his upbringing, defenceless. Like a fish on the quay, bewildered and out of his element, he floundered.

Moral judgements are inappropriate. The world needs both Bridgemans and Churchills. The latter type move things on, take risks, get things done and, if necessary, win wars. Their methods of operation are rarely pleasant and, thankfully, there are not many of them. But there are times when it is better to have a rule-breaker on your side than a rule-keeper. In normal circumstances men of Bridgeman's type ('true gentlemen', 'salt of the earth' – choose any of a number of laudatory epithets) are the people one wants in one's team: reliable, honest, self-sacrificing. Their morals are those of Kipling's 'If' (published in 1910) and St John: 'Greater love hath no man than this, that a man lay down his life for his friends.'

Never was the cult of the chivalrous gentleman stronger than in the years leading up the First World War. Its hero was Bridgeman's ex-Naval Assistant at the Admiralty, Captain Robert Falcon Scott. It was wholly appropriate, therefore, that in March 1912, as he lay slowly freezing to death in a distant storm-blown tent, he should have written a justificatory note to his First Sea Lord and not the First Lord of the Admiralty. Churchill, although sentimental like many ruthless men, had no time for losers, however gallant. 'My dear Sir Francis,' Scott wrote,

> 'I fear we have slipped up – a close shave. I am writing a few letters which I hope will be delivered some day – I want to thank you for the friendship you gave me of late years and to tell you how extraordinarily pleasant I found it to serve under you – that I am <u>not</u> too old for this job. It was the younger men that went under first. Finally, I want you to do your best

to secure a competence for my widow and boy. I leave them very ill provided for but feel that the country ought not to neglect them – After all, we are setting a good example to our countrymen, if not by getting into a tight place, by facing it like men when we were there. We could have come through had we neglected the sick –

Goodbye & goodbye to <u>dear</u> Lady Bridgeman.

Yours ever

R Scott

Excuse writing. It is -40 & has been for nigh a week.'[44]

Scott's spirit did not die with him. It grew steadily until, in the autumn of 1914, its 'gallant, uncompromising, uncerebral imperatives' became suddenly and horribly inappropriate, even irrelevant. In the new game the brave but ultimately hopeless last wicket partnership was as pointless as arriving second at the South Pole and dying on the return journey. Victory was all that mattered; only those who understood that and were prepared to use any means to achieve it were needed. They were the Churchills, not the Bridgemans.[45]

Captain Scott writing his diary at base camp, 1912

Herbert Ponting/Popperfoto

The Bridgeman-Churchill clash, therefore, was more than just a conflict of personalities. It was a meeting of two cultures, two ethical codes. In the context of a fighting Service Churchill's, however distasteful, was the more appropriate. It was also almost certain to triumph.

By March, when he complained at the way Troubridge was passing War Staff correspondence directly to the First Lord rather than through himself, Bridgeman was beginning to find Churchill's behaviour irksome. In April he was depressed and complained of having had 'an awful time of it' through illness.[46] A month later things had clearly taken a turn for the worse. Fisher noted that Bridgeman was finding resistance to Churchill impossible. On 20th he wrote to his protégé from the Hotel Excelsior, Naples, saying that he was not alone in finding the First Lord difficult. 'My relations with Winston have been strained to the breaking point,' Fisher complained. He went on to beg Bridgeman not to resign, 'regardless of every personal consideration. You're a rock that can't be displaced,' he flattered, 'no matter how the wind blows or the rain beats on you!'[47]

As we have seen, Second Sea Lord Bridgeman made a habit of threatening resignation. It now looks as if the old habit was returning. This prompted Fisher, keen to support Churchill's reforming administration, to write the agitated First Sea Lord another flattering, morale-boosting letter from Naples. Under his customary melodramatic heading – *'Private and confidential and please BURN'* – Fisher apologised for Churchill. His only fault, he explained, was that he 'cuts off more than he can chew'. With unseemly pleading, he added,

> 'I write to tell you that Winston *quite spontaneously* said to me (*he need not have said anything!*) that he had the very highest regard for you and intended to do his utmost to secure your remaining with him and added that if necessary you must be made admiral of the fleet.
>
> ... *I think you ought to hang on at all costs for the good of the Navy.*

... I only write my dear friend to urge you on my bended knees to *stick to your post to the bitter end* – and that *Winston loves you!*' [48]

Having already lost one First Sea Lord during his short stay at the Admiralty, Churchill clearly did not want to lose another unless he had to. It might seem more than carelessness. He did, however, suggest a less embarrassing way of getting Bridgeman out of the way: for the sake of his health he should take an extended holiday abroad. The idea was rejected.[49]

The extent of Bridgeman's isolation became more apparent in July when discussions were once again held with Saint-Seine on Anglo-French naval co-operation. This time Churchill was present and the cordiality of the previous meetings evaporated. The Mediterranean was discussed, obviously, and Bridgeman gathered that the French considered their forces there equal to those of Austria and Hungary combined (reinforcing his belief that the Royal Navy need not maintain capital ships at Malta). But Churchill was not prepared to take the matter further, saying he wished for only a non-obligatory agreement and could do little without Cabinet approval. Bridgeman, with an extraordinary admission of weakness, confessed to the French that decisions regarding the Mediterranean had been taken out of his hands and given to the Cabinet and the CID, i.e. Churchill. The First Sea Lord, who earlier had been so keen on sorting out some kind of co-operation for flotilla craft in the Channel, appeared even to lack the confidence to take up this issue again. When asked to consider a modification of the agreement worked out by Wilson in September 1911, he merely agreed to pass the matter over to the War Staff.[50] Which meant Troubridge, which in turn meant Churchill. Again, as he had done in his struggle with Heneage all those years before, it was beginning to look very much as if Bridgeman had given up.

If this was the case, then something happened to make Bridgeman change his mind. After several weeks recuperation at Copgrove, in September he returned to the Admiralty full of fight, determined to block the Churchillian steamroller. But in his absence it had gathered yet more momentum.

On 14 September Churchill circulated the Board with perfectly sensible proposals for reforming the Navy's ability to mobilise swiftly in event of a crisis. Unfortunately, the document, written on the headed notepaper of the *Enchantress* from which the First Lord was observing fleet exercises in the Mediterranean, read distinctly like an order. It began by pointing out that as the system now in operation had been drawn up 'when the crisis of war came much slower than now,' the Service was short of the men needed for a really swift emergency mobilisation. It was unwise, he noted, that 780 men skilled in torpedo and gunnery should be discounted because they were in shore-based schools; and that the 3,728 ratings allocated to 'Harbour Establishments at Home' and other institutions (including 307 qualified men in the yachts *Enchantress* and *Surprise*) should be similarly unavailable. His solution, which included all men below commissioned rank serving for at least one month a year in a warship, was reasonable. The tone in which he presented it was not: 'The old system is to be brought to an end forthwith; the following principles are to be observed ... no exception is to be made to these rules ... .'[51]

Bridgeman saw red. After talking to Battenberg, who was equally put out by the First Lord's peremptory manner, he replied on 16 September:

'First Lord. With reference to your minute enclosed – I feel obliged to draw your attention to paragraphs underlined which read to me like a direct order to be obeyed forthwith.

I desire to remind you that all orders such as these must emanate from the Board and be issued by the Secretary.

I find myself quite unable to concur in what appears to be your view of the position and authority of the Sea Lords who are your colleagues & *not* heads of departments as maintained in other offices of the State & who therefore are in the habit of receiving orders.

I take no exception to the matter of your minute, & I have given directions for a careful investigation on it which will be duly reported and considered by the 2nd Sea Lord & myself! As you will probably wish to recant your minute, I therefore enclose it.'[52]

We do not know when Churchill decided Bridgeman had to go. But if there was a turning point, a time when he concluded that his First Sea Lord was more trouble than he was worth, this was probably it.

But Churchill could not just dismiss Bridgeman because he found him awkward to work with. He needed a reason for asking him to step down and at the moment he did not have one to hand. So he replied to the First Sea Lord's blunt tirade with a conciliatory telegram – 'Will certainly meet your views about minute' – followed on the same day by an equally amenable letter:

> 'It is far from my wish to create disagreements where none exists. The minute was an expression of my views & wishes on a general question of policy, & it c[oul]d not from the nature of that question be "a direct order to be obeyed forthwith". I gladly amend it to make this clear.'[53]

The matter did not rest there. Apparently this was not the first time Churchill had 'outraged official decorum by the language of his official minutes', so on the First Lord's return from the Mediterranean Bridgeman confronted him, telling him 'he must mend his manners or his Board would have to take action'. Sandars, the source of the story, goes on,

> 'Bridgeman pointed out that Winston could not give a single order outside the Admiralty building without the consent of the Board & that [as] he was only *primus inter pares* the terms in which he had been addressing his colleagues was most improper. Winston at first contested this position; whereupon Bridgeman replied that in the event the Sea Lords would address themselves to Asquith and ultimately to the King. Winston then capitulated abjectly, broke into tears and talked in such a melancholy manner about himself that Bridgeman thinks he must be ill.'

Sandars knew Churchill better than that. 'I had never known the time when sympathy was asked for Winston on grounds of health,' he retorted.

At around this time Bridgeman led his Board in another successful revolt against their overbearing First Lord. Robert Borden, the distinguished Canadian Prime Minister, had suggested his country might help Britain by paying for three battleships and he wrote to the Admiralty requesting further information on British strength and deployment in the North Sea. Churchill took it upon himself to reply and with an unusual respect for formalities showed the letter to his Board before sending it. The Board was horrified at its contents. They 'begged and implored' him not to send it. It did not answer Borden's specific questions, revealed secret policy matters and was 'most dictatorial in tone'.

Churchill ignored them and sent the letter. Back came a reply from Borden, once again asking for answers to his questions. So Churchill wrote a second, different letter and again showed it to the Board. He agreed to listen to their comments, but refused to let them alter it. Rejecting this, the Board took it upon themselves to re-write the letter. Churchill was furious and referred the whole matter to Asquith, whom he expected to approve what he, not the Board, had written. To his intense chagrin, the Prime Minister preferred the Board's letter and it was that which was eventually sent to Canada![54]

Relations between Bridgeman and Churchill were fast approaching crisis point. One wonders, therefore, whether the series of confrontations from September onwards were deliberately engineered by Bridgeman to bring things to a head? That would certainly explain why after months of quiescence, he had suddenly turned so obstructionist. But it is unlikely he believed he could remove Churchill, or even wanted to. With most of the First Lord's ideas and policies he had no argument; it was his methods he could not stand. Therefore, as he was deeply unhappy with the way he was treated (which may or may not have contributed to his periods of sickness) and was increasingly drawn to the prospect of tranquil retirement at Copgrove, it is plausible that he had decided, perhaps only half-consciously, to go down fighting. Such a course was, after all, in the best tradition of the Royal Navy. Sir Richard Grenville and his ancestor Admiral Benbow had done it. Captain Scott had done it in the Antarctic only a few months earlier and Bridgeman's friend Kit Cradock would do it at Coronel two years hence.

In mid-October Bridgeman again called on his friend Jack Sandars and unleashed another bit of anti-Churchill venom. This time it concerned the Estimates. In the spring Churchill had told the Commons that if Germany added a ship to her programme, the Navy would respond by laying down two. He had now changed his mind and without telling the Board was proposing to ask for £1 million for submarines in lieu of an extra battleship.[55] Once more Bridgeman was being by-passed on a major policy issue. It says something for the First Sea Lord's discretion that Sir Francis Hopwood, one of the Civil Lords of the Admiralty, could tell Churchill on 24 October that although there were 'rumblings, grumblings and flatulence' among civilian members of the Board, the Sea Lords were 'very staunch to him'. He dismissed the row over Churchill's raw language as merely 'reflecting on the individuals who have grown up with the system & have not attempted to correct it'.[56]

Accompanied by his wife Clementine, Churchill arrives at Portsmouth Dockyard for the launch of the battleship Iron Duke, *12 October 1912*

In early November Churchill was 'confronted by the [threatened] resignation of the Sea Lords in a body,' led by Bridgeman, over the possibility of his failing to secure government approval for the Admiralty's proposed 1913-14 manning levels and improved pay for Able Seamen and Petty Officers. A watered down scheme was eventually accepted, but Churchill cannot have appreciated a threat that if carried out would have made his own position 'quite untenable'.[57] Incidentally, although the Board cared strongly about the pay reform, most of the credit for it should go to Churchill. The pay of senior seamen had risen by only one penny above the 1/7d fixed in 1852 and the 3d rise to 1/11 was long overdue.[58] It was only one item on a raft of measures (including fairer discipline and punishment, improved leave, easier promotion from the ranks) Churchill introduced to improve the life of the ordinary sailor and give the Service a more up-to-date career structure.[59]

Two more clashes arose in the first part of November, both over appointments. One flared when Churchill gave command of the 1st Cruiser Squadron to Troubridge, countermanding a promise Bridgeman had made to Rear-Admiral Rosslyn Wemyss. The second was a disagreement over Bridgeman's wish to keep Admiral Farquhar on the active list (and therefore drawing full-pay) by appointing him to command the Reserves and Coast Guard.[60] Bridgeman felt so strongly about this that he suggested resignation and Churchill backed down. By now neither man was making much of an effort to get on with the other and the tension at the Admiralty was embarrassing.[61]

On 17th Fisher intervened for the last time. 'I hope you're taking care of yourself,' he wrote to the harassed Bridgeman. 'Short of dying you've got to stay where you are!'[62] This was all very well, but the decision was not just Bridgeman's. The First Lord had a say in the matter, too.

Emily (second from left) among the guests at Powerscourt, Ireland, the home of her husband's niece, Sybil

NOTES

1   Bridgeman was officially First Sea Lord from 9 December 1911 to 28 December 1912.

2   14/12/1911, Sandars to Balfour, cited in Randolph Churchill, *Winston Churchill*, ii, p. 542.

3   30/11/1911, *Daily Mirror*.

4   4/12/1911, cited in Marder, ed., *Fear God*, ii, pp. 418-9.

5   *Ibid*., p. 439.

6   *Ibid*., p. 418.

7   'Bridgeman', pp. 61 & 58.

8   *Ibid*., p. 61.

9   *Ibid*., p. 59.

10   See Marder, ed., *Fear God*, ii, p. 439.

11   Lambert, 'Bridgeman', p. 63.

12   *Ibid*., p. 58.

13   *Ibid*.

14   Randolph Churchill, *Winston S Churchill*, ii, Companion III, p. 1506.

15   NMM, BTY/2/3/1.

16   This issue is dealt with by Lambert in 'Bridgeman', pp. 63-4.

17   Lambert, 'Bridgeman', p. 57.

18   Cited in Hattendorf, 'Battenberg', p. 78.

19   Nicholas Lambert has demonstrated that Churchill's Naval War Staff was largely a mythical creation. It was only the old Naval Intelligence Department, renamed, given three more clerks and a fresh face in charge. See Lambert, 'Wilson', p. 48 & 'Bridgeman', p. 57.

20 See below, pp. 251-2; PRO ADM 116/3096 & 3099.

21 13/11/1914, Bridgeman to Sandars, Sandars mss 767.

22 Marder, *From Dreadnought to Scapa Flow*, p. 231.

23 *Ibid.*, p. 277.

24 NMM BTY/2/3/5.

25 Marder, *From Dreadnought to Scapa Flow*, p. 283.

26 Marder, ed., *Fear God*, ii, p. 469.

27 The name 'battlecruiser' became official only in 1912. Before this they had been called 'fast armoured cruisers'.

28 Lambert, 'Bridgeman', pp. 61-2.

29 1/6/1912, Fisher to Bridgeman, L.L.P.P.

30 A pair of these awe-inspiring 15" guns are today on permanent display outside the Imperial War Museum.

31 *Ibid.*, pp. 64-67.

32 Marder, *From Dreadnought to Scapa Flow*, p. 291.

33 Halpern, *The Mediterranean Naval Situation*, p. 12.

34 *Ibid.*

35 *Ibid.*, p. 86.

36 Williamson, *The Politics of Grand Strategy*, p. 247.

37 Randolph Churchill, *Winston S Churchill*, ii, Companion III, pp. 1568-9.

38 Lambert, 'Bridgeman', pp. 65-6.

39 PRO ADM 116/3099. See also Brett, ed., *Letters and Journals*, iii, p. 103 and Lambert, *ibid.*, p. 67.

40 Lambert, *ibid.*, p. 66.

41 *Ibid.*

42 *Ibid.*, pp. 66-7; see also below, p. 251.

43 Bridgeman's charm rarely failed him. General Wilson passed the evening of 17 January 1912 discussing strategy with Bridgeman and Troubridge. After what he described as the 'most satisfactory meeting I have spent in years,' he declared himself 'greatly pleased with their outlook and their most kindly feeling to me personally.' Cited in Williamson, *The Politics of Grand Strategy*, p. 196.

44 An abridged version of this letter is to be found in Huxley, L, *Scott's Last Expedition*, vol. II, p. 600. The full (and rather less heroic) text quoted here is kindly provided by Sir James Graham Bt. News of Scott's death did not reach Britain until February 1913, after Bridgeman had left office. In accordance with her husband's request, Kathleen and Peter Scott were well provided for. On top of her Admiralty pension, she received £100 a year from the government and an £8,500 share of the Scott Memorial Fund. Peter was paid an allowance and, at the age of 25, came into £3,500 from the Fund. Interestingly, one of Scott's last requests of his wife was that Peter should be steered towards natural history rather than games. Kathleen did as he asked.

45 Gordon, *The Rules of the Game*, p. 380. I make no claims over the originality of the thesis expressed in the last three paragraphs. It will be found more eloquently expressed and better substantiated in Andrew Gordon's book.

46 Hough, *Admiral Lord Fisher*, p. 257.

47 Marder, ed., *Fear God*, ii, p. 462; L.L.P.P.

48   1/6/1912, L.L.P.P.

49   See below, p. 205.

50   Halpern, *The Mediterranean Naval Situation*, p. 90; Williamson, *The Politics of Grand Strategy*, p. 286.

51   L.L.P.P.

52   Hough, *Admiral Lord Fisher*, p. 252; L.L.P.P.

53   25/9/1912, L.L.P.P.

54   . 10/10/1912, to Asquith, cited in Randolph Churchill, *Winston S Churchill*, ii, p. 629.

55   16/10/1912, Sandars to Asquith, cited in Randolph Churchill, *Winston S Churchill*, ii, Companion III, pp. 1654-5.

56   *Ibid.*, pp. 1656-7.

57   Randolph Churchill, *Winston S Churchill*, ii, pp. 601-603.

58   Hough, *Admiral Lord Fisher*, p. 258.

59   Bridgeman himself was now on £1,500 a year. (PRO PMG 15/145).

60   Lambert, 'Bridgeman', p. 69.

61   14/11/12, Victoria Battenberg to Nora Kerr, cited in Hough, *Admiral Lord Fisher*, p. 257.

62   L.L.P.P.

11 'I have been meaning to write ...'

On 14 November 1912 Churchill told Battenberg in confidence that he wanted him to become First Sea Lord as soon as the awkward Bridgeman could be got rid of.[1] That they discussed how this might be done is clear from the letter Battenberg's wife wrote the same day to her friend Nora Kerr. 'Sir Francis Bridgeman has again been ill,' she observed. 'It is more than likely that he will resign his post before long & then the Prince, who is doing B's work as well as his own now, will succeed him.'[2] Now the plot was laid, all the conspirators had to do was wait until Bridgeman caught a cold before they struck.

They did not have long to wait. On 25 November, while he was taking a long-planned rest cure at Copgrove, Bridgeman unwisely confessed to Battenberg that he was 'very depressed' about his health, which had kept him away from the Admiralty longer than he had intended:

> 'two attacks of bronchitis within a few months, and coming on top of appendicitis, seems to have weakened my constitution, and I sometimes feel inclined to give up my post ... The fact is, I really ought to go somewhere warmer than England to spend the winter – an impossibility so long as one remains at the Admiralty.'[3]

Eager that the First Sea Lord should continue to think along these lines, Battenberg wrote back the very next day:

> 'Just a line ... as regards ... your health. I am so much concerned about what you say. You told me before that the doctor had wished you to have a spell abroad soon. Let me beg of you not to neglect his advice. You need have no compunction about me. I had no intention whatever of leaving London this winter & with the assistance of your

excellent staff I can perfectly attend to your papers whilst you are abroad.' [4]

Such a letter would have aroused immediate suspicion in the wary mind of a Fisher or a Churchill – or even the most humble backbencher. But not in Bridgeman's. Unable to read between the lines (a fault that he was to display even more openly a few days later) he accepted the letter for what it purported to be – a well-meant expression of concern.

He was clearly in low spirits and having shared his misery with the Second Sea Lord he now did the same with Beatty, Churchill's private secretary. The previous evening, he confessed, he had felt so rotten he had taken up his pen to write a letter of resignation. Then, changing his mind, he had decided to sleep on it. Feeling better the next morning had not taken the matter any further. Why Bridgeman confided thus to both Battenberg and Beatty we will never know. If he honestly believed his remarks would not get back to Churchill then he had learned nothing over the past year of the way the First Lord and his band of close colleagues operated. If, on the other hand, he was hinting that he would welcome a letter suggesting he retire on grounds of ill health, then how he reacted when one came does not make sense. Perhaps, therefore, this was just another of his resignation threats. If it was, then it was one too many.

Battenberg and Beatty liked Bridgeman but did not think much of him as First Sea Lord. Both showed their respective letters to Churchill.[5] Battenberg, as heir apparent, had obvious personal reasons for doing so. Seizing his opportunity, the First Lord immediately wrote to Bridgeman at Copgrove. Had he thought more carefully about the nature of the person he was addressing, he might have made a better job of it. He began innocently enough:

'I am very glad to hear from various sources that you have somewhat recovered from the chill which so unkindly spoiled your holiday, & I trust you will continue to make good progress in spite of the drop in the temperature.'

The 'somewhat' was ominous. The formal courtesies out of the way, Churchill came to the purpose of his writing. Or, more precisely, to what he thought was the purpose of his writing. He chose his words rather too carefully.

> 'I have been meaning for some time to write to you about your health which causes me concern both as a colleague & a friend. During the year that we have worked together I have seen how heavily the strain of your great office has told upon you & I know that only your high sense of duty & your consideration for me have enabled you successfully to overcome your strong inclination to retire. That strain will not I fear diminish in the future; & if, by any misadventure, we were to be involved in war, I feel that the burden might be more than you could sustain.
>
> If therefore you should feel disposed at this juncture to retire, I could not whatever my personal regrets oppose your wish, & I believe that such a step would be a relief to you.'

What Churchill meant to tell Bridgeman was that he was sacked, but to avoid scandal and embarrassment the First Lord was giving him an opportunity to make it seem as if he was retiring on grounds of ill-health. The next few weeks would have been much easier for both of them if Churchill had said precisely what he meant and not indulged in such misleading litotes, however well meant. Bridgeman was a direct, straightforward man and needed to be addressed as such.

In a paragraph that was omitted when the letter was later printed for presentation to Cabinet and Parliament, Churchill attempted to sweeten the bitter pill he believed he had just administered; or – a less flattering interpretation – he tried to bribe Bridgeman to swallow it:

> 'You have held so many great commands afloat & ashore, & I am so grateful to you for the aid you have given me, during what will certainly be regarded as a memorable year in naval administrations, that I should consider it my duty to

submit your name on retirement from your present office to the King for promotion to the rank of Admiral of the Fleet as an addition to the regular list.'

Such a promotion would have given Bridgeman an extra five years' full salary.

In another piece of delightful circumlocution, Churchill concluded by expressing the hope that Bridgeman would accept his decision gracefully and not use it as an excuse to drag up their past disagreements:

'It would be a cause of very great pleasure to me if I could feel that our association in so much important business had in no way been a cause of regret or dissatisfaction to you.
Believe me.
Yours very sincerely,
Winston S Churchill' [6]

On 29 November, before he had heard back from Bridgeman, Churchill wrote to the King. In a recent (but not his last) audition, he reminded His Majesty, he had expressed 'increasing anxiety about the state of Sir Francis Bridgeman's health'. He was now no longer satisfied that the First Sea Lord was 'capable of bearing the immense responsibility and strain' of his office. In the light of this he had 'suggested to Sir Francis Bridgeman in terms of high consideration [too high, as it turned out] the propriety of his retirement at an early date'. Churchill also mentioned, as he had promised Bridgeman he would, that the First Sea Lord might be made an additional Admiral of the Fleet. In conclusion, he put forward the names of Battenberg as First Sea Lord and Jellicoe as Second Sea Lord.[7]

Later in the day Churchill received Bridgeman's reply to his letter of 28th. It is not hard to imagine the First Lord's dismay when he read:

'I am in receipt of your kindly-meant letter, and I will give it careful consideration. I am much better, I am glad to say, and am coming to London as soon as the doctor [Wexley-Smith] will allow me.' [8]

Bridgeman was not playing ball at all! Had he really misunderstood the message of Churchill's letter or was he being deliberately awkward? The former is the more likely. Bridgeman was never deliberately awkward; he relished neither confrontation nor ill-feeling. Although he would one day co-author a slim booklet and tell the naval historian Corbett that he had a 'Nautical Library', he was not widely read.[9] His prose style, as befitted a man used to giving orders that needed to be understood, is direct and clear. Implication was as alien to him as dissimulation. In his eyes Churchill's expression 'feel disposed ... to retire' meant just that and at the moment he was not sure he did feel thus disposed. It would depend on what Dr Wexley-Smith had to say. Rarely can Churchill's illustrious prose have let him down so badly. He was due to leave for one of his jaunts in the *Enchantress* on 30th, so before he left he had a word with Battenberg asking him to give Bridgeman another push. But subtly. He knew how awkward Bridgeman could be if he felt he were being dictated to.

Battenberg's letter, written on 30 November, began by saying how 'troubled and concerned' he was at Churchill's mentioning the possibility that Bridgeman might want to 'give up' owing to his weak health. Knowing how poorly the First Sea Lord thought of Battenberg, the clumsy sentence that followed must have convinced Bridgeman to stay put:

> 'Should a change become inevitable I thought you might like
> to know that I have, provisionally and whenever it should be
> necessary, accepted the First Lord's offer to fill, to the best of
> my ability, your place.'[10]

Three letters that made the whole situation distastefully complicated were now written in quick succession. On 2 December Lord Stamfordham the king's Private Secretary replied to Churchill's letter of 29 November. His Majesty was clearly put out to hear that the First Sea Lord was being asked to retire without prior consultation with the Palace. The King had not forgotten his naval days and liked to have a say in what went on in the Senior Service. Churchill had talked with him in late November, when, significantly and contrary to the implication of his letter to the Palace, he had apparently made no mention of Bridgeman's health. Churchill had kept quiet probably because he anticipated royal opposition to his coup. The Admiral's leaving, Stamfordham reported, was 'a loss to the Navy which His Majesty much deplores'.

His Majesty was equally annoyed that Churchill had suggested Bridgeman might be made an Admiral of the Fleet. Stamfordham pointed out that the King had known Bridgeman 'for a great number of years' (at least since the First Sea Lord's time in the *Howe* in 1889) and had 'the highest possible regard for him' and fully appreciated his 'professional abilities'. Nevertheless, His Majesty was unwilling to promote Bridgeman above his seniors, Sir William May and Sir Hedworth Meux. The alternative – promoting all three – was equally unacceptable because he wished the list of Admirals of the Fleet to be kept short and exclusive.[11] The King certainly was a stickler for naval tradition and there may well have been some truth in what Stamfordham wrote. But a few days later Jack Sandars put a different gloss on the matter. As one who knew the King 'a great deal better than Winston does,' he told Bridgeman, he reckoned that His Majesty had such respect for the (now) ex-First Sea Lord, whose sterling qualities he had discussed with Sandars, that he would have been quite prepared to make him an Admiral of the Fleet. But he refused to do so because of Churchill's arrogance in mentioning the matter to Bridgeman before consulting with the Palace, in whose gift the appointment lay.[12]

While Stamfordham was conveying the King's displeasure to Churchill, the First Lord was conveying his to Bridgeman for not grasping the meaning of his last letter. 'Before writing to you,' he began sharply from his cabin in the *Enchantress*,

> 'I consulted the Prime Minister and informed the King. The conclusion at which I have arrived must necessarily be final; and I am confident that it will command your assent. I hope you will let me know your wishes in regard to any member of your staff for whom employment should be provided at the Admiralty or at sea.'

There was no question this time of Bridgeman not getting the message. But it was necessary for Churchill to keep playing the health card, so he ended his brief letter with another reference to Bridgeman's illness:

> 'I am very glad, indeed, to hear you are better. A warm climate during these winter months and relief from office cares will restore your health, I trust, for many honoured years.'[13]

Before he received this clarifying letter Bridgeman had given 'careful consideration' to the First Lord's original suggestion and after weighing the situation up had decided to stay where he was. He thanked Churchill for his 'very kind and sympathetic letter' (of 28 November) then announced:

> 'I have carefully thought the matter over, and as it seemed to be more a question for the doctors to give an opinion on, I have consulted them. Dr Wexley-Smith ... is of opinion that having now diagnosed thoroughly the malady, feels himself able to put me right, there being nothing organically wrong, but that I have been run down.
>
> The change to this place [Copgrove] has done me a lot of good, and I am returning to London on Monday next. I don't think there is a necessity to resign, neither do I think I need go abroad. I shall remain in London for a week or ten days, and then come back for Christmas and return for good to the Admiralty at the new year ...
>
> I wish I had taken your advice six or seven months ago and gone abroad. I should probably have avoided all this trouble.'[14]

On the same day Bridgeman wrote with the same message to Battenberg.[15]

The letter to Churchill is interesting on two counts. Bridgeman's statement that he had been no more than 'run down' lends further credence to the impression we have of his being something of a hypochondriac. He had obviously believed himself ill enough occasionally to absent himself from one of the most important positions in the country; and yet there was nothing 'organically' wrong with him. A few days later he would remind Battenberg that he had been away from the Admiralty 'for never more than the inside of a fortnight at a time and very few weekends'.[16] He had stayed at the Admiralty during the summer months, when most other members of the Board were away, so that he could be free in November. *The Times* revealed that he had been operated on for appendicitis some time before he was appointed First Sea Lord and while in office his only worrying illness had been a 'slight attack of bronchitis' early in the year.[17] His subsequent bouts of ill-health, such as they were, had probably been stress-related, induced by over-work and the tense atmosphere at the Admiralty. Dr Wexley-Smith was a man of his times and of course he did not diagnose stress as contributing to Bridgeman's malaise, but a doctor today would almost certainly do so. The First Sea Lord had been struggling to cope with a job that in the best of circumstances he would have found difficult. With Churchill breathing down his neck and the international situation liable to explode into crisis at any moment, at times it was all too much for him.

The second point is that Bridgeman was not (physically, at least) *that* unwell. He was certainly in much better shape than Churchill himself would be during the latter part of World War II and probably fitter than Fisher when he returned to the Admiralty, aged 73, in 1914. Had the First Lord wished Bridgeman to remain in office, there would have been no problem. But now he had decided to dismiss him on grounds of health, and Bridgeman had declared himself willing and fit enough to continue, the material was there for a spectacular scandal. Much depended on how the next steps were handled.

At first things seemed to be going quite smoothly. In possession of Churchill's abrupt letter of 2 December, on Wednesday 4th Bridgeman followed the only course open to him. 'My dear Mr Churchill,' he wrote sadly,

'I am in receipt of your letter ... written from the Admiralty yacht. I think our letters must have crossed.

I had no idea that my leaving the Admiralty had already been settled and that you had discussed it with the King and the Prime Minister; had I known this, I should not have written my letter in answer to yours of 28th November, in which you express anxiety as to my health and asked me what I am disposed to do.

I now understand that you expect me to resign, and I am happy to be able to meet your wishes.
Believe me,
Yours very sincerely,
F B Bridgeman' [18]

It is safe to assume that Bridgeman wrote immediately on receipt of Churchill's letter, before he had time to consult with anyone but Emily. Had he waited for the opinion of Sandars, for example, it is most unlikely he would have adopted so mild a tone.

At the same time as tendering his resignation, Bridgeman had explained to Sandars what had happened. Jack's reply was a snorter. He was 'very angry' at that 'poisonous and treacherous little brute' Churchill and begged his friend – 'in the interests of the Service & those who come after you' – to make a public statement about what had gone on. It had to be 'carefully worded', showing no feeling and 'coldly, officially and gravely composed'.[19]

Meanwhile, back from the *Enchantress* and unaware of the revolt stirring in Yorkshire, Churchill set about smoothing the ruffled royal feathers. In a letter of 5 December he explained to the Palace that he had not mentioned the Bridgeman affair when he met the King in November because he had not then finished arranging his new Board. (This was almost certainly untrue. Churchill had planned to have Battenberg as his next First Sea Lord even before appointing Bridgeman.) He mentioned Bridgeman's letter of resignation and said his retirement would be made public when he had received 'a telegraphic expression' of His Majesty's agreement. This was provided forthwith and Battenberg slipped behind

Bridgeman's desk, with which he was already deeply familiar, on 7 December. The timing could scarcely have been more cruel. It was Bridgeman's sixty-fourth birthday. Churchill ended his letter with an expression of regret that Bridgeman could not be made an Admiral of the Fleet and suggested as an alternative that he be created a GCB (Knight Grand Cross of the Bath) 'as a special mark of Your Majesty's favour to so distinguished an officer'.[20]

The following day Churchill wrote to Bridgeman again. Perhaps sensing that the matter was not yet quite closed and that there remained ample scope for one of his many political enemies to cause mischief, he was at his most eloquent best. His first, transparently flattering paragraph, clearly written with an eye to future publication should that become necessary, explained more carefully why he had asked Bridgeman to resign:

> 'I am very sorry indeed that the time has come when we should close our year of important and successful work. The general state of your health and vigour made me feel that if a war suddenly broke out upon us you would not be able to stand the tremendous strain that would fall on the First Sea Lord. The times are too critical to brook delay, and once this conviction had formed in my mind I was bound in duty to tell you, just as you would have been bound to tell me had our situations been reversed ... I am sure that this course on my part is only what you would wish and approve. The time comes to us all when the wheels begin to slow down, and when the burden becomes too heavy and the pace too hot. If a man has worked as you have done for so many years from a sense of duty, in spite of many attractions to ease and diversion, and have filled so many great commands and offices with conspicuous success, there is absolutely nothing to regret.'

If Churchill had bent the truth slightly thus far, it was nothing compared with the twisted wreck he made of it in his second paragraph. 'I hope that the warm personal regard which I have acquired for you during our year of co-operation will not be wholly unreciprocated,' he pleaded, no doubt wishing to emphasise the word 'personal' as distinct from 'professional'. He selected his next words even more felicitously:

> 'No one knows better than I do the soundness of your judgement in great matters of naval administration, or the value your personal and professional reputation has been to the Board of Admiralty over which I have presided.'

Poor Bridgeman! Churchill admitted he had sound judgement but had refrained from praising it. Instead, he had, quite correctly, singled out Bridgeman's reputation as the gift to the Board Churchill valued most highly.

A new, self-justificatory tone appears, too, no doubt added so that if rumours of his disagreements with Bridgeman got out he could shrug off responsibility for them. 'I have acted towards you with loyalty and sincerity,' he wrote, quite unnecessarily. 'When I was in the wrong I have admitted it. I feel no prick of conscience on account of our relations.' If he genuinely did not, then he ought to have done. Or perhaps he blamed Fisher for foisting Bridgeman on him under false pretences, a supposed yes-man who had not lived up to his billing?[21]

Bridgeman made a hasty visit to London around 6 - 7 December, no doubt to collect private possessions and papers from the Admiralty. It was hardly how he would have chosen to spend his birthday. Stirred by Sandars' comments, he felt angry, hurt and let down at Churchill's underhand behaviour. Neither he nor the First Lord made any attempt to meet. But the Admiral must have got wind of the rumours that were starting to circulate about his resignation and he almost certainly bumped into colleagues who urged him for the good of the Service and the nation at large not to let the high-handed young First Lord get away with it. Their exhortations fell on an increasingly bitter, receptive ear.

During the long train journey back to Yorkshire the 64-year-old admiral peered gloomily out of the carriage window at the barren winter landscape. Only a short while previously, he thought, it had been so full of life. Like his blighted career. Now both were dark and moribund. He paused to light his pipe. Then, pulling his coat more closely about him, he resumed his angry reverie. The metaphor was powerful but flawed. The countryside would come alive again in the spring, but not so his career. It was finished, cruelly pulled up at the roots with only a year to go. He would not now step down with the customary round of dinners, presentations and warm speeches of praise. Not for him the smiling reminiscence and glowing tribute. Instead he been pushed out early, ushered down the back stairs and away from the crowd. It was not the right or decent thing to do to a colleague. Why could Winston not have spoken to him face to face instead of resorting to those slippery, weasel-worded letters that went on about his health and ignored their clashes over appointment, policy and the way the Admiralty was being run? The man was a coward and a cad. He had to be checked. Bridgeman's friends were right: for the sake of the Royal Navy the arrogant First Lord had to be brought to book.

That evening Bridgeman must have shared his thoughts with Emily. She understood his distress but advised restraint. So soon after the Fisher-Beresford affair did he really think it wise to present the country with another inglorious story of naval backbiting and dissent? Would bringing down Churchill, which was what might happen, really benefit the Navy? Bridgeman, as he always did, listened carefully to what his wife had to say. They were wise words but they did not make his predicament any easier. They left him torn between counter-attack, as advocated by Sandars, and silence. Until the King eventually intervened on the side of the latter, he was never quite sure which plan to adopt and this uncertainty is reflected in his actions and words over the ensuing days. He did not withdraw, he did not press forward. He should have known that a commander who goes into battle without clear tactics or objective is almost bound to lose both the fight and the respect of those relying on his leadership.

The first tangible evidence that Bridgeman was not pleased with the way things had been handled appears in a letter he wrote from Copgrove on Sunday 8 December. To avoid the scandal of an unprompted resignation, he told Sandars, Churchill had 'struck first' by getting rid of him.[22] On the same day Bridgeman sent Churchill a telegram thanking him for the offer of the GCB. He followed this up with a much longer letter in which he gracefully accepted the GCB, put forward a list of those he recommended for special advancement and explained that promotion to Admiral of the Fleet would be unpopular with senior colleagues and the King. By this time Churchill had already heard through an unknown 'indirect channel' of Bridgeman's reluctance to be nominated as an additional Admiral of the Fleet because it would involve leapfrogging Beresford.[23] Perhaps the ex-First Sea Lord sensed he now might have more in common with Lord Charles than he had previously realised.

Then, after apologising that 'such a heavy cold' had made it impossible for him to call on the First Lord, Bridgeman finally got round to hinting that he believed he had been asked to resign for reasons other than ill-health,

> 'I feel that I ought to have explained to you my attitude and the reason for it at the meeting in your room on the discussion of appointments of flag officers. Perhaps my not having done so may have had something to do with the cause of my being asked to resign. I am sure that a holiday quite free from official worry is all I wanted. I had not had this.' [24]

But he did now, although it was not yet free from official worry.

Churchill replied by return of post. He was obviously worried by Bridgeman's change of tone. 'No,' he emphasised,

> 'there is absolutely no truth in the idea that any difference or incident between us influenced me at all. Honestly, I only thought about your health and the European situation and what would happen if war began and you broke down.' [25]

While Churchill clearly *had* been influenced by Bridgeman's resistance to his high-handed style of management, he must also have been genuinely anxious about how a self-confessedly infirm and cautious First Sea Lord would have managed if war had broken out. Unlike Churchill, Bridgeman did not thrive on pressure, and although his level head might have been a useful counterweight to the First Lord's impulsion, his somewhat tarnished medical record and patent dislike of administration would not have made him the Service's ideal wartime supremo.

A fair summary of how the First Lord and First Sea Lord had worked together, Churchill suggested, could be found in *The Times* leader of the previous Saturday, 7 December. He was bound to say that, as the information and tone of the piece had very likely been provided by himself.[26] He was too shrewd an operator not to take every opportunity to set out his side of the story in case the situation turned nasty. And there were now distinct signs that it might.

At the same time as Churchill's letter arrived, another came from Sandars. 'I can hardly refrain from proclaiming the iniquity of Churchill from the house tops,' he fumed. Questions on the First Sea Lord's resignation were going to be asked in the Commons. 'Churchill will lie — of that you may be assured,' Sandars explained, so the opposition had better prepare their tactics carefully.[27]

NOTES

1   Lambert, 'Bridgeman', p. 69.
2   Hough, *Admiral Lord Fisher*, p. 257.
3   Cited by Churchill in a letter to Bridgeman (14/12/1912), L.L.P.P.
4   L.L.P.P.
5   Roskill, *Churchill and the Admirals*, p. 53.
6   28/11/1912, Churchill to Bridgeman, L.L.P.P.
7   Randolph Churchill, *Winston Spencer Churchill*, ii, p. 631.
8   9.11.12, L.L.P.P.
9   NMM, MS82/006.
10 L.L.P.P.
11 Randolph Churchill, *Winston Spencer Churchill*, ii, Companion III, pp. 1676-7.
12 19/12/1912, Sandars to Bridgeman, L.L.P.P.
13 L.L.P.P.
14 3/12/1912. L.L.P.P.
15 Hough, *Admiral Lord Fisher*, p. 258.
16 Cited in Lambert, 'Bridgeman', p. 58.

17 14/12/1912.

18 L.L.P.P.

19 5/12/1912, L.L.P.P.

20 Randolph Churchill, *Winston Spencer Churchill*, ii, Companion III, pp. 1680-2.

21 L.L.P.P.

22 Cited in Lambert, 'Bridgeman', p. 58.

23 16/12/1912, Churchill to Bridgeman, L.L.P.P.

24 L.L.P.P.

25 9/12/1912, L.L.P.P.

26 This suggestion is made by Lombard-Hobson, *Never Go To Sea*, L.L.P.P.

27 8/12/1912, L.L.P.P.

12 'The Healthiest Invalid in England'

During the week of 8 - 14 December 1912 a dense winter smog blanketed central London. The atmosphere was thickest in the thin, vital triangle bounded by Westminster, the Admiralty and Fleet Street, where flying rumour and counter-rumour mingled with river mist and coal smoke. Had Bridgeman gone willingly or had he been pushed? If the latter, then why? One story circulating among junior naval officers and perhaps suggested by Churchill himself was that the First Sea Lord had wanted to retire for some time but had remained in office to see out the Balkans crisis.[1] More astute observers came nearer the truth. Lord Lytton, for example, a future Civil Lord of the Admiralty, wrote to Bridgeman saying he was sure he had been 'abominably treated' and that his 'resignation' had been forced upon him. 'I know that when you accepted the appointment,' he ended,

> '... it was prophesied that a certain gang would work for the result which has now come about. It is a disgusting business and I am more sorry for you than I can say.'[2]

Admiral Durnford, whom Churchill had come close to making First Sea Lord instead of Bridgeman, had no need to guess what had gone on. Bridgeman had already written to his 'sincere old friend' telling him that ill-health had not been the 'real cause' of his resignation. Durnford was sure he was 'well out of it', but regretted that Churchill had not treated 'an honourable man in an honourable manner'.[3] Fisher, too, learned the truth from Bridgeman's own hand. His reply found him at his most eloquently Pecksniffian:

> *'Private and secret, please BURN*
> My beloved Bridgeman
> ... I am *astounded*! Not even a faint hint was given me by W C when talking to him a few days ago.

As I once told you W C had said to me in confidence that he looked upon you as his sheet anchor and if necessary would arrange for you to be an admiral of the fleet. So you can imagine my astonishment at getting your letter!

... Well! I've nothing more to say. I shan't go near the Admiralty any more. Possibly I shall chuck the Royal Commission. *Please burn this.*' [4]

Fisher did not leave the Royal Commission on Oil Supply. Moreover, he not only went near the Admiralty again – in October 1914 he resumed the post of First Sea Lord. More significant than his wild and unkept resolution was his exhortation that Bridgeman keep quiet. He may or may not have wanted Bridgeman to go, but he certainly did not want Churchill to follow.

On the day that Lytton was sending Bridgeman his condolences, the issue of the First Sea Lord's resignation was being raised in the House of Commons. This was not what the ex-First Sea Lord wanted, partly for his own and Emily's sakes, but also to safeguard the good name of the Navy and to protect those of his friends whose promotion might otherwise be jeopardised.[5] The case for his doing otherwise was most eloquently expressed by the Conservative and Unionist Chief Whip Lord Balcarres in a note he sent Sandars on Monday 9 December. As he hoped, it was passed straight to Bridgeman:

'Acquiescence & silence in this case mean condoning a felony, and may well do more harm to the morale of the Fleet than all Fisher's extravagances.

But Beresford knows something, how much I can't make out. Rest assured that the matter cannot be completely suppressed – questions will be asked, & partial lying answers will ensue. It would at least be well if the comments of the injured man were recorded at the Admiralty.

In any case, Party & Admiralty apart, it's his duty to lay the facts before the King.' [6]

Bridgeman would not be persuaded. He wrote and cabled that he had no desire for 'public attention to be taken to what had happened' and refused Sandars' repeated requests for a public statement. On Tuesday 10th, to take his mind off the matter, he went out hunting.[7]

But Sandars, arguing that he was acting in the public interest on an issue that was now attracting a great deal of attention, had shown Bridgeman's letters to Balcarres. If the Whip was to handle matters properly and follow Bridgeman's wishes, Sandars explained, he had to be in possession of the facts. Without them he would not be able to direct his party and control his party's more fervent anti-Churchill-ites.[8] Even with them, he found the task impossible. The reason was simple – Lord Charles Beresford.

Hearts in the Tory hierarchy sank when Beresford rose to his feet. He was a loose cannon whose wild and random shots, like those of the ships he commanded, frequently went yards wide of their target and were as likely to injure friend as foe. He had originally set out no less than 20 questions to ask the First Lord. These had been trimmed, but despite the best efforts of Balcarres, Durnford and others to get him to hold his tongue, the self-appointed Tory watchdog over all naval matters, now a pale shadow (intellectually though not physically) of his former self, was determined not to 'lose the opportunity for an advertisement of himself'.[9] He could not resist picking up and playing with any scrap of scandal that might be useful in his campaign against the 'certain gang' whom he blamed for pushing him out of the Navy before his time. The Bridgeman resignation was too tempting an opportunity for him to ignore.

Beresford began by asking for the 'full circumstances' of the First Sea Lord's resignation. Churchill replied that, 'reasons of health led to the resignation' and 'no difference in view or policy had led to any disagreement' between himself and the 'distinguished officer' Sir Francis Bridgeman. Had he conveniently forgotten the time when confrontation with the First Sea Lord had reduced him to tears?

As a supplementary question Beresford asked whether the First Sea Lord's resignation had been due solely to reasons of health. Had there been 'no other cause at all?' As far as he was aware, Churchill answered carefully, there had been 'no other cause whatever'.

At this point George Lane Fox intervened. Having been hunting with Bridgeman on Tuesday, he was 'bursting with information and indignation'.[10] Did the First Lord speak with Sir Francis Bridgeman's authority? Sensing a trap, Churchill gave an evasive reply.

Before Lane Fox could come back at him, Beresford jumped in again: 'May I ask on which side the proposal for resignation emanated – from the Admiralty or from the First Sea Lord?'

It was a good question. Churchill needed to find out how much his opponent knew. Before answering, therefore, he asked whether Beresford was 'speaking on behalf of Sir Francis Bridgeman'. The Noble Lord replied honestly that he had not had 'any communication from Sir Francis Bridgeman of any sort or kind since his resignation'.

Lane Fox now managed to ask his original question again, to which Churchill replied that he took 'full responsibility' for *his* statements on the First Sea Lord's resignation. Then pressed by Beresford to answer his last question, Churchill admitted that the resignation suggestion had emanated from himself. Beresford and Lane Fox clearly felt they were on to something now, but they were put off their stride when the Ulster Unionist Kinloch-Cooke, who made a point of tackling Churchill on naval matters, unwisely asked whether it were true that more than once over the last months the Sea Lords had threatened to resign. It was the wrong question, too specific and obviously based on rumour. The First Lord was able to reply, quite correctly: 'There is absolutely no truth in that suggestion'. Before Lane Fox could re-join the fray, the speaker ruled that as eight supplementary questions had been asked the matter was now closed.[11]

Round One to Churchill. In a statement to the House the following day he repeated his insistence that Bridgeman's health and strength had become 'no longer sufficient to enable him ... to sustain the responsibilities of his great office'. He had had no difference of 'view or policy' with him and was filled with the 'greatest regret' that their official association should have come to an end.[12]

Sandars pleaded that the Commons clash had not been his fault and he had done his best to stop it. Even so, he warned Bridgeman, the fat was now in fire. As Churchill had 'made a grievously bad impression as regards his own veracity,' he explained, 'the matter does not end here.' Once again he begged his friend to come clean and make a statement to the *Yorkshire Post* about his health. He even went as far as writing out the announcement for him![13] Bridgeman did not take his advice.

The 'topic of the hour' took another twist when a Special Correspondent' of the *Standard* reported from Harrogate on Friday 13 December 1912:

> 'I have just seen the healthiest invalid in England – Sir Francis Bridgeman. Whatever may have been the mysterious cause of the First Sea Lord's resignation, certainly it was not ill-health. The admiral refused to discuss the circumstances of his retirement, but could not disguise the fact that he was in vigorous health.
>
> Asked if his demise was voluntary or on grounds of sickness, he replied smilingly: 'The answer is in the negative.'

Ignoring this Delphic pronouncement, the correspondent went on to labour the point about Bridgeman 'enjoying the best of health and all the robust pleasures of an English country gentleman,' explaining that he rode to hounds three times a week when he was 'generally well up to the front'. He concluded, 'Mr Churchill's excuses are ridiculed by all who know Sir Francis'.[14]

If Bridgeman had really wanted to scotch all rumours, he could have made a much better job of it. By carrying on with his hunting and making enigmatic statements to the press, he had succeeded only in stoking a fire which he supposedly wished to extinguish. Such contradictory behaviour stemmed from his inability to make up his mind what he really wanted to do. In the end it would be made up for him. Until then the untidy scandal rumbled inexorably on.

On Saturday 14 December *The Times* picked up the *Standard*'s story and ran with it. Under substantial headlines – 'Mr Churchill Refuted', 'Why Sea Lord Resigned', 'No Ill-Health', 'Flat Contradiction By Sir Francis Bridgeman' – it spoke of the deepening mystery of the First Sea Lord's retirement, about which 'a vast number of people' were dissatisfied. Bridgeman was not ill, the paper explained:

> 'As a matter of fact he was suffering from a slight chill some weeks ago, but that fact merely coincided with his visit to Yorkshire, which was arranged months ago.'

Sounding remarkably Beresford-esque, the paper's Naval Correspondent broadened the issue into a full-scale attack on 'the dictatorial methods of Mr Churchill's Admiralty regime'. He declared:

> 'It is well known in Admiralty circles that Mr Churchill objects to the First Sea Lord having any views of his own, and rupture with a strong man like Sir Francis Bridgeman, it was clear from the first, was sure to come. Under present methods the First Sea Lord's position is untenable except by a man prepared to bow to Mr Churchill and accept the new tyranny.'

Bridgeman's dismissal for refusing to accept 'amateur ideas' was 'a positive danger to the country'. Then followed criticism of Churchill's *Enchantress* trips and his habit of gathering ideas from junior officers 'over port at dinner and elaborating them in Whitehall,' causing 'a lot of useless and stupid enquiries and investigations'. It was wholly unacceptable, the correspondent said, to have 'the most serious and important position the country has to offer in the hands of an impetuous amateur,' for all his brilliance as a politician, author and letter-writer. He ended up in stentorian tones worthy of his paper's nickname:

> 'Sir Francis Bridgeman's ejection from the Admiralty is a scandal and display of tyranny; and the official explanation given is not only 'meaningless and silly', but it is a frigid,

calculated and deliberate 'terminological inexactitude', for which the Royal Navy fortunately has no equal ... [Churchill's] continuation at the Admiralty is not only a danger to the respect and tradition of English public life, but a real and dangerous menace to our life as a powerful nation.'

It is significant and rather sad that the article, like virtually all material written on the subject, makes much of Churchill's wickedness but little of Bridgeman's virtues apart from his 'robust health'. No one was prepared to say that in dismissing his First Sea Lord Churchill had deprived the Navy of a fine commander at a time of national peril. In the end, Bridgeman's modest personality and unspectacular virtues were among the First Lord's most powerful weapons.

There was nothing in the thundering of *The Times* to suggest that its accusations arose out of discussion with Bridgeman. Its criticism, though strident, is expressed in general terms unsubstantiated by specific evidence. This was not the case with the piece that appeared in the *Morning Post* the same morning. Claiming that its correctness was 'vouched for on the very best authority', the paper put forward a piece of information that seemed 'in obvious conflict' with the gist if not the precise meaning of Churchill's reply to Kinloch-Cooke's question in the Commons:

'Some time ago the late First Sea Lord took the initiative in urging his colleagues on the Board of Admiralty to tender their resignations on the subject of Pay and Manning in the Navy. This resolution was conveyed to the Prime Minister by Mr Winston Churchill, and it is not unreasonable to suppose that the result was the recent statement by the First Lord providing a general increase of pay.'[15]

The First Lord was furious at the *Post* not only for making public the Board's threat of mutiny but also for implying that it was they, not he, that had stood firm over improved manning and pay. He was equally annoyed by an announcement at the end of the article that he had offered Bridgeman the honour of Admiral of the Fleet. The last thing he wanted was for the Crown to become involved in the unsavoury fracas now rapidly developing.

As the *Post* had obviously had access to inside information, Churchill wrote to Bridgeman at once. The letter and the offending newspaper article were delivered to Copgrove at 2 am on Sunday morning. Such was Churchill's determination to arm himself for the coming fray, the delivery boy was under instruction not to leave until he had a reply.

The First Lord's tone was tough and businesslike. The flattery of his earlier letters was quite gone, replaced by a mix of condescension and threat that in places verged on blackmail. He began by admitting that the 'gross breach of official confidence' had not emanated from Bridgeman himself. Nevertheless, as the matter was now certain to be debated in Parliament, he wished to be free 'to deal fully and plainly with the facts' in order to 'guard and sustain' Bridgeman's 'professional reputation and personal dignity'. By suggesting that the ex-First Sea Lord's reputation needed guarding, he had cleverly if unscrupulously seized the higher ground.

He then asked for Bridgeman's concurrence on three statements. The first two were uncontentious: that they had been in full agreement over the manning and pay proposals. 'If the matter is disputed,' he warned unkindly,

> 'I should be forced to state that during your whole tenure as Second Sea Lord you made no proposals for increasing the pay, and that no proposals for increasing the pay either of officers or of men emanated from you during your tenure as First Sea Lord.'

The third statement was less straightforward:

> 'I have your authority in saying that no other cause of difference or disagreement in policy or view existed between us which had led, or was about to lead, to your resignation.'

As Bridgeman had, as far as we know, only threatened resignation, technically speaking this was correct. But such a blanket declaration disguised the truth of what had passed between the two men over the last year. Once again, to win compliance with his wishes Churchill bullied. If Bridgeman would not endorse the three statements, Churchill said it would be 'necessary' for him to publish their correspondence since 28 November, together with the 'confessional' letters Bridgeman had written to Battenberg and Beatty prior to this. His letter ended with a repetition of the statements Bridgeman was required to accept and a postscript wondering if he had any idea who had leaked the admiral of the Fleet proposal.[16]

It was an exemplary piece of prose – clear, forthright and brilliantly conceived. Churchill had in his possession evidence in Bridgeman's own hand of his wish to retire. He could argue, therefore, that in asking his First Sea Lord to step down he had merely been fulfilling the Admiral's own wish. Bridgeman could have countered this only by explaining that ill-health alone had not caused his disillusionment, and then listing all the other reasons. That would have shaken the Admiralty – indeed, the whole Royal Navy – to its very core. It would have been a very painful act for a man of Bridgeman's integrity at any time, but when international tension was so high it was inconceivable. Whatever his personal feelings, could he at the end contemplate damaging the Service to which he had devoted his entire career?

Not for the first time in his life Bridgeman had been out-manoeuvred by a more agile, more politically astute mind. By the time he had read Churchill's letter and thought through its implications, it must have been three o'clock in the morning, hardly the best time to make level judgements. Should he resist, and so risk ruining his reputation and undermining the position of the Admiralty? Or should he let Churchill have his way, even though he knew this would mean being party to half-truths and leaving in power a man whose impetuosity and amateurisms might one day bring real disaster on his country? In the end, no doubt having chatted the matter over with Emily, he cabled Churchill:

'Absolutely agree to all you say. I don't know where the 'Morning Post' article came from, but it's untrue. Am coming to London today; address Grosvenor Hotel; if you wish to see me will call tomorrow. – Bridgeman.' [17]

A few hours later, comfortably settled in the Grosvenor, he changed his mind.

'I now have time to amplify my telegram,' he wrote to Churchill, although 'amplify' hardly described the back-peddling he was about to indulge in. His cabled response to the pay and manning issues, delivered in what he now considered to have been 'general terms', still held good.

'But with regard to your third question, as to whether we have had no other causes of difference or disagreement in policy or view which might have led to my resignation, you will recollect that on more than one occasion such differences have arisen on matters of serious importance. For example, I need only refer to a recent question of an appointment which involved so grave a conflict of opinion that I felt obliged to suggest my resignation.'

He added a request that if Churchill published his previous 'private' letters, this letter should be made public too. A postscript, in which he said he had had 'no communication with the press' and had not 'authorised' (strange word) Beresford's questions in Parliament but had 'made no secret of the fact that I declined your offer to submit my name to His Majesty for the promotion to Admiral of the Fleet,' was deleted by Churchill before the letter was printed.[18]

Why the change of heart? The only realistic reason, the one that Churchill himself accepted, was that at some time on 15 December Bridgeman had once again been got at by Churchill's political opponents and persuaded it was his duty not to let the First Lord get away with 'terminal inexactitude'.[19] It is fair to assume that Bridgeman agreed to this only reluctantly. His amplification letter to Churchill had been moderate and at no time in the stormy days ahead, when he could easily have made the First Lord's position a great deal more difficult by writing to the press, did he break his silence. As a result, yet again he provided potential allies with sufficient ammunition to start a fight, but not enough to win it.

If Bridgeman thought his latest turn in the epistolary skirmish would give him the upper hand, he was wrong. Churchill dismissed his reservations as immaterial. 'It is quite true,' he pointed out,

> 'that differences of view have from time to time arisen between us as, between all persons who work together in the difficult business of government; but none of these differences led to your tendering your resignation, and all were adjusted to our mutual satisfaction by the ordinary process of frank and friendly discussion. None were [later corrected to 'was'] outstanding between us at the time of your departure to Copgrove.'

That there were no outstanding differences between them, he went on, was confirmed by Bridgeman's letter of 3 December in which he had declared himself willing to continue in office.

In a 'Most Secret' postscript that Churchill had erased from the correspondence printed for the Cabinet, he reprimanded Bridgeman for talking openly about the Admiral of the Fleet suggestion. This had placed the First Lord in 'particular embarrassment' regarding the King who 'may feel aggrieved that a proposal which he had disapproved should be represented in the press as having been offered and rejected'. Finally, still hoping to bring the whole business to a conclusion 'thoroughly agreeable' to Bridgeman's 'dignity and reputation', Churchill said he thought it would not be necessary for him to publish their correspondence and suggested they meet in the First Lord's room at the Admiralty at 4.40 pm to iron out any remaining difficulties.[20]

Unfortunately, by the time this letter reached the Grosvenor, Bridgeman had already gone back to Yorkshire in a huff. He left Churchill this curt note:

'Since I have not received any reply to my telegram to you asking whether you desired to see me, I am returning to the country this morning [Monday 16th].'[21]

Churchill responded the same day. He began by apologising for his part in their failure to meet. It is possible, however, that he had deliberately stayed out of Bridgeman's way. He did not like confrontation and had, it will be recalled, got Bridgeman to take Wilson his letter of dismissal rather than deliver it himself. The parallels between the two occasions are intriguing.

The second part of Churchill's letter put further pressure on Bridgeman to agree some form of words regarding his resignation as reports of 'fundamental differences' between them over Admiralty policy were likely to be exploited by the opposition to Prime Minister Borden in Canada.[22] Bridgeman, clearly fed up with bandying words, replied curtly that he had set out his position in his Grosvenor Hotel letter of Sunday and had nothing to add to it. With that, he dashed off a quick note to Sandars saying he wanted his 'affairs leaving alone', swapped his pen for a gun and went out shooting.[23]

Bridgeman's irritated tone may have owed something to a fawning letter of support he had just received from Beresford. After expressing 'entire sympathy' for his old colleague over the 'villainous' way he had been treated, Lord Charles declared that he had taken up the case not so much on Bridgeman's behalf but to defend the Navy from a 'young, arrogant and ignorant individual' who had created a 'serious danger to the State' by dismissing a First Sea Lord merely because he disagreed with him 'on questions of a technical character in which expert knowledge is essential'. Beresford was intelligent enough to realise Bridgeman would have been unimpressed if his new ally had pretended they had not had their differences. If anything was to win him over it would be an appeal to put the Service before personal feelings.

The main purpose of Beresford's writing, however, was not to let Bridgeman know of his support. Lord Charles wanted information to use in Parliament. Knowing his correspondent's integrity, he put his request as subtly as he knew how:

The First Lord of the Admiralty to Sir Francis:

"Then you don't agree with my notions:
"Then you must be very ill and unfit for your post."

C.W.C. Chapman   17.12.1912

This cartoon, apparently never before published, found among Bridgeman's papers

'If I can be of any use to you in any way in this matter please let me know, and whatever you tell me to prove the case you can rely upon me not to mention those things you do not want mentioned; but you will see that as the case of going to a lawyer, the person who fights the case must know as much as possible.'

He ended with gentlemanly courtesy, sending Emily his compliments and his sympathy 'in an affair which must give her great anxiety'.[24] In all his correspondence Churchill never mentioned Lady Bridgeman once.

Bridgeman passed on no information to enable Beresford, the honest lawyer, to fight his case. But he did send Churchill an irate telegram reminding him that if their correspondence was to be published,

'you must not omit the reference in my letters to the fact that on other matters we have differed to the extent that I suggested resignation.'[25]

Back came Churchill at once. The gloves were now off and the friendly 'My Dear Sir Francis' and 'Yours very sincerely' of his early letters had now become the formal 'Dear Sir Francis Bridgeman' and 'Yours very truly'. Whereas Bridgeman had said he had *suggested* resignation, Churchill deliberately ignored this:

'I cannot accept the statement contained in your telegram just received by me. You have never on any occasion tendered your resignation to me. No resignation by you was threatened or impending at the time of your retirement.'

The positions of both men were technically correct. Bridgeman had threatened resignation without ever officially tendering it. He had last done so in early or mid-November but the matter had been cleared up before he retired to Copgrove, so was not outstanding at the time of his dismissal.

After going over old ground yet again, Churchill criticised

Bridgeman as 'unworthy' for not disassociating himself publicly from unfounded statements in the press. He ended in angry voice:

> 'I shall certainly not place any reliance upon your authority in any statement I may have to make, or quote you in any way as agreeing with me.' [26]

Rumours and leaks were now coming thick and fast. Old Sir Michael Culme-Seymour had briefed a friendly Tory MP, Edward Fitzroy, with suitable parliamentary questions and someone was passing information out of the Admiralty so fast that Churchill was threatening to use the Official Secrets Act to plug the leak.[27] On Wednesday 18th he was again challenged in Parliament, this time by Beresford and Kinloch-Cooke in conjunction with Fitzroy. There was a good deal of wrangling and Churchill managed to avoid Beresford's only useful question – had Bridgeman ever threatened to resign 'on questions of difference of opinion between himself and the First Lord connected with technical matters regarding expert opinion' – by saying he required prior notice before answering. He did, however, admit to having consulted with the Prime Minister about Bridgeman's health before asking him to resign. Dissatisfied with what he had heard, Fitzroy stated that he would raise the whole issue again in Friday's Adjournment Debate.[28]

With the Bridgeman Question now on the agenda for a full Parliamentary debate, the Opposition were desperate for further revelations. After Wednesday's exchange of questions in the House, Beresford once more pressed Bridgeman for 'any points ... particularly with regard to facts connected with the affectionate letter of 28th November and the insolent letter which followed'.[29] As on the last occasion, Bridgeman kept his own counsel. He did so again when approached by the Hon William Bridgeman, a distant cousin and leading Tory backbencher, who wrote that as it would not be in the public interest for Churchill to 'get out free from blame' at his ex-First Sea Lord's expense, Bridgeman should make a 'full statement'.[30]

It is difficult to work out quite what Bridgeman *did* want at this stage. He clearly abhorred the idea of a debate and would not meet the Opposition's requests for information. At the same time he did not want Churchill to get away with having been sparing with the truth. Since Churchill had made his side of the story public, it is difficult to see how Bridgeman hoped to challenge him only in private correspondence. Did he really think the First Lord could admit privately that they had, after all, had their differences at the Admiralty, while at the same time holding publicly to his line that Bridgeman had retired for health reasons? If he did that, when the truth got out, as it inevitably would, Churchill's political career would be finished. Perhaps as he cantered gently about the Yorkshire countryside Bridgeman genuinely did not realise what he had done. By not openly supporting the First Lord, he had allowed him to be driven into a corner from which he now had to fight his way out. And when it came to fighting, there was no better man than Churchill.

NOTES

1. 8/12/1912, Sandars to Bridgeman, L.L.P.P.
2. 11/12/1912, *ibid.*
3. 10/12/1912, *ibid.*
4. Undated, *ibid.*
5. 12/12/1912, Sandars to Bridgeman, *ibid.*
6. L.L.P.P.
7. 11/12/1912, Balcarres to Sandars, *ibid.*
8. 9/12/1912 & 11/12/1912, Sandars to Bridgeman, *ibid.*
9. 16/12/1912, Durnford to Bridgeman, L.L.P.P., 11/12/1912 & 12/12/1912, Sandars to Bridgeman, *ibid.*
10. 11/12/1912, Sandars to Bridgeman, *ibid.* Durnford says Churchill had asked Lane Fox to bowl him an easy question but he had refused after reading the First Lord's correspondence with Bridgeman; 16/12/1912, Durnford to Bridgeman, L.L.P.P.
11. 14/12/1912, *The Times.* The Parliamentary exchange was recorded in manuscript on House of Commons notepaper, L.L.P.P. See also *Hansard*, 11/12/1912, vol. XIV, 1912.
12. *Hansard*, 12/12/1912, *ibid.*
13. 11/12/1912 & 12/12/1912, Sandars to Bridgeman, L.L.P.P.
14. 14/12/1912, Sandars to Bridgeman, *ibid.*
15. See above, p. 195.
16. 14/12/1912, L.L.P.P.
17. 15/12/1912, *ibid.*
18. *Ibid.*
19. 21/12/1912, Churchill to Bridgeman, *ibid.*

20   16/12/1912, *ibid.*

21   *Ibid.*

22   *Ibid.* The reference to the situation in Canada did not appear in the version of the letter printed for the cabinet.

23   17/12/1912, *ibid.* 17/12/1912 & 18/12/1912, Sandars to Bridgeman, *ibid.*

24   16/12/1912, *ibid.*

25   18/12/1912, *ibid.*

26   *Ibid.*

27   18/12/1912 & 19/12/1912, Sandars to Bridgeman, *ibid.*

28   *Hansard*, 18/12/1912, vol. XIV, 1912.

29   18/12/1912, Beresford to Bridgeman, *ibid.*

30   18/12/1912, Hon W C Bridgeman to Sir Francis Bridgeman, *ibid.*

13 Party Purposes

The Bridgeman Question was raised by the Opposition during the adjournment debate on the morning of Friday 20 December, 1912.[1] As Bridgeman feared, although a sensational political occasion, it was in Lord Wemyss' words 'damnable, undignified and extremely bad for the Service in particular'.[2] The debate was opened by Culme-Seymour's friend, the future speaker Edward Fitzroy. He was acting, he said, because of the 'uneasy feeling' in the Navy and the country at large 'as to the fairness of the treatment which Sir Francis Bridgeman has received'. Two questions needed answering: Did the First Lord believe he alone could be the judge of whether Bridgeman had been fit enough to continue at his post? And had he had differences of opinion with the admiral that had led to his threatening resignation?

After a brief Liberal intervention that sought to belittle Beresford and make out that the resignation issue had been raised not for the good of the Navy but 'merely for party purposes', the Irish peer himself rose to his feet. This was the moment MPs had been waiting for. The Commons was always good theatre when Beresford was around. Following a few introductory remarks, during which Churchill laughed and expressed surprise that the Noble Lord should be speaking on behalf of someone with whom he was known not to be friends, Beresford came round to his main point.[3] Although put with little eloquence, wit or incisiveness, he got to the heart of the matter reasonably well. But he was severely hampered by lack of specific evidence.

'I want to know whether the First Lord of the Admiralty misled the Crown, misled the Prime Minister and the Cabinet,' he drawled with an effort at oratory, 'into believing that the First Sea Lord was unfit to carry out his duties'. He then talked vaguely of Churchill's letters to Bridgeman, of which he clearly had only second-hand knowledge, claiming that the second said in effect:

'You are ill; you shall be ill; I order you to be ill.' Then: 'If
you keep silent' – I do not say he said this, but it is the
inference I draw – 'If you keep silent I will make you a GCB
and an Admiral of the Fleet.' ... The First Lord's policy is one
of bribes and threats. It has occurred before ...'

After an interruption he went on:

'What was the real reason why Sir Francis Bridgeman had to
go? Because he would not agree with the autocratic methods
of the First Lord and because he thought on technical
questions expert opinion should be taken.'

With perfect timing, Churchill now intervened. 'What questions?' he
asked. Of course Beresford did not know the answer and he was not
nimble-minded enough to think of a way round it. Churchill intervened
on several more occasions, each time throwing the Noble Lord out of his
uncertain stride. Beresford huffed and puffed but was unable to get going
again. His statements grew more and more vague, until he was drawn to
confess that the First Lord of the Admiralty was 'an extremely clever
person'.

Churchill relaxed. He knew now that he was safe and began to enjoy
himself. 'What I ask the Noble Lord to do,' he quipped, 'is to state
specifically what he has in his mind – if he has anything in his mind.'
Unable to think of a suitable reply, Beresford resorted to general
accusations about Churchill's conduct as First Lord. He waffled on about
Churchill not behaving in a 'gentlemanly' or 'statesmanlike manner' and
about him undermining the Navy's 'good comradeship' and finally sat
down muttering darkly that it would all lead to disaster if the country
went to war. Sandars' understatement that Bridgeman's case was not in
'clever hands' needed no other vindication.[4]

Churchill began his reply with a few comments on Beresford's
'insinuations of a very gross character'. He would, however, choose to
ignore them. 'I am not one of those who take the Noble Lord too seriously,'

he admitted cruelly, 'I know him too well. He does not mean to be as offensive as he often is when he is speaking on public platforms.' Turning to the specific question of Bridgeman's resignation, Churchill emphasised yet again that it had been 'due to reasons of health, and to reasons of health alone'. He then gambled on Bridgeman and other members of the Board holding their tongues by saying he had been asked:

> '... whether differences had arisen between me and Sir Francis Bridgeman on matters of expert opinion. I know of no such differences, apart from the ordinary discussions which take place between colleagues in the transaction of official business.'

On the matter of resignation threats he was equally bold. 'I do not remember being threatened with his resignation on any occasion', he ventured. 'We were in agreement on all fundamental matters of naval policy.' There was sufficient leeway in both statements to enable him to escape if further information came to light.

Gathering momentum, Churchill gave an edited version of the resignation story. He 'knew nothing of the state of [Bridgeman's] health when he came to the Admiralty, he confessed, and proceeded to Bridgeman's letters to Battenberg and Beatty and his own, 'expressed in terms of the highest consideration,' asking him to retire. The current situation arose, he explained, because his letter was 'so considerately expressed that Sir Francis Bridgeman misapprehended its character'. The admiral was 'a simple man, and thought the letter left him an option'. The First Lord had not told the whole story at first because he had hoped to shield Bridgeman, 'whose health was rapidly reducing him to an invalid's condition,' from public embarrassment. Any other version of events was 'utterly false'.

When he sat down, the issue was as good as dead. Without more specific information on what had gone on at the Admiralty over the past year there was very little the Opposition could do. But Bonar Law did make one last, half-hearted effort. While accepting much that Churchill had said, he pressed two points. The first was,

> 'whether or not it was a fact there had been a difference of opinion sufficiently wide to make him [Sir Francis Bridgeman] say, that if the right hon Gentleman carried out his view he would resign.'

Churchill, perhaps recalling Bridgeman's own admission that he had suggested resignation, replied, 'Sir Francis Bridgeman never made any statement such as that to me'. Instead of taking the matter further by asking Churchill whether the question of the First Sea Lord's resignation had arisen in any form at any time, after a few further comments Bonar Law moved on to his second point, the manner in which Bridgeman's resignation had been demanded.

Churchill's first letter, Bonar Law admitted, had been 'very nice'; but the follow up, clarifying Churchill's desire that the First Sea Lord step down, 'was one that Sir Francis Bridgeman could not but regard as insulting'. It would have been fairer and more courteous to have seen him and talked to him face to face. In case Churchill thought these remarks unmerited, Bonar Law asked him to let the House decide by producing the resignation correspondence. Churchill readily agreed and read the letters, but only as far as Bridgeman's of 4 December that had ended, 'I am happy to be able to meet with your wishes'. The contentious and potentially much more damaging later exchanges he left unread.

The Government benches gave Churchill vociferous support when he finished. They knew the First Lord had ridden out the storm. Bonar Law had to content himself with the observation that Bridgeman had received 'brutal treatment'. Churchill had misled him with his first letter, which contained no more than a suggestion, and then hit him with the second by declaring his 'decision' was final. It was a fair point, but hardly one over which Churchill could be forced to resign.

Reactions to the debate were mixed. The press reported along party lines. The Liberals and their supporters (which now included *The Times* – 'got at' by Churchill 'very early in the proceedings') were obviously delighted with the First Lord's performance.[5] The Opposition, staunchly backed by the *Morning Post*, were more critical. The *Globe* denounced Churchill's methods as 'wholly unfitted for the great Service of which for the time being he is the responsible head'.[6] Beresford thought Bonar Law's intervention had been 'quite excellent' and looked forward to discovering much more about the 'disgraceful affair'.[7] He was right in thinking there was more, but wrong in believing it could be got hold of. Perhaps sensing this, after a few days he took himself off to Cannes for a holiday.[8]

Bridgeman did not accede to the requests from the Opposition Chief Whip and his old commander-in-chief, Sir Michael Culme-Seymour, that he ask Churchill to publish all their correspondence. Neither would he do so himself, nor would he permit anyone else to urge Churchill to do so.[9] On 23 December he wrote to Bonar Law thanking him for what he had 'very kindly' said on his behalf. But there he now wished the matter to stop.

> 'I now desire to say that I am still more anxious that the case should not be re-opened: no good from my point of view could result and these unhappy differences do much harm to the great Service I have the honour to belong [to]. I feel that you will agree with me that the welfare of the Navy is a matter of first class importance, and that many things should be sacrificed to the maintenance of its hitherto high traditions. I am seeing Balcarres shortly and propose repeating this to him.' [10]

In the best cloak-and-dagger tradition, the meeting with Balcarres took place clandestinely at either Manchester Exchange or Leeds Central railway station.[11] Within a few weeks most people had lost interest in the Bridgeman affair. It was old news. Churchill had survived and the focus of public attention turned to far weightier matters at home, across the Irish Sea and in continental Europe.

Some naval men believed the crisis had been mishandled. Sir Michael Culme-Seymour blamed Beresford:

> 'I cannot but feel that Charlie Beresford got a proper dressing down from Churchill & that it was quite deserved: it is such a pity that with all his charming personality, he is such a fool without any common sense whatever.' [12]

The Culme-Seymours were not altogether happy with Bonar Law's flabby performance, either. Two-and-a-half years later Sir Michael Culme-Seymour wrote to his father: 'You will recollect how he [Bonar Law] messed up the Bridgeman case & let it go ... [He] never took the trouble to understand it'.[13] This is true. But in defence of Bonar Law it should be pointed out that when he heard Bridgeman was not prepared to help by providing further information, he tried to get the subject of the Adjournment Debate changed. Beresford was the sticking point. Despite a half-hour chat with Lord Balcarres, Lord Charles believed he had Churchill on the rack and insisted on going ahead.[14] As a result he was humiliated. Bonar Law avoided a similar fate by limiting himself to minor points. He knew that only if Churchill slipped up would the Opposition be able to press home their attack. Churchill did not slip and so Bonar Law did not press. The First Lord may have cursed Bridgeman for behaviour that brought him to court; but he should also have been grateful to him for the silent part he played in getting him acquitted.

And what of Bridgeman himself? We don't know whether he was in London on the Friday of the debate, but he was certainly there on the Saturday. And he was not happy. He was particularly annoyed that Churchill had cited his private correspondence but had not followed his request also to read the Grosvenor Hotel letter of 15 December in which he had talked of their differences and of his suggesting resignation. As a consequence, he felt he 'had no choice' but to urge Churchill to publish all their correspondence forthwith.[15]

Churchill wrote back at once saying that he saw 'no reason to object to a further publication of [their] correspondence'. He then went through all their letters one by one, saying that references to the King and other persons not relevant to the argument should be omitted and adding his own interpretations. These included:

> '... in its proper place will come your letter written from the Grosvenor Hotel ... , when under what influence I cannot determine you go back on your spontaneous first thoughts and allow yourself to become the tool of party attack. My letter of 16th December must be published, as it deals with the alleged incident of your threatening resignation, and shows the proper proportions of the affair. In this connection I may remind you that it is the Naval Secretary, and not the First Sea Lord, who by long-established custom advises the First Lord on naval appointments, and even if it were true that you threatened to resign, which I was certainly not aware of, it would have been a most unreasonable and improper occasion. Had your resignation been tendered on such a subject I should have been bound to accept it forthwith.'

Needless to say, he also asked that this letter too be included in those published. In case Bridgeman chose to go ahead, he added a further paragraph on the question of his health. As well as going over the old ground, he added the fact that the First Sea Lord had missed half of the CID meetings he was supposed to have attended and on one occasion when he was present he had been 'forced to leave from sudden faintness'. He reinforced still further his self-generated image as the honourable guardian of the older man's good name by ending:

> 'If you desire that a further publication shall be made I shall not resist your wishes. But I warn you most earnestly that I would be deeply injurious to your reputation. That is the last service which I can render you.' [16]

The letter was undoubtedly a gamble on Churchill's part. Although publication of the correspondence, particularly the Grosvenor Hotel letter in which he went back on his earlier agreement with Churchill, would have discredited Bridgeman, the whole unseemly wrangle would have reflected poorly on Churchill. Although he claimed not to have remembered Bridgeman's offer to resign, there was enough in Bridgeman's letters to indicate that the First Lord had not been quite straight when he told the Commons his disagreements with Bridgeman had been no more than 'ordinary discussions which take place between colleagues in the transaction of official business'. Churchill knew this and he followed his latest letter to Bridgeman with one to the King asking him to warn Bridgeman 'of the deplorable folly of persisting further on disclosures damaging only to himself'. He also sent the resignation correspondence to the Palace, asking that the King should look through it before receiving Bridgeman. It would show, he explained, how the ex-First Sea Lord had been repeatedly making small and false points 'to lend colour to vague insinuations,' and how he had also 'allowed his mind to be poisoned by persons who wish to make party attacks in Parliament'. Stamfordham replied that the King did not want to become involved in the matter but would leave it in Churchill's hands to deal with as he deemed best.[17]

The King might not have intervened directly, but he did have some influence on events. At his audience with Bridgeman on the afternoon of Saturday 21 December he deplored the way the resignation issue had become 'not only public property but a party question' and urged Bridgeman to act with restraint for the good of the Navy and the country at large.[18] Bridgeman duly obliged. Hence his letter to Balfour and his secret assignment with Balcarres in a station buffet. When he had returned to Copgrove he wrote to Churchill saying he wished to reply to his 'threatening' letter 'with emphasis'.

> 'However after consulting with a High Personage I had already been led to the conclusion that the publication of our correspondence would not conduce to the interests of the Service.
>
> I accordingly withdraw my claim that the complete and unedited correspondence which has passed between us should be published.'[19]

On Christmas Eve Churchill wrote back endorsing Bridgeman's decision not to bring their correspondence into the public domain. Even now he would concede not an inch. 'The matter was however one for you to decide,' he wrote.

> 'I have not desired for any reason which concerns myself to prevent a publication. I wished you to decide freely. I am glad you have decided rightly.' [20]

Typically, he had to have the last word.

The Palace was delighted that the matter had been resolved without further scandal. The relief in Stamfordham's letter from Buckingham Palace was palpable:

> 'His Majesty wishes me to say that he is very glad that you have abandoned the idea of a further publication of correspondence and that he thinks your letter to Churchill a very dignified one –
>
> If I may be allowed to say so, your decision to let the matter drop is the best thing you could have done for the name of the Service; and you have subordinated your own feelings to the interest of the Navy. I only hope Churchill will realize this and appreciate your action ...
>
> I am convinced that you have done the right and the unselfish thing – I trust you will have no further worry and that you have a peaceful and happy new year in store.
>
> Please give my kind regards to Lady Bridgeman ...' [21]

The matter was not quite dead. After Christmas Battenberg warned Churchill that Admiral Meux was continuing to stir up trouble by saying that Bridgeman had gone 'for reasons beside health'. There are some indications that Bridgeman himself was not quite as discrete as he might have been. Admiral Durnford wrote to him on Boxing Day offering to delve further into the matter at the ex-First Sea Lord's request.[22] The new First Sea Lord was also worried that his predecessor's inaccurate statements 'based on recollections' were conveying 'an altogether wrong impression'.[23] He need not have worried. Only Beresford, when he returned from the Mediterranean, was still hopeful of discomforting Churchill. Bridgeman and Balcarres were keen that the whole sorry business be forgotten. Even the vituperative Sandars could see 'no further advantage to be gained by extending the controversy in the Commons'. Nevertheless, he still hoped that one day perdition would 'seize that ... lying scoundrel who sits in the name of First Lord'!

On 29 December Bridgeman told Stamfordham that he was using every bit of influence he possessed to arrest 'deep-laid agitation against Churchill'. He was almost certainly exaggerating and this one remark is hardly convincing evidence for Randolph Churchill's assertion that he bore Churchill no malice.[24] He did, but for the moment was prepared to keep it to himself. By way of consolation, as he settled down to a life of retirement with Emily, he convinced himself that his sacking had been a sort of back-handed compliment. 'I was fired *without* warning,' he told Additional Sea Lord Sir Francis Hopwood, ' ... not because I was too weak, but because I was too strong!'[25] It was not a completely erroneous judgement.

It is not immediately apparent today why for a few hectic days the Bridgeman Question should have caused such a furore. We need to see it in the context of the extremely bitter party conflict that had arisen since the Liberal landslide of 1906 and the sequence of radical measures introduced by the administrations of Campbell-Bannerman and Asquith. The Lord's opposition to Lloyd George's budget of 1909, leading to two elections in 1910 and the curbing of the Upper House's powers, left the Opposition feeling intensely angry and frustrated. The political temperature had been further raised by the looming crisis over the Liberal's Irish Home Rule, introduced in the spring of 1912. In all this Churchill, the brilliant, taunting orator, was a *bête noire* to many on the opposite side of the House and they eagerly seized any opportunity, however slight, to try to damage him.

The fact that the Bridgeman Question was a naval scandal was also important. As a result of the rapid expansion of the German fleet and the series of dangerous international crises, the nation's interest in the Royal

Navy was higher than at any time for more than a century. Its financial commitment to the Service was even greater. In 1901 the Army and Navy had shared some £61 million equally between them. By 1913 the Naval Estimates were £51.5 million (approximately one-quarter of the government's total revenue budgeted for) compared with the Army's £28.8 million. That such a hugely costly and militarily vital Service might be anything other than expertly manned and professionally managed was extremely alarming.

In some ways the whole business did not matter. Bridgeman would have retired anyway in 1913, before the outbreak of hostilities. Battenberg, his replacement, blamed for the Navy's patent unpreparedness for modern warfare and unfairly hounded because of his German ancestry, submitted his resignation in October 1914. But from another point of view the scandal over Bridgeman's resignation was important. Churchill had survived and dominated the Admiralty in a manner rarely, if ever, seen before by a First Lord. Had Bridgeman been more of a politician or less of a gentleman, the outcome of his tussle with the First Lord might have been different. If Churchill and his First Sea Lord had fallen together, the history of Britain, even of the whole world, would have been very different.

Churchill inspecting cadets of HMS St Vincent, *c.1913*

NOTES

1   The full report is in *Hansard* vol. XIV, 1912, from which all extracts are taken.

2   Lady Wemyss, ed., *Lord Wester Wemyss*, p. 141.

3   Bridgeman was supposed to have opposed Beresford being made an Admiral of the Fleet. Perhaps he recalled the incident with the Russians off Tangier?

4   19/12/1912, to Bridgeman, L.L.P.P.

5   21/12/1912, Captain E A Fitzroy to Sir Michael Culme-Seymour, L.L.P.P.

6   21/12/12.

7   20/12/1912, Beresford to Bonar Law, cited in Randolph Churchill, *Winston S Churchill*, ii, pp. 636-7.

8   27/12/1912, Balcarres to Bridgeman, L.L.P.P.

9   20/12/1912, Balcarres to Bridgeman, *ibid.*; 22/12/1912 Sir Michael Culme-Seymour to Lady Bridgeman, *ibid.*

10 *Ibid.*

11 22/12/1912, Bridgeman to Balcarres, *ibid.*

12 22/12/1912, Sir Michael Culme-Seymour to Lady Bridgeman, *ibid.*

13 April 1915, S.W.P.C.

14 22/12/1912, Sir Michael Culme-Seymour to Lady Bridgeman, L.L.P.P.

15 *Ibid.*

16 *Ibid.*

17 Randolph Churchill, *Winston S Churchill*, ii, p. 637 and *Companion* III, p. 1690.

18 *Companion*, p. 1691.

19 Randolph Churchill, *Winston S Churchill*, ii, p. 640.

20 L.L.P.P.

21 24/12/1912, *ibid.*

22 *Ibid.*

23 Randolph Churchill, *Winston S Churchill*, ii, Companion III, p. 1994.

24 Randolph Churchill, *Winston S Churchill*, ii, pp. 640-1

25 Cited in Marder, *From Dreadnought to Scapa Flow*, p. 259.

14 Bitter-sweet

Bridgeman retired from the Royal Navy altogether on 11 December 1913, almost exactly a year after he had left the Admiralty. We do not know what he did with that year on half-pay, but it would be heartening to think he took Emily on the extended holiday for which he had been longing for several years. Even if the couple just stayed peacefully at home, the chance to relax, free from the worry and hassle that had driven him to depression and illness, must have been very welcome.

In all likelihood Bridgeman had by now had enough of the Navy. For Fisher, who revelled in theory, planning, grand strategy and debate but was unremarkable as a practical sailor, the years at the Admiralty were the apogee of his career; all his life he had longed to be First Sea Lord and

By courtesy of the National Portrait Gallery, London

Ernest Moore's portrait of Bridgeman, 1925. It appeared in the Illustrated London News, *Exhibition of Country Portraiture: Men of Yorkshire*

when the chance came he seized it with all the fire and verve of a revolutionary. Bridgeman's Navy was primarily about ships, sailors and the sea, and his happiest years were those spent in command of great fleets. So when the hands-on pleasures which he had enjoyed for most of his career were denied him, replaced by paperwork and politics, his desire to remain in the Service had withered.

This sad, unspoken disillusionment may help explain his contradictory behaviour during the final weeks of 1912. The sense of duty and propriety that had kept him at his desk had inspired his half-hearted, incoherent resistance to Churchill's attempt to prize him from it. Yet there must have been a part of him that saw resignation as bringing welcome relief from the nightmare his career had become. So when obedience to duty, in the form of a request from the King that he drop his feud with the First Lord, coincided with his innermost inclination, he instantly withdrew and left the field to his political master. Perhaps behind his extreme reluctance to take on the job of First Sea Lord in 1911 lay an instinctive feeling, shared by others, that something like this might happen.

From Christmas 1912 onwards Bridgeman disappeared from the national consciousness even quicker than he had slipped into it. When still a serving officer he had put down strong roots in his adopted Yorkshire community and retreated to Copgrove whenever the opportunity arose. His fleeting visits to the capital during the resignation affair suggests that he did not enjoy London and he remained there for as short a time as possible. He had been born and raised in the country, surrounded by farms and woods, and it was in the country that he now intended to pass his remaining years, enjoying the rural pursuits that hitherto he had been able to indulge in only intermittently.

His withdrawal from the public eye was largely self-imposed. Unlike Beresford, he did not take up a second career in national politics (although, as we shall see, he was given an opportunity to do so); nor, as Fisher could not help doing, did he adopt the role of backstage sage, prompter and critic. He wanted to be left alone and those who approached him in the hope of catching some controversial off-the-cuff remark were disappointed.

Finding a 'silent man' who 'shunned publicity', before long they learned to leave him be.[1] If he had something to say, and occasionally he was drawn to break his silence to comment on events (but never on his own resignation), it would be on his own terms, when he chose.

There is every reason to believe Bridgeman mastered his resentment sufficiently to enjoy himself in his declining years, at least until Emily's death deprived him of his best friend and companion. Beatrice, his sole surviving sister, and his brothers George, William and the ebullient Orlando called at Copgrove from time to time. Orlando's three daughters, now married and raising families of their own, also visited. So too did the Pleydell-Bouverie nieces and step-nieces. Emily had always felt that Copgrove's ample rooms and broad gardens were a privilege to be shared and now that her husband was always at her side not many weeks passed without some branch of the family arriving at the doorstep with boxes and suitcases to stay with the ageing but well-loved Uncle Francey and Aunt Emmy.

The Pleydell-Bouverie's at ease, Chiddingford, 1894: Nell the dog, FW the governess, Mildred, Sybil (standing), Edith and her son Humphrey

The *Yorkshire Post* obituary, written by someone who clearly knew Bridgeman well in his later years, remarked how well he adapted to the life of a 'fine type of country gentleman' after more than 50 years in the Navy. His love of sport remained undiminished and although there is no evidence that he ever took up his cricket bat again, he regularly rode with the Bramham Moor and the York and Ainsty Hounds. Only over Christmas in 1913 was he out of the saddle for long, and then only because of an accident.[2] He continued to shoot, too. The obituary remarked that he was 'an expert with the gun', which was either flattery or meant that he had improved after his less than outstanding marksmanship in Australia all those years ago.

More interesting are the *Yorkshire Post*'s observations on Bridgeman's personality, the closest we get to a contemporary character sketch. He had a certain 'breeziness', which the author attributed to 'half a century's life as a sailor'. By this he presumably meant the Admiral's self-protective, cheerful, no-nonsense manner, perhaps occasionally tinged with irritation for those who did not say what they meant. That would certainly be the Bridgeman who struggled so forlornly to cope with the circumlocution and double-speak of officialdom. However, his breezy manner was not cutting; it was 'blended with a gentleness of disposition and courtliness of manner that gained for him' the affection of friends and the admiration of neighbours'.[3] Here too is a portrait we recognise. The more sensitive Bridgeman, the well-mannered gentleman, in the best sense of that word. More than any other qualities, it was his gentleness and ability to get on with everyone he met that had carried him to the highest position in the Navy – but left him sadly ill-equipped when he got there. Ultimately perhaps that did not matter. He might not have shaken up the world or even the Royal Navy, but he had stirred the hearts of hundreds, probably thousands, and given them an example of civilised, decent and considerate behaviour they would not forget. If all the world were populated by Bridgemans, there would be no need for Churchills.

The Copgrove estate required a great deal of management and when not following one of his sporting pleasures Bridgeman spent a lot of time overseeing the team in his employment. Within the house this included at least half-a-dozen maids, kitchen staff, his personal valet, a butler and an odd-job man. The estate was managed by an agent, under whom worked a bailiff, a stud groom, head gardener, head gamekeeper, woodsman, carpenter and several boys and other labourers. As getting this crew working efficiently was not dissimilar from running a ship, Bridgeman cannot have found it too taxing. It may even have helped ease the transition from Service to civil existence.

Bridgeman maintained the tradition, established by James Brown in the first half of the nineteenth century and generously continued by Emily and her mother, that it was the duty of the owners of Copgrove to support and protect the local community. In 1915 he got working conditions at a local armaments factory improved.[4] Although we know nothing of his musical taste or abilities, as an ex-sailor he undoubtedly enjoyed a lusty sing-song. It was appropriate, therefore, that he crowned Emily's refurbishment of the tiny Copgrove Parish Church, scarcely more than a chapel to the Hall, with the gift of a new organ.[5] Acting in consort, Emily and he paid for the village pump at nearby Burton Leonard to be refurbished and planted new trees on the green.[6] The pump and the trees survive to this day.

In a broader sphere Bridgeman took up again his work as a JP and chairman of the Parish Council. No doubt fired by the treatment he had received at the hands of a radical Liberal First Lord, he also became heavily involved in local politics. As in the Navy, he seems to have positioned himself just to the right of centre – not instinctively opposed to change but believing the status quo satisfactory until proved otherwise. Accordingly, he gave active support to the Primrose League, an organisation established in 1883 to promote Disraeli's democratic, one-nation Conservatism. Francis' reforming outlook coincided happily with Emily's, who served as Dame President of the St Wilfrid's Habitation, the Harrogate branch of the League, for some 40 years.[7]

The year after his formal retirement, on the death of Andrew Lawson, Bridgeman was elected Chairman of the Yorkshire Division of the Conservative and Unionist Association. Although there appears to be no record of what he got up to with the local party, he clearly went down well. Early in 1917, on the death of the sitting Conservative and Unionist MP for York, he was asked to fill the vacant seat in the House of Commons. The place would be his without a contest, and although nearing 70 and well past what Jack Sandars wistfully called 'the meridian of life', Bridgeman gave the offer serious consideration. He wrote asking Jack for his opinion.

The reply, written from Torquay, was masterly. It began with a little flattery. Sir Francis was a man of 'local distinction' inspired only by 'public interest' and not personal gain, who would make a 'popular candidate in the best sense of the word'. Then, gently at first but with mounting firmness, came the objections. Would Bridgeman's health (a delicate subject this) stand the strain of Parliamentary hours and prolonged stays in the unwholesome London atmosphere? Did the admiral realise that in the Commons he would get a chance to use his naval expertise only very rarely? Could he tolerate being subject to the demands of the party whip, 'driven to attend debate after debate ... division after division'? Did he want to 'jostle in the competition for place and preferment', swapping the saddle and the pheasant shoot for the thronging lobby and smoky bars filled with middle-aged barristers on the make? 'Frankly', Sandars concluded,

> 'I don't think the life will suit you. I don't think it will suit your health. I don't think the work will be agreeable to you. I don't think you will find the task imposed worth the sacrifice involved'.[8]

Bridgeman did not become Conservative and Unionist MP for York.

Although he continued to fulminate against Churchill in private, Bridgeman made no public pronouncements on naval matters for a year-and-a-half after leaving office. He emerged in June 1914 to engage Percy Scott briefly in the columns of *The Times* on the extent to which submarines and aircraft would revolutionise naval warfare. Afterwards

Scott would criticise Bridgeman unfairly for being against the submarine.[9] He was not. As we have seen, he had a higher opinion of the vessel's capacity than many of his contemporaries and certainly should not be included among the dinosaurs like Sir A K Wilson.[10]

When war came in 1914, as Fisher had so uncannily predicted, many retired flag officers offered their services to the Admiralty and went on to serve both ashore and afloat. Strangely for one of his seniority who had left the active list only in 1913, Bridgeman was not among them.[11] His absence is one of several unexplained mysteries of his career. Was it the continued presence of Churchill or embittered disillusionment that prevented him from putting his name forward officially? And why did the Admiralty apparently not make the first move and seek to take formal advantage of his vast experience, even when Churchill had gone? Certainly, having served for so long and worked so hard to prepare the Home Fleet for action, he found it irksome to stand impotently by and watch events unfolding. 'I long to be afloat, and with my old comrades,' he wrote sadly to Admiral Sir Walter Cowan in 1915.[12]

For the Western Front he advocated a far-sighted strategy of 'restraint', cutting out useless advances, building up defences and relying on the naval blockade to bring Germany to her knees.[13] In 1916 he considered it his duty to write to General Haig warning him about the underhand methods of his latest star recruit, the ex-First Lord of the Admiralty![14] He took great interest, obviously, in the Dardanelles campaign and although we have no precise information he seems to have been somehow involved in post-Jutland naval re-organisation, anti-submarine strategy and plans to put the merchant marine under the control of the Royal Navy.[15] He went down to London only infrequently, however, and although Sandars insisted he must be 'wanted on some committee' and in 1917 he was in discussions with Jellicoe, he took up no formal post.[16]

The ex-First Sea Lord's injured pride may have been eased when he saw what the war did to the reputations of all who had either helped dislodge him or been regarded as his betters. Neither Churchill, nor Battenberg, nor Troubridge, nor Jellicoe escaped unscathed. Battenberg, 'completely broken down' and held responsible for the Navy's obvious unpreparedness for technological warfare, left the Admiralty a couple of months after the outbreak of war.[17] Writing to Bridgeman on 12 November, Sandars agreed that it had been right for Battenberg to go. But he fumed against Churchill for offering Battenberg's unpopular German ancestry as the reason for his resignation rather than the Navy's unsatisfactory performance. As always, Churchill wanted no admissions that might reflect poorly on his work as First Lord. It was the same sort of underhand tactic he had used over Bridgeman's resignation two years previously. 'Doesn't it make you furious,' Sandars growled, 'even if all you can say is it is just like Churchill.'[18] No doubt Bridgeman agreed with him. As we shall see, Troubridge was also brought low, perhaps with the connivance of the same First Lord who had raised him high. Jellicoe's glittering career was tarnished, albeit unfairly, by the events of the Battle of Jutland, 1916. Churchill, having failed to work with Fisher, was ejected from the Admiralty after the Dardanelles disaster. In all likelihood Bridgeman would have performed no better than any of them. But at least by 1916 his very human frailties had been put into a more realistic focus.

Troubridge, Bridgeman's ex-sparring partner from the Navy War Staff, was the first to fall. At the outbreak of war he commanded the British cruiser squadron based at Malta. The revised 'Malta compromise', it will be remembered, envisaged a major force in the eastern Mediterranean, but not before 1915. Fisher's plan, which Bridgeman had tacitly supported, to protect British interests with a considerable torpedo-launching force of submarines and destroyers had been rejected. Until the reinforcements arrived, therefore, the fate of British interests in the area rested with Troubridge's cruisers, although in certain circumstances they might receive support from Sir Archibald Milne's battlecruisers based at Gibraltar.

Sensing British weakness in the region, before the outbreak of war the Germans sent to the Mediterranean their massive battlecruiser *Goeben*, a still larger and more powerful version of the awesome *Von der Tann* that had raised eyebrows at the 1911 Naval Review. Accompanied by the light cruiser *Breslau*, the *Goeben* shelled Algerian ports to hamper French troops crossing to Europe. She then eluded the Gibraltar-based battlecruisers *Indomitable* and *Indefatigable* and headed for neutral Constantinople. *En route*, after refuelling in Messina, off the western coast of Greece, she was confronted by Troubridge's four cruisers, for which the German's ten 11" guns were more than a match. Troubridge was aware of this and stuck to his somewhat unhelpful Admiralty orders requiring him not to engage an enemy more powerful than himself. The *Goeben* and the *Breslau* got away. Two-and-a-half months later, following a surprise raid on Sebastopol by the *Goeben*, Turkey declared war on the Allies.[19]

A court of enquiry declared Troubridge's action 'deplorable and contrary to the traditions of the British Navy'. The effects of this harsh pronouncement, which read like a public school housemaster's rebuke to a rugby team that had not shown enough 'guts', were felt by every captain, every officer in the Service. They may even have reverberated to the other side of the world, where Rear-Admiral Sir Christopher Cradock was steaming south towards the Falkland Islands in search of enemy raiders.

Troubridge was charged with 'not pursuing the flying enemy by negligence or default'. Balfour, echoing Bridgeman's sympathies entirely, 'simply *could not* believe it'. Talk of hushing the matter up was set aside and Troubridge was hauled before a court martial under Sir George Egerton on 5 November 1914.[20] Sir Francis and Lady Bridgeman attended to lend him their support and share his delight when five days later the 'triumphant' verdict was announced. The charges were 'not proved' and Troubridge was 'fully and honourably' acquitted.[21] Nevertheless, he never again held a sea-going command. In the Navy and beyond there were those who believed he had been made a scapegoat for Admiralty (i.e. Churchill's) errors of both strategy and command. Troubridge himself was highly indignant that his 'real accuser' had not been his fellow sailors 'but an *amateur*'.[22] Accusing fingers were pointed at imprecise orders and the decision neither to entrust the Eastern Mediterranean to flotilla craft (Fisher's proposal) nor to reinforce the Malta squadron until 1915. This was the situation which Bridgeman described as a 'mess'.[23]

When his ordeal was over, Troubridge thanked Sir Francis and 'dear Lady Bridgeman' for their belief and trust in him, as well as their 'kind sympathy and support ... [when his] silent endurance was becoming almost more than [he] could bear.' He was reduced to tears when, in a letter from Bridgeman, he read what Cradock had written just before his death. 'Good, God what a cruel shame!' wrote Troubridge. 'They say in the Fleet "[Cradock] lost his squadron because Churchill court martialled Troubridge for not losing his." '[24]

Rear-Admiral Sir Christopher ('Kit') Cradock was an able and upright sailor of the old school. The strength of the Royal Navy, he wrote in a little book for aspiring officers, rested on comradeship, loyalty and 'the sacred laws of naval discipline'.[25] As a lieutenant he had been a junior member of the 'band of brothers' assembled to take the *Howe* through her paces in 1889. Bridgeman knew him well and had a high regard for his abilities and upright character. He therefore took a close personal interest in the tragedy that unfolded off South America in October and November 1914.

The outbreak of hostilities found Cradock in command of the North America and West Indies Station. He was notably successful in clearing the raiding German cruisers *Dresden* and *Karlsruhe* from the North Atlantic, almost sinking the *Karlsruhe* and driving them both down south away from the busiest shipping corridors. In some ways, though, he had only made his task more difficult. He was now sent into the South Atlantic with the dual role of finding the raiders and protecting Allied shipping over thousands of square miles of ocean. There was also the possibility that he might run into Admiral von Spee's powerful German Far East squadron, which had sailed east into the Pacific in June and had subsequently been reported in the vicinity of New Guinea.

Cradock's squadron comprised the *Good Hope*, an armoured cruiser, the cruiser *Monmouth*, the light cruiser *Glasgow* and the armed merchantman *Otranto*. It was a doughty enough collection of warships for general duties, but no match for von Spee's armoured cruisers *Scharnhorst* and *Gneisenau* supported by three light cruisers, *Dresden*, *Leipzig* and *Nürnberg*. The principal German vessels carried eight 8" guns and were manned by first-rate crews. The *Good Hope*, Cradock's flagship, was an elderly vessel with unreliable engines. In September the port engine broke down and she lay idle for a week while it was repaired.[26] She was armed

National Maritime Museum, London

The pre-dreadnought battleship Canopus *at Portsmouth, 1909*

with many 6" guns, only half of which could be brought to bare on a target at any one time, and two 9.2" guns mounted fore and aft. Her weapons were ancient, her crew largely reservists. The lightly-armoured *Monmouth* was similarly crewed and boasted no guns larger than 6".

On 14 September the Admiralty told Cradock it was very likely that von Spee was heading in his direction. At first the Rear-Admiral's orders seemed contradictory:

> 'Concentrate a squadron strong enough to meet *Scharnhorst* and *Gneisenau*, making Falkland Islands your coaling base, and leaving sufficient force to deal with *Dresden* and *Karlsruhe*.'

With the forces at his disposal how could Cradock both challenge the superior German force approaching across the Pacific and leave 'sufficient force' to deal with the raiders? The situation was clarified in the next paragraph. Cradock would be joined by the modern armoured cruiser *Defence* from the Mediterranean and by the antique battleship *Canopus* from Brazil.[27] In the eyes of Charles Gould, the *Good Hope's* wireless operator, the arrival of 'more powerful ships' was essential if Cradock was to stand any chance of successfully 'seeing off' the *Scharnhorst* and *Gneisenau*.[28]

Although promised more ships, Cradock was still confused. Was he supposed to divide his squadron, leaving some to protect shipping and look for the *Dresden* and *Karlsruhe*, and take the rest to hunt von Spee? If so, then neither force, even with the promised reinforcements, would be sufficient to guarantee success. His position was only slightly clarified in early October when the Admiralty told him to be prepared to meet von Spee 'in company' (a very Churchillian phrase!) with *Canopus* escorted by *Glasgow*, *Monmouth* and *Otranto*. They were also to 'search and protect trade in combination'.[29] No mention was made of the *Defence*.

On 8 October (received at the Admiralty four days later, the usual delay at that time) Cradock pointed out that in case von Spee slipped by his pursuers to the west of South America, a second powerful force was needed to the east of the Straits of Magellan. In the meantime, he sent another cable to propose concentrating all his ships on the Falkland Isles and asked anxiously, ' ... does *Defence* join my command?'[30] The answer was sent on 14 October: *Defence* was now in Montevideo under the command of Admiral Stoddart and she was staying there. Ten years later the *Morning Post* (hardly the most Churchill-friendly newspaper) reported that Cradock asked for the *Defence* three times in all and was told after his last request he would be replaced if he asked again.

By mid-October Cradock was at Port William in the Falkland Isles where she was joined on 18th by the chugging *Canopus*. The old lady's arrival hardly filled the anxious British squadron with joy. The 13,000-ton pre-dreadnought battleship was now 14 years old and her intended 18-knot top speed had fallen away sharply. Her Krupp armour and four 12" guns (two forward, two aft) had once made her the pride of the Navy, but she was now too old and her armament too obsolete for her to pose much threat to a more modern ship of similar size. She had been relegated to the Reserves before the war and was now manned by part-timers. Most worrying of all, her slow speed (which Cradock said would reduce his squadron's to no more than about 12 knots) meant she would be useless in trying to catch the speedy German squadron.

On 20 October Gould was still expecting the *Defence* to join them. Cradock knew she never would. When his squadron left the Falklands and steamed west for the Straits of Magellan and the Pacific, he was angry and bitter. His mission, he told his flag captain, was 'suicide' without the *Defence*. The officers were thin-lipped and silent. 'There is, I believe, something in the wind, which they are trying to keep from us,' Gould noted ominously in his diary. '[We have] ... a sporting chance ... [but] I think those at home should give us more modern ships to back us up.' The *Canopus*, too slow to keep up with the rest of the squadron, was left behind to follow with the colliers, 'the only thing she [was] fit for,' remarked Gould bitterly.[31]

The men were going to their deaths and they knew it. On Sunday 25th, on taking out a picture of his wife and children to illustrate a point in his sermon, the *Good Hope*'s chaplain burst into years. An air of terrible foreboding descended over the doomed ship and by the time the last hymn had been sung the entire crew was weeping.[32] The following day Cradock telegraphed the Admiralty to inform them of his decision regarding the *Canopus*. Again he requested the presence of the *Defence*. He said, significantly, that he did so because he believed he was under orders to 'search for enemy' and bring about 'early success'. With the words of Troubridge's inquiry nagging at the back of his mind – 'deplorable and contrary to the traditions of the British navy' – he knew these orders had to be obeyed, however senseless they might seem. He was that sort of man. Like Bridgeman, he believed the Navy came before self and duty came before all. Even unto death.

On receiving the telegram, Churchill, who was in the throes of swapping Battenberg for Fisher and for the time being taking most decisions himself, declared it 'very obscure', adding 'I do not understand what Admiral Craddock intends and wishes'.[33] He did not release the *Defence* until 3 November and he sent no precise orders to Cradock telling him not to engage the enemy without the *Canopus*.

And so the tragedy of misunderstanding and pointless heroism continued to unfold.

On 27 October Gould and a small party from the *Good Hope* were put ashore on the island of Auchilu Veshupi. They built a hut and installed their radio equipment. The enemy's signals came through loud and clear but there was no news from Cradock.[34] The following day Fisher became First Sea Lord for the second time. Appraising the situation off the coasts of South America, he ordered two battlecruisers from the Grand Fleet (as the Home Fleet was now known) to the region and told Cradock specifically not to fight von Spee without the *Canopus*. The command never reached him.

Von Spee's squadron arrived at Valpariso at the end of the month and hearing that the British light cruiser *Glasgow* was 200 miles to the south at Coronel, they steamed off to find it. Their course took them straight into the path of Cradock, who was now in the Pacific and proceeding anxiously north. The two squadrons met 50 miles off Coronel at five in the afternoon of 1 November. The sea was rough. When the first shots were fired two hours later the light was fading fast.

It was all over in about an hour. Von Spee used his ships' superior speed to keep the enemy silhouetted against the horizon. The inexperienced and under-trained British gunners, with only gun flashes and vague shapes in the darkness to aim at, scored not a single hit. The swell was too high for their secondary armament to be used. Repeatedly pounded by the enemy guns, the *Good Hope* blew up and went down with all hands. Shortly afterwards the *Monmouth*, trapped by the *Nürnberg* and refusing to surrender, suffered a similar fate. In all 1,600 men were lost. As night closed in, the *Glasgow* and the *Otranto* fled south into the gathering gloom.

The following morning Gould and his band, the only members of the crew of the *Good Hope* left alive, were collected by the *Canopus* which was now running for her life towards the Straits of Magellan. Fearing the worst, Gould scribbled incoherently in his diary:

'It's a bit rough, old scrap iron to fight up-to-date ships. They had no chance ... we are running away, our turn if they catch us, not a gun with anything like the range of theirs and the old crock steaming 14 knots, the enemy 22 knots ... a disgrace to any navy ... well, we will take our chance, only got to die once.'[35]

He did not die. The venerable *Canopus* got away and on 8 December a powerful British force, including the two battlecruisers, destroyed von Spee's squadron off the Falkland Islands. The Battle of Coronel had been avenged, but it was not forgotten.

Because the country was at war, open criticism of the circumstances that had caused the Coronel disaster was muted. Private comments, however, were less restrained. Writing to Bridgeman on 12 November Sandars spoke of Cradock as having been 'sacrificed' by Churchill. He went on in no less bitter a tone:

'Now we must await the usual string of mendacities which will be served out by Churchill in order to cover up his follies and blunders.

Altogether I am unhappy about naval affairs; but this is partly due to the fact that its administration in high places is in hands that are not the best, and that the best could have been found had Churchill only been left in an Antwerp trench or had been interned in Holland.' [36]

The wise and humane Captain Oliver Andrews criticised Churchill for shrugging off defeat as merely the loss of useless ships, ignoring the fates of the families and men who had died in them.[37] For the moment Bridgeman kept quiet. His only extant wartime thoughts on Coronel are found in a letter he wrote to Kit Cradock's brother, Sheldon, on 23 September 1917. Although the ex-First Sea Lord held Battenberg and Admiral Sturdee, von Spee's eventual vanquisher, primarily responsible for the disaster, he sensed the ubiquitous hand of the First Lord had played some part in events:

'Churchill however may and possibly did influence their better judgement! But to send three old crocks to meet von Spee was the highth [sic] of folly – for which in my opinion there was no excuse! Jack Fisher ... finally saved the situation on the East Coast by sending a couple of good ships to the Falkland Ids.

I dare not write more on the subject – but you can realise my feelings when I tell you that my strategy was upset for that particular region [word illegible], when Battenberg took my place at the head of the War Staff – with the result we so painfully have experienced.' [38]

It is worth examining the claim made in the last sentence. Had Bridgeman's strategy for the region not been changed by Battenberg might the disaster have been avoided? It is not clear what region Bridgeman was referring to – the South Atlantic or the Pacific. If the latter, then there is no evidence to support his assertion. When First Sea Lord, Fisher had planned for a new and powerful Pacific Fleet of battlecruisers comprising two British ships and one each from Australia and New Zealand.[39] Searching for economies, Churchill had abandoned this idea. He considered old armoured cruisers sufficient to safeguard Britain's Pacific interests, particularly as she would be able to call on powerful naval assistance from her ally Japan. According to Nicholas Lambert,

'Bridgeman placed no obstacles in front of Churchill, honestly believing that such powerful warships as battlecruisers were not really needed in the Pacific at that time.' [40]

This may, of course, not be the whole story. But as far as we know the man who had patrolled the Pacific to good effect in a tiny steam corvette probably did not envisage the need for dreadnought-type ships in that vast, empty ocean. In which case, he must bear at least some indirect responsibility for what happened at Coronel.

Whether his strategy might have prevented Cradock's death or not, Bridgeman was deeply concerned about the way the Admiralty was being run. The problem, he confided in a letter to his old commander, Sir Michael Culme-Seymour, was the extent to which all power had concentrated into the hands of the First Lord. The letter is a rare insight into Bridgeman's thinking. After three years at the Admiralty with two very different First Lords, during which time he discussed widely the relative roles of Board members with various colleagues, he declared the First Lord to be,

> '*primus inter pares* in all matters other than those of Cabinet rank – which being put in plain English means – Cabinet policy must be followed & the 1st Lord represents the views of the Cabinet at the Admiralty.'

This 'mode of action', he said, he 'never ceased to preach ... to all concerned, and most particularly to Winston Churchill!'. (If he really did preach at Churchill, no wonder he was sacked!) Bridgeman's recipe for an Admiralty running 'smoothly and well' was for his definition of the First Lord's duties to be adhered to. It had been thus under McKenna, he controversially suggested, who although weak in Cabinet had done more for the Navy than the more forceful and confrontational Churchill:

> 'Churchill when he became 1st Lord reversed or tried to reverse that policy. He desired executive control in every department, which resulted in confusion, overlapping of offices & much discontent – & one was frequently faced with the difficulty of not knowing what was happening in one's own department! I could quote many cases of this happening in my own time – & they have occurred much more frequently since I left!'

He did not mention the Coronel fiasco, but it must certainly have been one of the examples he had in mind.

Things would improve now that Fisher was back at the Admiralty, he believed. But the outstanding First Sea Lord of his generation had 'aged greatly' and the man who had once thought nothing of talking all night now went to bed in his suite in the Ritz before 10 pm.[41] Moreover, he did not have eyes at the back of his head,

> 'with the result that executive orders to the fleet are sent out secretly – anything more dangerous & likely to lead to disaster with a man like Churchill cannot be imagined.'

Interestingly, the executive qualities Bridgeman said Churchill most lacked – 'stability and judgement' – were those for which he was most frequently praised.[42]

Although purporting to be objective analysis, one cannot help feeling that Bridgeman's remarks are too deeply scarred with resentment to be of much value. Michael Culme-Seymour junior immediately identified the flaw in his argument. Writing to his father from the *Centurion* on 27 April, he observed that 'of Cabinet rank' was a meaningless phrase as 'different cabinets, different 1st Lords & different 1st Sea Lords will take different views of what constitutes a question of Cabinet rank'. Commenting on his father's intention of taking up Churchill's behaviour with Bonar Law, Michael went on,

> 'Under the present regulations the First Lord has no doubt unlimited powers & can do anything he likes – legally. So if you have a First Lord who has not the sense to take the advice of the naval members of the Board, you have executive orders in naval matters given by a civilian & that can only, as we have seen recently [at Coronel and the Dardanelles], lead to disaster.'

The 'best thing for the country' he declared, getting crosser as he went on, would be for Churchill to be removed from office and replaced as First Lord by Fisher. Churchill's administration was full of 'errors, mistakes & want of knowledge' and it was the 'universal opinion ... to get rid of W C at any price'. By '*universal*' he admitted he meant the opinion of senior officers; some junior officers 'put W C on a pedestal'.

The letter ends with a request that Sir Michael approach Bonar Law speaking for himself only. Bridgeman should not be mentioned, he told his father, as 'your opinion, without his, would carry far greater weight than if his was tacked onto it'.[43]

Sir Michael had no need to go to Bonar Law. In one cataclysmic three-day period in May 1915 Fisher resigned, unable to work with Churchill any longer, a coalition government was formed under Asquith and Churchill, complaining bitterly, moved out of the Admiralty. He had survived Coronel by barely six months. Fisher replied to Bridgeman's letter of sympathy with his usual vigour:

> 'Your dear letter has touched my heart very deeply! *It is all as you say*! Sir E Grey said to me 'You have ruined the Government' – I replied it was better to wreck the government than wreck the Navy! So of course the Prime Minister wrecked me!
> Of course it's a bitter pill being out of it all! But silence is the *only* thing!' [44]

As Fisher's tirade indicates, a balanced estimation of Churchill's contribution to the Service he had come to love was largely drowned by a chorus of relief and long-suppressed disapproval. 'We can now breath more freely to be ridden of the succubus,' sighed Beatty. Grand Fleet commander Jellicoe admitted, 'I have for long thoroughly distrusted Mr Churchill because he constantly arrogated to himself technical knowledge which, with all his brilliant qualities, I know he did not possess,' while from the Palace Sir Stanley Colville admitted, 'We all considered that he was a danger to the Empire'.[45]

Bridgeman's old friend Jack Sandars was even more forthright. Churchill's final speech to the Commons as First Lord, he wrote, was, 'after his own manner and substance. It was vulgar, vainglorious, egotistical and mendacious – careless of any reputation but his own – injurious to officials and unjust to colleagues in office.'

He hoped that in the Army, where the ex-First Lord proposed to serve, he would be subject to 'the rules of ordinary discipline' which he had so flouted at the Admiralty. 'The price put on his head by the Boers when he escaped from prison was £20,' he concluded spitefully. 'I think that still represents his full value.'[46]

Bridgeman's reaction to the news of his old adversary's fall is not recorded. One would hope it was not unmitigated glee. For all his impetuosity and self-centredness, Churchill was the age's most dynamically original and devoted First Lord. The Royal Navy may not have been prepared for modern warfare in 1914, but it was in vastly better shape than it had been before the Churchillian gale started to blow two years earlier. Nemesis had answered Bridgeman's prayers, but her gifts were bitter-sweet.

NOTES

1   From a newspaper obituary in the Wakefield Archives, QD1/151, wrongly attributed to *Yorkshire Post*.
2   1/1/1914, Sandars to Bridgeman, L.L.P.P.
3   4/3/1929.
4   7/4/1915, Sandars to Bridgeman, L.L.P.P.
5   Leaflet outlining the history of St Michael and All Angels, available in the church. N.D.
6   Diggle, *Burton Leonard Past and Present*, p. 93.
7   4/3/1929, *Yorkshire Post*.
8   8/1/1917, Sandars to Bridgeman, L.L.P.P.
9   *Fifty Years in the Navy in the Royal Navy*, p. 279.
10 See above p. 119.
11 I am indebted to Mr R Suddaby of the Imperial War Museum for drawing my attention to this point.
12 NMM COW/6.
13 27/2/1915 & 4/9/1915, Sandars to Bridgeman, L.L.P.P.
14 30/1/1916, *ibid.*
15 14/12/1916 & 22/1/1917, *ibid.*

16   30/1/1916 & 12/7/1917, *ibid*. In a letter of January 1917 Jack Sandars referred tantalisingly to Bridgeman's 'pressing Admiralty problem'. How one would love to know what it was! 8/1/1917, *ibid*.

17   12/11/1914, *ibid*.

18   *Ibid*.

19   Although damaged later in the war, the *Goeben* was repaired and amazingly remained in commission until 1960.

20   11/1/1913, Sandars to Bridgeman, L.L.P.P.; 10/11/1914, Troubridge to Bridgeman, *ibid*.

21   *Ibid.*; typescript of court-martial, *ibid*.

22   10/11/1914, Troubridge to Bridgeman, *ibid*.

23   See p. 186.

24   10/11/1914 & 14/11/1914, Troubridge to Bridgeman, L.L.P.P.

25   *Whispers from the Fleet*, p. 28.

26   *True Copy of Rough Diary of Chas W Gould Lieut. RN "Last Journey of* **HMS Good Hope** *August 2nd 1914 to December 25th 1914"*, G.B.P.P.

27   Cited in Winston Churchill, *World Crisis*, I, p. 365.

28   30/9/1914, Gould, *Diary*, G.B.P.P.

29   Cited in Winston Churchill, *World Crisis*, I, p. 367.

30   *Ibid*.

31   22/10/1914, Gould, *Diary*, G.B.P.P.

32   25/10/1914, *ibid*.

33   Cited in Winston Churchill, *World Crisis*, I, p. 372.

34   28/10/1914, Gould, *Diary*, G.B.P.P.

35   2/11/1914, *ibid*.

36   L.L.P.P. The last sentence refers to the First Lord's controversial personal involvement in the defence of Antwerp at the start of the war.

37   *Seamarks and Landmarks*, p. 285.

38   G.B.P.P.

39   See Lambert, 'Bridgeman', pp. 68-69.

40   *Ibid.*, p. 68.

41   12/11/1914, Sandars to Bridgeman, L.L.P.P.

42   2/4/1915, S.W.P.P.

43   S.W.P.P.

44   16/8/1915, L.L.P.P.

45   Cited in Lombard-Hobson, *Never Go To Sea*, pp. 98-99, L.L.P.P.

46   18/11/1915, to Bridgeman, L.L.P.P.

15 'A Noble Example'

K nowing what we do, it is pleasantly ironic but no surprise to learn that Bridgeman hunted, shot and sailed for at least a dozen years after he had been obliged to retire from the Navy on grounds of ill-health. He continued with his community work, too. In 1918-19 he helped sort out the inevitable chaos and disruption that followed the cessation of hostilities by chairing the Yorkshire and East Midlands Division of the Council for Demobilisation and Resettlement. By July 1919, once again Chairman of the Parish Council, he was again heavily involved in local affairs. It must have felt strange for a man who had once commanded thousands and handled budgets of many millions of pounds to find himself worrying over broken footbridges and village seats, organising footpath clearance, trying to get the people of Burton Leonard to agree on the best form of war memorial and reprimanding the

Bridgeman: A fine type of country gentleman in retirement

inefficient clerk who had failed to inform him he had been re-elected to lead the Parish Council! But he went about his business with a will, serving Copgrove and Burton Leonard as once he had served His Majesty and his Royal Navy.[1] He knew no other course.

Each summer after the war he travelled down to the Solent to race with the Royal Yacht Squadron. His magnificent 68-ton cutter *Susan*, although not often a winner, never failed to impress with her immaculate appearance and the professional way she was handled. But even here, on the clear, breezy waters of the Solent, the old resentments lingered on. It was Bridgeman, apparently, who was the driving force behind the move to have his successor's son, Prince Louis Mountbatten, blackballed from the Royal Yacht Squadron, even though he had been put up by the then First Sea Lord David Beatty.[2]

As the years slipped by, so Bridgeman's old friends and comrades began to leave the scene. Sir Michael Culme-Seymour died at the beginning of 1920, leaving a vacancy in the list of vice-admirals of the United Kingdom that was appropriately filled by Sir Francis himself. Fisher passed away that summer and was buried with much majesty in Westminster Abbey. Bridgeman attended both funerals. Lord Charles Beresford died the following year and Bridgeman, in a final gesture of solidarity with the man who had huffed and puffed in the Commons on his behalf, travelled down from Yorkshire to act as pall-bearer at the grand funeral in St Paul's. No such pomp marked the next funeral he attended.

Emily (Lady Bridgeman) died on 22 November 1922, aged 80. She was laid to rest in a simple grave at the eastern edge of the churchyard of St Michael and All Angels, Copgrove, the church to which she had devoted so much of her time and money. Nearby lay the bodies of her sister Anne (Lady Graham) and brother-in-law, Sir Reginald Graham 8th Bt, and their son Nigel.

Even today the profound tranquillity of this small, remote graveyard is broken only occasionally by the noise of a passing car or the chug of a tractor labouring in a nearby field. 75 years ago it was a haven of peace in a broad green Yorkshire landscape. On many occasions, perhaps even daily, Sir Francis made his way slowly between the tall trees of the Copgrove estate to stand in silent, sorrowful gratitude over the grave of the woman who had meant so much to him. Whose advice he had always sought, whose companionship he had cherished above all others, whose love had never failed him. When it seemed as if he was destined to spend the rest of his life in inner solitude, she had brought him with the warmth, gentleness and inner security for which he had secretly yearned from the moment he joined *Britannia* as a boy. Profound mutual respect and affection, not quick-burning passion, had underpinned their relationship.[3] Her unselfish presence had made everything bearable – even the painful humiliation of his dismissal. Now she was gone he was but half a man again and wished for little else than to be reunited with her in death. From this time forward every letter he wrote, every card he sent, was bordered in black.

The simple Bridgeman tomb in the churchyard of St Michael and All Angels, Copgrove,
beneath which Francey and Emmy were buried side by side

Emily's death turned Bridgeman's thoughts towards his own and in July 1923 he made his will. He appointed his solicitors, Charles Nicholl and Edward Manisty, his sole executors and trustees and left them £200 each for their pains. He asked to be buried beside his wife beneath a modest memorial stone. £200 was to be spent on their shared grave and a further £150 set aside for its upkeep.

To his unmarried step-niece Nancy Pleydell-Bouverie, the nurse who was to tend him in Brown's Hotel, he left £1,000. His remaining estate was also to provide independent incomes for his sister Beatrice and his nieces Mildred Hingston and Sybil Powerscourt. The Shiffner money that he had acquired through marriage he honourably left to his wife's side of the family. The original Brown estate was divided between his sister-in-law's remaining children, Sir Reginald Guy Graham and Lieutenant-Colonel Malise Graham. Malise would inherit Copgrove, its contents and money on trust.

No member of the household was forgotten. Some were bequeathed as much as £100. Senior staff were to receive ten shillings a week for life and everyone who had been in his employment for ten years or more was to receive five shillings on the same terms. The estate carpenter and his wife were given use of their tied cottage for the remainder of their days. As he grew more infirm, Bridgeman came to rely more and more on his personal valet Christopher Oates. Originally bequeathed £100, a codicil appended to the will in 1926 raised this to a considerable £1,000 and also stipulated that he could have the Admiral's clothes and other apparel. Unlike some with whom he had worked, Bridgeman saw it as his duty to care for those who had served him to the best of their ability.

Bridgeman's will mentions few household effects individually. Obviously the list is by no means complete. We know, for example, that he left his letters and medals to his favourite niece Sybil, but there is no reference to this in the will. Nor is mention made of valuable items like dinner services, cutlery and the library. Nevertheless, the evidence we have suggests that for a house of its size and grandeur Copgrove was not lavishly furnished. This is no surprise as far as the Admiral was concerned; after half a century in the Navy he was accustomed to the most Spartan conditions. As far as we know before his marriage he owned no property in which he could display treasures and souvenirs collected on his travels. It is more surprising that Emily, a very wealthy woman, did not furnish her home more luxuriously. Perhaps, being a deeply Christian woman, she scorned worldly ostentation?

The pictures show that neither Sir Francis nor Emily was a serious collector. Apart from a portrait of Queen Caroline and a painting of cattle by Cooper, all the other pictures related either to the family or to the admiral's career. There was a portrait of Addison by Kneller, another of Nelson and assorted likenesses of various members of the Brown and Shiffner families. The only other painting mentioned was a watercolour of Edward VII inspecting the Home Fleet, presumably done in 1907.

Two photographs commemorating Captain Scott were listed, one of the *Discovery* locked in the ice and another of the polar explorer himself. His last letter to Bridgeman was also preserved in a frame. A photograph of Emily was framed in gold, beside one of her husband as a sub-lieutenant. No furniture is mentioned apart from some Spanish leather chairs, a single Chippendale chair and a writing table given to Thomas Shiffner by William IV. The only recorded silverware is that inherited from Bridgeman's uncle, Sir William Eyre. The inventory is completed by the model of the *Dreadnought* presented to the Admiral when he went aboard her in 1907, a screen decorated with some of the ships in which he served, and a motley collection of books that included a leather-bound Shakespeare, Gould's *Birds* [of the British Isles] and Scott's *Furthest South*.[4]

After the war Bridgeman spent most of his time in Yorkshire. Inevitably, with the passing of the years he lost touch with old friends and colleagues. In 1920 he even came close to falling out with Fisher. Shortly before his death, Britain's most famous sailor wrote wildly to *The Times* about the 'plutocratic, effete, despicable' nature of the post-war House of Commons. He went on to castigate continued use of the word 'Empire', claiming it was an undemocratic 'Hun word'. Moving on to the Armed Services, he condemned high expenditure on the Army as it ignored the 'one thing needful' to the country's defence, 'air supremacy'. (Fisher's gift of prophesy had not deserted him, even in his dotage.) He dismissed the War Office as nincompoops and the Board of Admiralty as asses who possessed no vision and rounded off his tirade with a quotation from the Book of Proverbs: 'Where there is no vision the people perish'.[5]

Fisher the inveterate radical and Bridgeman the natural conservative had never seen eye to eye on politics. The iconoclasm of Fisher's letter was too much for Bridgeman, even though it came from an ex-comrade, and he took up his pen to reply. 'Dear Admiral', he began with his customary formality. For the sake of 'old friends, old memories and old records' he could not let a 'dear old friend' get away with what he had written:

> 'When I read this letter [to *The Times*], I confess I was fairly aghast! ... Surely it is enough to inveigh against waste and extravagance without employing argument and vituperation to pull down the whole system of government for a substitute that must inevitably mean ferment, chaos, then anarchy!'[6]

In its way Bridgeman's ripost was just as blinkered as Fisher's, but without the latter's redeeming insight. Fisher had not sought revolution; all he had asked for was a substitution of 'Commonwealth' for 'Empire'. Age and retirement were beginning to erode Bridgeman's flexibility and willingness to consider new ideas. But to his credit his warmth and humanity remained intact – his angry rejoinder remained unsigned on his desk.

In 1923 Bridgeman returned publicly to naval matters for the last time. The occasion was the publication of *The World Crisis 1911-1918*, Winston Churchill's highly readable but very personal and frequently self-justificatory two-volume history of the First World War. Steadfast in his undertaking to the King not to re-open the controversy surrounding his resignation, Bridgeman did not take issue with Churchill over the way that incident was handled in the book. He did not return to the Troubridge court martial, either. The passages to which he chose to take public exception dealt with the lead up to the Battle of Coronel and the death of his old friend Kit Cradock.

Not surprisingly, Bridgeman aired his views in the *Morning Post*.[7] His position had changed somewhat since he had written to Sheldon Cradock during the war.[8] Now he was quite clear that the blame for the Coronel disaster fell squarely on Churchill's shoulders. Central to the issue were the Admiralty's opaque orders and decision:

> 'to divide Admiral Cradock's whole force into two weak squadrons, one under Admiral Stoddart to be based at Montevideo in the north, the other under Cradock at the Falklands Islands in the south.'

'The wisdom of this decision of Mr Churchill's,' he challenged, 'seems very doubtful.' In support of this assertion Bridgeman quoted a letter 'written by a brother officer of [Cradock's] just after the disaster':

> 'I happen to know that Cradock wired to the Admiralty for the *Defence* to be allowed to join him and was told that his present force was sufficient ... Poor Cradock, when the Admiralty refused to let him have the *Defence*, he knew he would never get back, and buried his medals and decorations in the Governor's garden at [the] Falkland[s], and left a large sealed packet ... to send home when his death was confirmed.
>
> It does seem hard luck on Cradock to give him inferior ships off the dockyard wall, manned by coastguards, boys straight from the training ships, reserve men, bandsmen and naval cadets, and putting them up against ships manned by the pick of the German Navy and a long time in commission; it is a horrible libel if the blame is put on Cradock for the disaster, as we all feel out here that any brave man would have done the same as he did.'

Anticipating a rejoinder that Cradock would have had no problem had he moved in conjunction with the *Canopus*, instead of leaving her to convoy the colliers, Bridgeman challenged Churchill's description of the battleship as 'a citadel around which all our cruisers in those waters could find absolute security'.[9] The Admiral was 'amazed' to read this description of the ship. He suggested it was merely 'a clever bit of journalism' intended for an uninformed public 'who attach the greatest value to the magic term "battleship"'. His own description of the *Canopus* was quite different and supported Gould's disparaging remark that she was 'old scrap iron'.

> 'The *Canopus*, aged 14, was one of a class built for foreign service, and like most [such?] ships, was a compromise. She was given a narrow belt of armour ... the same as the *Good Hope* ... She had long been in the Reserve, and throughout her career frequently developed many engine room weaknesses, and had always been unreliable as a steamer when called upon to make an effort. Her armament of four twelve-inch guns were of an obsolete mark and short range ... [and] her crew composed largely of Reservists had had no opportunity of being trained in the use of them ...
>
> In fact, she was neither ... a battleship, nor a cruiser, but just a useful conglomerate of old-fashioned ideas that made a good show in peacetime!
>
> I feel it quite safe to say that the *Canopus* would have had no chance at all in an engagement with the two, or even one, of von Spee's heavy cruisers with their long range guns and that she was nothing but an encumbrance to Cradock in his search for von Spee's powerful squadron.'

The rest of the letter was taken up with an analysis of the 'appalling dilemma' in which Cradock was put by the Admiralty's contradictory orders and a brief eulogy on the Admiral's brave personality. Never in his career had Bridgeman written so powerfully or used his wide knowledge with such skill. Recognising this, a few weeks later he confessed,

> 'I don't know that I ever enjoyed writing a letter more than I did this one; to be able to state facts in contradiction of what [Churchill] says in his book is a real delight.' [10]

Churchill replied, also in the *Morning Post*, on 28 April 1923. He made no attempt to contradict Bridgeman's criticisms. Indeed, he would have found it very difficult to have done so. He tried instead to pass responsibility for the pre-Coronel decisions and orders on to Admiral Sturdee and First Sea Lord Battenberg. He did, however, launch one fresh dart in the direction of his recalcitrant ex-First Sea Lord. British weakness in the Pacific, he suggested, was not his fault but Bridgeman's:

> 'One of the first acts of Sir Francis Bridgeman, when he became First Sea Lord at the end of 1911, was to cancel the order which Sir Arthur Wilson had given to send the *Indomitable* [battlecruiser] to the China Station.'

As Nicholas Lambert has shown, the cancellation order may have been issued in Bridgeman's name but the initiative for not building up a battlecruiser fleet in the Pacific was certainly the First Lord's.[11] If Bridgeman was guilty, it was only of a sin of omission.

Bridgeman wrote one more public letter on the subject, this time to the *Yorkshire Post* on 30 April. It contained nothing he had not said before. It did not need to. Given the atmosphere created by the treatment of Troubridge and Cradock's reckless gallantry, the reasons for the disaster at Coronel were now clear. For the first and only time in his life Bridgeman had prevailed over his old master.

The Bridgeman-Churchill confrontation was widely read and drew some unexpected correspondence. One letter in particular caught Bridgeman's eye. Dated 19 April 1924, it came from a Wing Commander Stanley Turner, then based with the Royal Air Force in Cairo. At the time of Cradock's last visit to the Falkland Islands Turner had been the officer commanding the troops there. He had met the admiral almost every day while his ships were in Port Stanley and was responsible for the wireless station that received and transmitted the squadron's signals. Two of his revelations struck Bridgeman as particularly significant. They are both contained in this section of Turner's letter:

'I well remember that after Cradock's signal asking for reinforcements, he finally received a definitive order. I cannot pretend after this period to remember what the exact wording of the signal was, but ... it was to the effect that he was to proceed to sea forthwith, seek out the enemy and engage him ... Cradock had stayed the night at Government House; and was in my opinion worried, although he largely concealed it under his usual cheerful manner. I remember that he wrote two letters; one ... to Admiral Meux, and the other ... to a relative ... These two letters were put on the mantelpiece in the Governor's office, and they were to be posted when the news came along that the *Good Hope* had been sunk. I also remember that that morning at breakfast Cradock said 'Winston has always borne a grudge against me, ever since the ...... affair.' (I forget the name of the ship, but it was, I think, a P&O – the one which was wrecked with the Duke and Duchess of Fife on board.[12]) He then said: 'This is Winston's doing' – referring apparently to the order which I have mentioned above. He seemed very worried.'

Had Cradock really been told clearly to 'proceed to sea at once' and engage a superior enemy? And what was this grudge Churchill was supposed to have borne Cradock? Turner's half-remembered recollections, written down almost ten years after the event, are scarcely reliable evidence. Nevertheless, they raise fascinating, if unanswerable, questions about the dynamics of what was going on in the lead up to Coronel.

Turner's long letter threw further light on the pessimistic mood of Cradock's second-rate squadron during its last hours in the Falkland Islands. The *Good Hope* he remembered as being 'very old and ... full of defects'. A Royal Marines captain, heavily critical of the amount of wood used in the ship's construction, commented, 'If we meet the Hun, this is going to be my frying pan'. The traversing mechanism on one of the 6" guns was malfunctioning. The ship's range-finder was defective. Just before she put to sea, the crew were allowed a final trip ashore. 'It was common talk among them,' Turner went on, 'that it was the last chance they would have, and they proceeded to drink Port Stanley dry and to smash up the public houses. I well remember the trouble we had gathering them up and getting them into their launches at the Town Jetty. A number of them (eight I think) fell into the water and were picked out half-drowned.'

Cradock was upset that his lucky mascot, a piece of old black pottery he had picked up in China, had broken when he transferred to the *Good Hope*. The Falkland Islands' tug *Samson*, which took the Admiral back to his ship, lost control in the gale-force winds and damaged one of the warship's screws as she came alongside. As there was insufficient time for repairs, the *Good Hope* was obliged to leave with a bit missing from one of her propellers.[13] Turner had never met a 'more knightly soul' than the Admiral who sailed so steadfastly to his certain death.

At Turner's request, Bridgeman told no one what had been revealed to him in the strictest confidence.

By kind permission of the Dean and Chapter of York

*The memorial to Admiral Cradock, York Minster. Bridgeman
took a strong personal interest in its erection*

The controversy with Churchill made Bridgeman a bit of a hero in the Falklands. The islands' Dean, J Stanley Smith, wrote to thank him for his letter to the *Morning Post* and revealed that Churchill's book had caused 'intense indignation amongst the people here who know the truth'.[14] When the Falkland Islanders wanted a picture of the Cradock memorial that had been erected in York Minster, it was to Bridgeman they wrote and he was only too pleased to oblige.[15]

After this a curtain of silence descends over Bridgeman's life. Now in his mid-seventies, he had dropped most of his voluntary political and community activities and hunted less frequently. In its place he took up gardening. In late September 1926 he asked Jack Sandars about Clematis plants. Which variety would be best suited to Copgrove's soil and the Yorkshire climate? And when should it be planted? Sandars recommended 'Lady Northcliffe' and suggested a nursery in Surrey that provided good specimens. They should be planted in February, he advised, in well-drained soil that had been lightly manured.[16] How strangely touching it is to read the correspondence of men who not many years before had been talking of wars and strategies now exchanging tips on the cultivation of Clematis!

Bridgeman probably did not see his new plants until well into the following year. 50 years of pipe smoking had made him prone to a range of respiratory complaints and he was now wintering in the Bahamas to escape the snows and bitter east winds that buffeted Copgrove during the less clement months of the year. In 1928 he delayed his retreat to the sunshine to be at home for his eightieth birthday, when his friends clubbed together to present him with a Chippendale-style gold salver. Shortly afterwards the *Yorkshire Post* published a photograph of him seated by his fireside at the time of the presentation. He still retained the handsome features and good figure of his youth. His face, if understandably careworn and tired, bears the look of a man at peace with himself, knowing he had done his duty.

Bridgeman died suddenly of heart disease at Nassau in the Bahamas on 17 February 1929.[17] His estate, proved on 31 July, was valued

£138,354-5-11d. His body was brought back to Southampton by steamer. From here it was taken by road to Copgrove, where it rested in the library over the weekend. The funeral reflected the man – modest, straightforward, homely. The coffin, unpolished English oak draped with his flag and surmounted by his admiral's sword and hat, was taken to the church on a plain farm wagon drawn by two working horses from the estate. The floor of the wagon was carpeted with a Union Jack. Unlike most of his distinguished contemporaries, Bridgeman asked for no medalled dignitaries as his pall bearers but chose instead ordinary Yorkshire farm hands who returned to the plough and the granary when their task was done.

The mourners were drawn mostly from the local community. The family was represented by his sister, Mrs Beatrice Duncombe, Sir Guy and Lady Graham, Lieutenant-Colonel Malise Graham, his nieces Lady Powerscourt and Mrs Mildred Hingston, accompanied by her husband Charles, and Viscount Lascelles. The sole representative of the Royal Navy was Admiral Stanhope Hawke, a frequent guest at Copgrove in earlier days. The local MP, Major J W Hills, was there, accompanying several members of the Ripon Division of the Conservative and Unionist

Bridgeman's body arrives at Southampton after the long voyage from the Bahamas on the steamship Olympic

Association. Lord Stamfordham kindly telegrammed Beatrice Duncombe to convey the King and Queen's sympathy at the passing of 'an old and valued friend'.[18] But if Winston Churchill set aside past differences and came to pay his last respects, he kept his presence a secret.

Dr White, the Rector of Copgrove, took the service. The organist from Christ Church, Harrogate, played Chopin's *Funeral March* and Schubert's *Solemn March* on the instrument which the Admiral himself had given to the church 30 years before. The uncertain singing of the Copgrove Village Choir was supported by imported choristers, also from Harrogate. After the short service the body was laid to rest beside Emily's in a flower-lined grave.[19] As he had requested, the spot was later marked by a simple flat slab of dark stone carved with a cross and his own and Emily's name and dates. That was sufficient.

A service commemorating the Admiral's life and work was held in Copgrove Church on 4 March. The congregation sang the *Nunc Dimittis* and Psalm XV:

> 'Lord, who shall dwell in Thy tabernacle:
> Or who shall rest upon Thy holy hill?
> Even he that leadeth an uncorrupt life:
> And doeth the thing which is right, and speaketh the truth
> from his heart.'

It was, in its understated way, as fitting a conclusion as Bridgeman could have wished for.

A visitor to the pretty parish church of St Michael and All Angels will find two white marble plaques on the west wall above the font. That on the left is inscribed with a name followed by these words:

> 'A faithful Christian, a kind friend, a generous helper of every good cause, she was esteemed & beloved by all her neighbours in the country she loved so well.'

Beneath the name and titles on the right-hand tablet is carved:

'Prompt, Practical, Patient, he set a noble example of loyal and disinterested public service.'

The names, of course, are Dame Emily Charlotte and Admiral Francis Charles Bridgeman, GCB, GCVO. Neither is forgotten.

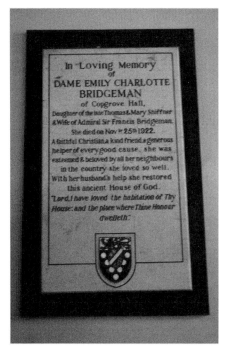 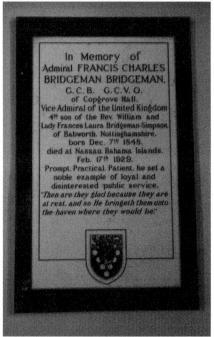

NOTES

1   13/7/19, *Burton Leonard Parish Council Minute Book*.

2   Lombard-Hobson, *Never Go To Sea*, p. 64, L.L.P.P. Hough, Admiral Lord Fisher, p. 260.

3   From the evidence of his will, as was customary for Edwardian couples of their standing, they each had their own bedroom. L.L.P.P.

4   L.L.P.P.

5   15/6/1920.

6   16/06/1920, Bridgeman to Fisher, L.L.P.P.

7   20/4/1923; the version used here is the draft mss. in L.L.P.P.

8   See pp. 257-8.

9   *World Crisis*, i, p. 370.

10   25/4/1923, Bridgeman to Mrs Straker (Cradock's sister), G.B.P.P.

11   See above, p. 186.

12   The P&O liner *Delhi* which went down off Tangier on 13 December 1911.

13   L.L.P.P.

14   27/7/1923, G.B.P.P.

15   4/11/23, Bridgeman to Mrs Straker, G.B.P.P.

16   4/10/1926, Sandars to Bridgeman, L.L.P.P.

17   4/3/1929, *Yorkshire Post*. The paper gave the cause of death as arteriosclerosis, so he may have had either a heart attack or a stroke.

18   L.L.P.P.

19   5/3/1929, *Yorkshire Post*.

Select Bibliography

MANUSCRIPT SOURCES

Public Record Office, Kew – Admiralty Records
  Paymaster General Records
Imperial War Museum – Troubridge Papers
Bodleian Library, Oxford – Jack Sandars Papers
National Maritime Museum, Greenwich –
  Brent Papers
  Bridge Papers
  Corbett Papers
  Domvile Papers
  Houston Papers
  Markham Papers
  Richmond Papers
  Sisson Papers
  Stokes-Rees Papers
  Wrey Papers
Burton Leonard Parish Council Records
Gore-Booth Private Papers (G.B.P.P.)
Loch Private Papers (L.L.P.P.) – to be entrusted to the Imperial War
  Museum in 1998.
Saunders Watson Private Papers (S.W.P.P.)
Sheffield City Archives – Eyre and Bridgeman-Simpson diaries
Wakefield City Archives

PRINTED SOURCES

Andrews, Captain O W, *Seamarks and Landmarks*, London, 1927.
Bacon, Admiral Sir Reginald, *From 1900 Onward*, London, 1940.
Bacon, Admiral Sir Reginald, *A Naval Scrapbook*, London, 1925.

Beresford, Lord Charles, *The Betrayal*, London, 1912.

Beresford, Lord Charles, *Memoirs*, London, 1914.

Brett, M V, ed., *Journals and Letters of Reginald Viscount Esher*, London, 1934.

Bridgeman, Admiral Sir Francis, and James, Captain W M, *HMS Dreadnought Her Place In History*, Leeds, 1926.

Chambers, Admiral B M, *Salt Junk – Naval Reminiscences, 1881-1906*, London, 1927.

Chatfield, Lord, *The Navy and Defence*, London, 1941

Cradock, Christopher, *Whispers From the Fleet*, London, 1907.

Dewar, K G B, *The Navy from Within*, London, 1939.

Dundas, C, *An Admiral's Yarns*, London, 1922.

Fisher, Lord John, *Memories*, London, 1919.

Fisher, Lord John, *Records*, London, 1919.

Fitzgerald, Admiral Penrose, *Memories of the Sea*, London, 1913.

Fleet, H L, *My Life and a Few Yarns*, London, 1922.

Fortescue, Sir Seymour, *Looking Back*, London, 1920.

Freemantle, E R, *The Navy as I Have Known It*, London, 1934.

Freemantle, S, *My Naval Career, 1880-1928*, London, 1949.

Hansard Official Report, Commons.

Keppel, Henry, *A Sailor's Life Under Four Sovereigns*, 3 vols, London, 1952.

Kerr, Mark, *The Navy in My Time*, London, 1933.

Keyes, Admiral Sir Roger, *Adventures Ashore and Afloat*, London, 1939.

Keyes, Admiral Sir Roger, *Naval Memoirs*, 2 vols, London, 1934.

King Hall, Admiral Sir Herbert, *Naval Memories and Traditions*, London, 1926.

King-Hall, Louise, ed., *Sea Saga*, London, 1935.

Marder, A, ed., *Fear God and Dread Nought The Correspondence of Admiral of the Fleet Lord Fisher of Kilverstone*, 3 vols, London, 1951-9.

Peterson, T, ed., *The Jellicoe Papers*, 2 vols, London, 1966 & 1968.

Ranft, B, *The Beatty Papers*, 2 vols, London, 1989 & 1992.

Riddell, *More Pages from my Diary*, London, 1926.

Royal Navy List.

Scott, Sir Percy, *Fifty Years in the Navy*, London, 1919.

Seymour, Sir Michael, *My Naval Career and Travels*, London, 1911.

Smith, Humphrey H, *A Yellow Admiral Remembers,* London, 1932.

Sumida, J T, ed., *Pollen Papers*, Navy Records Society, 1984.

Usborne, Vice-Admiral C V, *Blast and Counter-Blast,* London, 1935.

Wemyss, Lady Victoria, ed., *Life and Letters of Lord Wester Wemyss*, London, 1935.

Willis, G H A, *The Royal Navy As I Saw It*, London, 1924.

Yexley, Lionel, *Our Fighting Seamen*, London, 1911.

Yexley, Lionel, *The Inner Life of the Navy*, London, 1908.

SECONDARY SOURCES

Anon, *Guide to Copgrove Church.*

Bacon, Sir Reginald, *Life of John Rushworth Earl Jellicoe*, 1936.

Barnett, Correlli, *The Sword Bearers*, London, 1969.

Bennett, Geoffrey, *Charlie B*, London, 1968.

Bonnett, Stanley, *Price of Admiralty An Indictment of the Royal Navy 1805-1966*, London, 1968.

Bradford, Admiral Sir E E, *Life of Admiral of the Fleet Sir Arthur Knyvet Wilson*, London, 1923.

Briggs, J H, *Naval Administrations*, Marston, 1897.

Chalmers, W S, *Life and Letters of David, Earl Beatty, London*, 1951.

Churchill, Randolph, *Winston S Churchill*, vols i & ii, London, 1966, 1967.

Churchill, Winston, *World Crisis 1911-1918*, London, 1923.

Diggle, H F, *Burton Leonard Past and Present*, 1951.

Dorling, Taprell, *Men O' War*, London, 1929.

Ensor, R C K, *England 1870-1914*, Oxford, 1936.

Fincham, J, *History of Naval Architecture*, London, 1979.

Gollin, A, *Impact of Air Power on the British People and Government, 1909-1914*, London, 1989.

Gordon, Andrew, *The Rules of the Game – Jutland and the British Naval Command*, London, 1996.

Haggie, P, '*The Royal Navy and War Planning*', in *Journal of Contemporary History, VIII*, 1973.

Halpern, Paul G, *A Naval History of World War I*, London, 1994.

Halpern, Paul G, *The Mediterranean Naval Situation 1908-1914*, Oxford, 1971.

Hattendorf, John B, 'Admiral Prince Louis of Battenberg' in Murfett, *The First Sea Lords*, pp. 75-90.

Herwig, H H, '*Luxury' Fleet': The Imperial German Navy, 1888-1918*, London, 1980.

Hough, R, *First Sea Lord, An Authorised Biography of Admiral Lord Fisher*, London, 1969.

Hough, R, *Louis and Victoria*, London, 1974.

James, R R, *Churchill: A Study in Failure 1900-1939*, Penguin, 1973.

Kerr, M, *Prince Louis of Battenberg*, London, 1934.

Lambert, Nicholas A, 'Admiral Sir Arthur Knyvet Wilson, VC' in Murfett, *The First Sea Lords*, pp. 35-53.

Lambert, Nicholas A, 'Admiral Sir Francis Bridgeman-Bridgeman' in Murfett, *The First Sea Lords*, pp. 55-74

Lambert, Nicholas A, *Influence of the Submarine Upon Naval Strategy, 1898-1914*.

Lowis, G L, *Fabulous Admirals*, London, 1957.

Mackay, Ruddock, F, *Fisher of Kilverstone*, Oxford, 1974.

Magnus, Philip, *King Edward the Seventh*, London, 1964.

Manning, Frederick, *Life of Sir William White*, London, 1923.

Marder, Arthur J, *The Anatomy of British Sea Power ... 1880-1905*, New York, 1940, reprinted 1964.

Marder, Arthur J, *From Dreadnought to Scapa Flow*, 5 vols, Oxford, 1961-70.

Marder, Arthur J, *Portrait of an Admiral: The Life and Papers of Sir Herbert Richmond*, London, 1952.

Markham, M E & F A, *Life of Sir Albert Markham*, Cambridge, 1927.

Memorials of Copgrove, ND

Moresby, J, *Two Admirals*, London, 1909.

Morris, J, *Fisher's Face*, London, 1996.

Murfett, Malcolm H, ed., *The First Sea Lords from Fisher to Mountbatten*, London, 1995.

Ollard, R, *Fisher and Cunningham: A Study in the Personalities of the Churchill Era*, London, 1991.

Partridge, Michael S, *Military Planning for the Defence of the United Kingdom, 1814-1870*, London, 1989.

Patterson, A Temple, *Tyrwhitt of the Harwich Force: the Life of the Admiral of the Fleet Sir Reginald Tyrwhitt*, London, 1973.

Penrose, Fitzgerald, C C, *From Sail to Steam*, London, 1916.

Pollen, A, *The Great Gunnery Scandal*, London, 1980.

Rasor, E I, *Reform in the Royal Navy*, London, 1976.

Rogers, N A M, *Naval Records for Geneaologists*, HMSO, 1988.

Roskill, S, *Earl Beatty*, London, 1981.

Roskill, S, *Churchill and the Admirals*, London, 1977.

Schurman, D M, *The Education of a Navy*, London, 1965.

Sumida, J T, 'British Naval Administration and Policy in the Age of Fisher', *Journal of Military History*, January 1990.

Sumida, J T, *In Defence of Naval Supremacy: Finance, Technology and British Naval Policy, 1889-1914*, London, 1989.

Williamson, Samuel R, *The Politics of Grand Strategy: Britain and France Prepare for War 1904-1914*, Oxford, 1969.

Woodward, Sir Llewellyn, *The Age of Reform 1815-1870*, Oxford, 1962.

Index

Page numbers in italics refer to illustrations

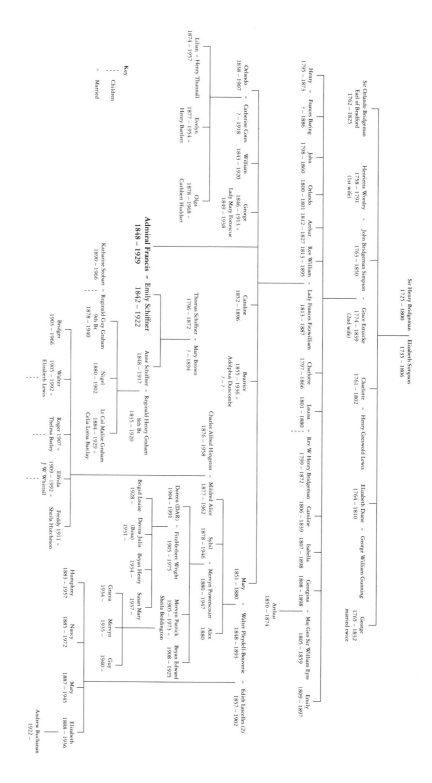

Key

——— Children

= Married